POLITICAL THEORIES OF
THE MIDDLE AGE

THIS re-issue of F. W. Maitland's translation of a vital section from Otto Gierke's monumental *Das Deutsche Genossenschaftsrecht* makes available once again one of the seminal texts in the historiography of political thought. Famed, *inter alia*, for the elegance and lucidity of Maitland's own expository introduction, *Political Theories of the Middle Age* is concerned in essence with the medieval development of the doctrine of State and Corporation – a concept which, as Maitland indicates, has been prone to misunderstanding by English minds versed in the tradition of the common law.

Gierke identifies the peculiar characteristic of medieval political thought as its vision of the universe as one articulated whole, and every being, whether a joint-being (community) or a single-being – as both a part and a whole: his text examines the potentially revolutionary effect upon this of certain crucial intellectual intrusions, derived in part from Roman Law, described by Gierke as 'ancient-modern'. He highlights the fundamental medieval tendency, familiar to generations of students of European absolutism, towards the concentration of right and power in the highest and widest groups on the one hand, and the individual man on the other, at the expense of all intermediate groups. In Maitland's words 'the ideas that are to possess and divide mankind from the sixteenth until the nineteenth century . . . are the ideas whose early history is to be detected, and they are set before us as thoughts which, under the influence of classical antiquity, necessarily shaped themselves in the course of medieval debate'.

POLITICAL THEORIES OF THE MIDDLE AGE

OTTO GIERKE

TRANSLATED
WITH AN INTRODUCTION
BY
FREDERIC WILLIAM MAITLAND

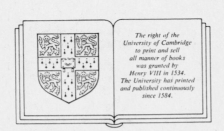

*The right of the
University of Cambridge
to print and sell
all manner of books
was granted by
Henry VIII in 1534.
The University has printed
and published continuously
since 1584.*

CAMBRIDGE UNIVERSITY PRESS

CAMBRIDGE
NEW YORK   NEW ROCHELLE
MELBOURNE   SYDNEY

Published by the Press Syndicate of the University of Cambridge
The Pitt Building, Trumpington Street, Cambridge CB2 1RP
32 East 57th Street, New York, NY 10022, USA
10 Stamford Road, Oakleigh, Melbourne 3166, Australia

First published 1900
Reprinted 1913, 1922, 1927, 1938, 1951, 1987
First paperback edition 1987

Printed in Great Britain by the University Press, Cambridge

British Library cataloguing in publication data
Gierke, Otto
  Political theories of the Middle Age.
  1. Political science—History
  I. Title   II. Deutsches Genossenschaftsrecht. *Vol. 3. English*
  320′.01   JA82

Library of Congress cataloguing in publicaiton data
Gierke, Otto Friedrich von, 1841-1921.
  Political theories of the Middle Age.
  Translation of: Die publicistischen Lehren des
  Mittelalters.
  Includes index.
  1. Political science—History.   2. Civilization,
  Medieval.   I. Title.
  JA82.G413   1987   320′.09   87-6590

    ISBN 0 521 34534 0 hard covers
    ISBN 0 521 34764 5 paperback

CONTENTS.

ERRATUM.

p. 150, note 158. Add to what is said of the opinions of Baldus the following :—

'But in Rubr. C. 10, 1, nr. 12, he holds that the *camera imperii* may in a secondary sense be said to belong to the Roman people; quia princeps repraesentat illum populum et ille populus imperium etiam, mortuo principe.'

INTRODUCTION.

HAD what is here translated, namely, a brief account of the political theories of the Middle Ages, appeared as a whole book, it would hardly have stood in need of that distorting medium, an English translation. Englishmen who were approaching the study of medieval politics, either from the practical or from the theoretical side, would have known that there was a book which they would do well to master, and many who were not professed students or whose interests lay altogether in modern times would have heard of it and have found it profitable. The elaborate notes would have shewn that its writer had read widely and deeply; they would also have guided explorers into a region where sign-posts are too few. As to the text, the last charge which could be made against it would be that of insufficient courage in generalization, unless indeed it were that of aimless medievalism. The outlines are large, the strokes are firm, and medieval appears as an introduction to modern thought. The ideas that are to possess and divide mankind from the sixteenth until the nineteenth century—Sovereignty, the Sovereign Ruler, the Sovereign People, the Representation of the People, the Social Contract, the Natural Rights of Man, the Divine Rights of Kings, the Positive Law that stands below the State, the Natural Law that stands above the State—these are the ideas whose early history is to be detected, and they are set before us as thoughts which, under the influence of Classical Antiquity, necessarily shaped themselves in the course of medieval debate. And if the thoughts are interesting, so too are the thinkers. In Dr Gierke's list of medieval publicists, beside the divines and schoolmen, stand great popes, great lawyers, great reformers, men who were clothing concrete projects in abstract vesture, men who fashioned the facts as well as the theories of their time.

Moreover, Englishmen should be especially grateful to a guide who is perhaps at his strongest just where they must needs be weak : that is, among the books of the legists and canonists. An educated Englishman may read and enjoy what Dante or Marsiglio has written. An English scholar may face Aquinas or Ockham or even the repellent Wyclif. But Baldus and Bartolus, Innocentius and Johannes Andreae, them he has never been taught to tackle, and they are not to be tackled by the untaught. And yet they are important people, for political philosophy in its youth is apt to look like a sublimated jurisprudence, and, even when it has grown in vigour and stature, is often compelled or content to work with tools—a social contract for example—which have been sharpened, if not forged, in the legal smithy. In that smithy Dr Gierke is at home. With perfect modesty he could say to a learned German public 'It is not probable that for some time to come anyone will tread exactly the same road that I have trodden in long years of fatiguing toil.'

But then what is here translated is only a small, a twentieth, part of a large and as yet unfinished book bearing a title which can hardly attract many readers in this country and for which an English equivalent cannot easily be found, namely *Das deutsche Genossenschaftsrecht*. Of that work the third volume contains a section entitled *Die publicistischen Lehren des Mittelalters*, and that is the section which is here done into English. Now though this section can be detached and still bear a high value, and though the author's permission for its detachment has been graciously given, still it would be untrue to say that this amputating process does no harm. The organism which is a whole with a life of its own, but is also a member of a larger and higher organism whose life it shares, this, so Dr Gierke will teach us, is an idea which we must keep before our minds when we are studying the political thought of the Middle Ages, and it is an idea which we may apply to his and to every good book. The section has a life of its own, but it also shares the life of the whole treatise. Nor only so ; it is *membrum de membro*. It is a section in a chapter entitled 'The Medieval Doctrine of State and Corporation,' which stands in a volume entitled 'The Antique and Medieval Doctrine of State and

Corporation and its Reception in Germany'; and this again is part of *Das deutsche Genossenschaftsrecht.* Indeed our section is a member of a highly organized system, and in that section are sentences and paragraphs which will not yield their full meaning except to those who know something of the residue of the book and something also of the controversial atmosphere in which a certain *Genossenschaftstheorie* has been unfolding itself. This being so, the intervention of a translator who has read the whole book, who has read many parts of it many times, who deeply admires it, may be of service. In a short introduction, even if his own steps are none too sure, he may be able to conduct some of his fellow-countrymen towards a point of view which commands a wide prospect of history and human affairs.

Staats- und Korporationslehre—the Doctrine of State and Corporation. Such a title may be to some a stumbling-block set before the threshold. A theory of the State, so it might be said, may be very interesting to the philosophic few and fairly interesting to the intelligent many, but a doctrine of Corporations, which probably speaks of fictitious personality and similar artifices, can only concern some juristic speculators, of whom there are none or next to none in this country. On second thoughts, however, we may be persuaded to see here no rock of offence but rather a stepping-stone which our thoughts should sometimes traverse. For, when all is said, there seems to be a genus of which State and Corporation are species. They seem to be permanently organized groups of men ; they seem to be group-units ; we seem to attribute acts and intents, rights and wrongs to these groups, to these units. Let it be allowed that the State is a highly peculiar group-unit; still it may be asked whether we ourselves are not the slaves of a jurist's theory and a little behind the age of Darwin if between the State and all other groups we fix an immeasurable gulf and ask ourselves no questions about the origin of species. Certain it is that our medieval history will go astray, our history of Italy and Germany will go far astray, unless we can suffer communities to acquire and lose the character of States somewhat easily, somewhat insensibly, or rather unless we both know and feel that we must not thrust our modern 'State-concept,' as a German would call it, upon the reluctant material.

Englishmen in particular should sometimes give themselves

this warning, and not only for the sake of the Middle Ages.
Fortunate in littleness and insularity, England could soon exhibit
as a difference in kind what elsewhere was a difference in degree,
namely, to use medieval terms, the difference between a community or corporation (*universitas*) which does and one which
does not 'recognize a superior.' There was no likelihood that
the England which the Norman duke had subdued and surveyed
would be either *Staatenbund* or *Bundesstaat*, and the aspiration
of Londoners to have 'no king but the mayor' was fleeting.
This, if it diminished our expenditure of blood and treasure—
an expenditure that impoverishes—diminished also our expenditure of thought—an expenditure that enriches—and facilitated
(might this not be said?) a certain thoughtlessness or poverty
of ideas. The State that Englishmen knew was a singularly
unicellular State, and at a critical time they were not too well
equipped with tried and traditional thoughts which would meet the
case of Ireland or of some communities, commonwealths, corporations in America which seemed to have wills—and hardly fictitious
wills—of their own, and which became States and United States[1].
The medieval Empire laboured under the weight of an incon-
gruously simple theory so soon as lawyers were teaching that the
Kaiser was the Princeps of Justinian's law-books. The modern
and multicellular British State—often and perhaps harmlessly called
an Empire—may prosper without a theory, but does not suggest
and, were we serious in our talk of sovereignty, would hardly
tolerate, a theory that is simple enough and insular enough, and
yet withal imperially Roman enough, to deny an essentially state-
like character to those 'self-governing colonies,' communities,
commonwealths, which are knit and welded into a larger sovereign
whole. The adventures of an English joint-stock company which
happed into a rulership of the Indies, the adventures of another
English company which while its charter was still very new had
become the puritan commonwealth of Massachusett's Bay should

---

[1] See the remarks of Sir C. Ilbert, The Government of India, p. 55: 'Both the
theory and the experience were lacking which are requisite for adapting English institutions to new and foreign circumstances. For want of such experience England was
destined to lose her colonies in the Western hemisphere. For want of it mistakes were
committed which imperilled the empire she was building up in the East.' The want
of a theory about Ireland which would have mediated between absolute dependence and
absolute independence was the origin of many evils.

be enough to shew that our popular English *Staatslehre* if, instead
of analyzing the contents of a speculative jurist's mind, it seriously
grasped the facts of English history, would shew some inclination
to become a *Korporationslehre* also.

Even as it is, such a tendency is plainly to be seen in many
zones. Standing on the solid ground of positive law and legal
orthodoxy we confess the king of this country to be a 'corporation
sole,' and, if we have any curiosity, ought to wonder why in the
sixteenth century the old idea that the king is the head of a 'corporation aggregate of many[1]' gave way before a thought which
classed him along with the parish parson of decadent ecclesiastical
law under one uncomfortable rubric. Deeply convinced though
our lawyers may be that individual men are the only 'real' and
'natural' persons, they are compelled to find some phrase which
places State and Man upon one level. 'The greatest of artificial
persons, politically speaking, is the State': so we may read in an
excellent First Book of Jurisprudence[2]. Ascending from the legal
plain, we are in a middle region where a sociology emulous of the
physical sciences discourses of organs and organisms and social
tissue, and cannot sever by sharp lines the natural history of the
state-group from the natural history of other groups. Finally, we
are among the summits of philosophy and observe how a doctrine,
which makes some way in England, ascribes to the State, or, more
vaguely, the Community, not only a real will, but even 'the' real
will, and it must occur to us to ask whether what is thus affirmed
in the case of the State can be denied in the case of other organized
groups: for example, that considerable group the Roman Catholic
Church. It seems possible to one who can only guess, that even
now-a-days a Jesuit may think that the will of the Company to
which he belongs is no less real than the will of any State, and, if
the reality of this will be granted by the philosopher, can he pause
until even the so-called one-man-company has a real will really
distinct from the several wills of the one man and his six humble
associates? If we pursue that thought, not only will our philosophic *Staatslehre* be merging itself in a wider doctrine, but we
shall already be deep in the *Genossenschaftstheorie.* In any case,
however, the law's old habit of co-ordinating men and 'bodies

[1] A late instance of this old concept occurs in Plowden's Commentaries, 234.
[2] Pollock, First Book of Jurisprudence, 113.

politic' as two kinds of Persons seems to deserve the close attention
of the modern philosopher, for, though it be an old habit, it has
become vastly more important in these last years than it ever was
before.   In the second half of the nineteenth century corporate
groups of the most various sorts have been multiplying all the
world over at a rate that far outstrips the increase of 'natural
persons,' and a large share of all our newest law is law concerning
corporations[1].   Something not unworthy of philosophic discussion
would seem to lie in this quarter : either some deep-set truth which
is always bearing fresh fruit, or else a surprisingly stable product of
mankind's propensity to feign.—Howbeit, this rare atmosphere we
do not easily breathe and therefore will for a while follow a lower
road.

I.

A large part in the volume that lies before the translator is
played by 'the Reception.'   When we speak of the Renaissance
and the Reformation we need not be at pains to name what was
reformed or what was born anew, and even so a German historian
will speak of the Reception when he means the Reception of
Roman law.   Very often Renaissance, Reformation and Reception
will be set before us as three intimately connected and almost
equally important movements which sever modern from medieval
history.   Modern Germany has attained such a pre-eminence
in the study of Roman law, that we in England may be pardoned
for forgetting that of Roman law medieval Germany was innocent
and ignorant, decidedly more innocent and more ignorant than
was the England of the thirteenth century.   It is true that in
Germany the theoretical continuity of the Empire was providing
a base for the argument that the law of Justinian's books was or
ought to be the law of the land ; it is also true that the Corpus
Iuris was furnishing weapons useful to Emperors who were at strife
with Popes ; but those weapons were fashioned and wielded chiefly
by Italian hands, and the practical law of Germany was as
German as it well could be.   Also—and here lay the possibility of

---

[1] In 1857 an American judge went the length of saying 'It is probably true that more
corporations were created by the legislature of Illinois at its last session than existed
in the whole civilized world at the commencement of the present century.'   Dillon,
Municipal Corporations, § 37 *a*.

a catastrophe—it was not learned law, it was not taught law, it was far from being *Juristenrecht.* Englishmen are wont to fancy that the law of Germany must needs savour of the school, the lecture room, the professor ; but in truth it was just because German law savoured of nothing of the kind, but rather of the open air, oral tradition and thoroughly unacademic doomsmen that the law of Germany ceased to be German and that German law has had to be disinterred by modern professors. Of the geographical and historical causes of the difference we need not speak, but in England we see a very early concentration of justice and then the rapid growth of a legal profession. The Year Books follow and the Inns of Court and lectures on English law and scholastic exercises and that 'call to the bar' of the Inn which is in fact an academically earned degree. Also long before Germany had universities, Roman law was being taught at Oxford and Cambridge, so that it would not come hither with the glamour of the Renaissance. A certain modest place had been assigned to it in the English scheme of life ; some knowledge of it was necessary to the students of the lucrative law of the Church, and a few civilians were required for what we should call the diplomatic service of the realm. But already in the fourteenth century Wyclif, the schoolman, had urged that if law was to be taught in the English universities it ought to be English law. In words which seem prophetic of modern 'Germanism' he protested that English was as just, as reasonable, as subtle, as was Roman jurisprudence[1].

Thus when the perilous time came, when the New Learning was in the air and the Modern State was emerging in the shape of the Tudor Monarchy, English law was and had long been lawyers' law, learned law, taught law, *Juristenrecht.* Disgracefully barbarous, so thought one enlightened apostle of the New Learning. Reginald Pole—and his advice was brought to his royal cousin—was for sweeping it away. In so many words he desired that England should 'receive' the civil law of the Romans : a law so civil that Nature's self might have dictated it and a law that was being received in all well governed lands[2]. We must not endeavour to tell

[1] Wyclif, De Officio Regis (ed. Pollard and Sayle, 1887), p. 193 : 'Sed non credo quod plus viget in Romana civilitate subtilitas racionis sive iusticia quam in civilitate Anglicana.'

[2] Starkey's England (Early Eng. Text Soc. 1878), 192—5.

the story of the danger that beset English law when the future Cardinal Archbishop was speaking thus: a glance towards Scotland would shew us that the danger was serious enough and would have been far more serious but for the continuous existence of the Inns of Court, and that *indoctissimum genus doctissimorum hominum* which was bred therein.   Then late in the sixteenth century began the wonderful resuscitation of medieval learning which attains its completion in the books and acts of Edward Coke. The political side of this movement is the best known.   Antiquarian research appears for a while as the guardian and renovator of national liberties, and the men who lead the House of Commons are becoming always more deeply versed in long-forgotten records. However, be it noted that even in England a certain amount of foreign theory was received, and by far the most remarkable instance is the reception of that Italian Theory of the Corporation of which Dr Gierke is the historian, and which centres round the phrase *persona ficta*.   It slowly stole from the ecclesiastical courts, which had much to say about the affairs of religious corporations, into our temporal courts, which, though they had long been dealing with English group-units, had no home-made theory to oppose to the subtle and polished invader.   This instance may help us to understand what happened in Germany, where the native law had not reached the doctrinal stage of growth, but was still rather 'folk law' than lawyers' law and was dissipating itself in countless local customs.

Italian doctrine swept like a deluge over Germany.   The learned doctors from the new universities whom the Princes called to their councils, could explain everything in a Roman or would-be Roman sense.   Those Princes were consolidating their powers into a (by Englishmen untranslatable) *Landeshoheit*: something that was less than modern sovereignty, for it still would have the Empire above it, but more than feudal seignory since classical thoughts about 'the State' were coming to its aid.   It is noticeable that, except in his hereditary dominions, the Emperor profited little by that dogma of continuity which served as an apology for the Reception.   The disintegrating process was so far advanced that not the Kaiser but the Fürst appeared as 'the Prince' of political theory and the Princeps of the Corpus Iuris. The doctors could teach such a prince much that was to his advantage. Beginning late in the fifteenth century the movement accomplished itself in the sixteenth. It is catastrophic when compared with the slow and silent process whereby the customary law of northern France was partially romanized. No legislator had said that Roman law had been or was to be received in Germany; the work was done not by lawgivers but by lawyers, and from age to age there remained some room for controversy as to the exact position that the Corpus Iuris occupied among the various sources of law actual and potential. Still the broad fact remains that Germany had bowed her neck to the Roman yoke.

In theory what was received was the law of Justinian's books. In practice what was received was the system which the Italian commentators had long been elaborating. Dr Gierke frequently insists that this is an important difference. In Italy the race of glossators who were sincerely endeavouring to discover the meaning of classical texts had given way to a race of commentators whose work was more or less controlled by a desire for practically acceptable results, and who therefore were disposed to accommo-date Roman law to medieval life. Our author says that especially in their doctrine of corporations or communities there is much that is not Roman, and much that may be called Germanic. This facilitated the Reception: Roman law had gone half-way to meet the facts that it was to govern. Then again, at a later time the influence of what we may call the 'natural' school of jurists smoothed away some of the contrasts between Roman law and German habit. If in the eyes of an English lawyer systems of Natural Law are apt to look suspiciously Roman, the modern Romanist will complain that when and where such systems were being constructed concrete Rome was evaporating in abstract Reason, and some modern Germanists will teach us that 'Nature Right' often served as the protective disguise of repressible but ineradicable Germanic ideas.

With the decadence of Nature Right and the advent of 'the historical school' a new chapter began. Savigny's teaching had two sides. We are accustomed to think of him, and rightly, as the herald of evolution, the man who substitutes development for manufacture, organism for mechanism, natural laws for Natural Law, the man who is nervously afraid lest a code should impede the beautiful processes of gradual growth. But then he was also the great Romanist, the great dogmatist, the expounder of classical texts according to their true—which must be their original—intent and meaning.   There was no good, he seemed to say, in playing at being Roman.   If the Common Law of Germany was Roman law, it ought to be the law of the Digest, not the law of glossators or commentators or 'natural' speculators.   This teaching, so we are told, bore fruit in the practical work of German courts.   They began to take the Corpus Iuris very seriously and to withdraw concessions that had been made—some will say to national life and modern fact, others will say to slovenly thought and slipshod practice.

But that famous historical school was not only a school of historically minded Romanists.   It was also the cradle of Germanism.   Eichhorn and Grimm stood by Savigny's side.   Every scrap and fragment of old German law was to be lovingly and scientifically recovered and edited.   Whatever was German was to be traced through all its fortunes to its fount.   The motive force in this prolonged effort—one of the great efforts of the nineteenth century—was not antiquarian pedantry, nor was it a purely disinterested curiosity.   If there was science there was also love.   At this point we ought to remember, and yet have some difficulty in remembering, what Germany, burdened with the curse of the translated Imperium, had become in the six centuries of her agony.   The last shadow of political unity had vanished and had left behind a 'geographical expression,' a mere collective name for some allied states.   Many of them were rather estates than states; most of them were too small to live vigorous lives; all of them were too small to be the Fatherland.   Much else besides blood, iron and song went to the remaking of Germany.   The idea of a Common Law would not die.   A common legislature there might not be, but a Common Law there was, and a hope that the law of Germany might someday be natively German was awakened. Then in historical retrospect the Reception began to look like disgrace and disaster, bound up as cause and effect with the forces that tore a nation into shreds.   The people that defied the tyranny of living popes had fallen under the tyranny of dead emperors, unworthily reincarnate in petty princelings.   The land that saw Luther burn one 'Welsh' Corpus Iuris had meekly accepted another.   It seemed shameful that Germans, not unconscious of their mastery of jurisprudence, should see, not only in England, but in France and even the France of Napoleon's Code the survival of principles that might certainly be called Germanic, but could not be called German without a sigh. Was not 'a daughter of the Salica,' or a grand-daughter, reigning over the breadth of North America? And then, as might be expected, all manner of causes and parties sought to suck advantage out of a patriotic aspiration. The socialist could denounce the stern and bitter individualism, the consecrated selfishness, of the alien slave-owners' law, and the Catholic zealot could contrast the Christiano-German law of Germany's great days with the Pagano-Roman law in which disruptive Protestantism had found an unholy ally.

In all soberness, however, it was asserted that old German law, blighted and stunted though it had been, might yet be nursed and tended into bearing the fruit of sound doctrine and reformed practice. The great men were neither dreamers nor purists. Jacob Grimm once said that to root out Roman ideas from German law would be as impossible as to banish Romance words from English speech. The technical merits of Roman law were admitted, admired and emulated. Besides Histories of German Law, Systems were produced and 'Institutes.' The Germanist claimed for his science a parity of doctrinal rank with the science of the Romanist. He too had his theory of possession; he too had his theory of corporations; and sometimes he could boast that, willingly or unwillingly, the courts were adopting his conclusions, though they might attain the Germanic result by the troublesome process of playing fast and loose with Ulpian and his fellows.

Happier days came. Germany was to have a Civil Code, or rather, for the title at least would be German, a Bürgerliches Gesetzbuch. Many years of keen debate now lie behind the most carefully considered statement of a nation's law that the world has ever seen. Enthusiastic Germanists are not content, but they have won something and may win more as the work of interpretation proceeds. What, however, concerns us here is that the appearance of 'Germanistic' doctrines led to controversies of a new and radical kind. It became always plainer that what was in the field was not merely a second set of rules but a second and a disparate set of ideas. Between Romanist and Germanist, and again within each school, the debate took a turn towards what we might call an ideal morphology. The forms of legal thought, the 'concepts' with which the lawyer 'operates,' were to be described, delimited, compared. In this work there was sometimes shewn a delicacy of touch and a subtlety of historical perception, of which in this country we, having no pressing need for comparisons, can know little, especially if our notion of an analytical jurisprudence is gathered from Austin's very 'natural' exploits. Of special interest to Englishmen should be the manner in which out of the rude material of old German law the Germanists will sometimes reconstruct an idea which in England needs no reconstruction since it is in all our heads, but which bears a wholly new value for us when we have seen it laboriously composed and tested.

II.

At an early moment in the development of Germanism a Theory of the Corporation, which gave itself out to be the orthodox Roman Theory and which Savigny had lately defined in severe outline, was assailed by Georg Beseler who lived to be a father among Germanists[1]. You will never, he said in effect, force our German fellowships, our German *Genossenschaften*, into the Roman scheme: we Germans have had and still have other thoughts than yours. Since then the Roman Corporation (*universitas*) has been in the crucible. Romanists of high repute have forsaken the Savignian path; Ihering went one way, Brinz another, and now, though it might be untrue to say that there are as many doctrines as there are doctors, there seems to be no creed that is entitled to give itself the airs of orthodoxy. It is important to remember that the materials which stand at the Romanist's disposal are meagre. The number of texts in the Digest which, even by a stretch of language, could be said to express a theory of Corporations is extremely small, and as to implied theories it is easy for different expositors to hold different opinions, especially if they feel more or less concerned to deduce a result that will be tolerable in modern Germany. The admission must be made that there is no text which directly calls the *universitas* a *persona*, and still less any that calls it *persona ficta*[2].

---

[1] Beseler, Volksrecht und Juristenrecht, Leipzig, 1843, pp. 158—194.

[2] It does not seem to be proved that the Roman jurists went beyond the 'personae

According to Dr Gierke, the first man who used this famous phrase was Sinibald Fieschi, who in 1243 became Pope Innocent IV.[1] More than one generation of investigators had passed away, indeed the whole school of glossators was passing away, before the Roman texts would yield a theory to men who lived in a Germanic environment, and, when a theory was found, it was found by the canonists, who had before their eyes as the typical corporation, no medieval city, village or gild, but a collegiate or cathedral church. In Dr Gierke's view Innocent, the father of 'the Fiction Theory,' appears as a truly great lawyer. He really understood the texts; the head of an absolute monarchy, such as the catholic Church was tending to become, was the very man to understand them; he found the phrase, the thought, for which others had sought in vain. The corporation is a person; but it is a person by fiction and only by fiction. Thenceforward this was the doctrine professed alike by legists and canonists, but, so our author contends, it never completely subdued some inconsistent thoughts of Germanic origin which found utterance in practical conclusions. In particular, to mention one rule which is a good touchstone for theories, Innocent, being in earnest about the mere fictitiousness of the corporation's personality and having good warrant in the Digest[2], proclaimed that the corporation could commit neither sin nor delict. As pope he might settle the question of sin, and at all events could prohibit the excommunication of an *universitas*[3], but as lawyer he could not convince his fellow lawyers that corporations must never be charged with crime or tort.

Then Savigny is set before us as recalling courts and lawyers from unprincipled aberrations to the straight but narrow Roman road. Let us bring to mind a few of the main traits of his renowned doctrine.

vice fungitur' of Dig. 46, 1, 22. Any modern text-book of Pandektenrecht will introduce its reader to the controversy, and give numerous references. Here it may be enough to name Ihering, Brinz, Windscheid, Pernice, Dernburg and Regelsberger as prominent expositors of various versions of the Roman theory. Among recent discussions may be mentioned, Kniep, Societas Publicanorum, 1896; Kuhlenbeck, Von den Pandekten zum bürgerlichen Gesetzbuch (1898), I. 169 ff.

[1] Gierke, Genossenschaftsrecht, III. 279.

[2] Dig. 4, 3, 15 § 1.

[3] Gierke, Genossenschaftsrecht, III. 280.

Besides men or 'natural persons,' the law knows as 'subjects[1]' of proprietary rights certain fictitious, artificial or juristic persons, and as one species of this class it knows the corporation. We must carefully sunder this ideal person from those natural persons who are called its members. It is capable of proprietary rights; but it is incapable of knowing, intending, willing, acting. The relation between it and the corporators may best be compared to that between *pupillus* and *tutor*, or that between a lunatic and the committee of his estate. By the action of its guardians it can acquire property, and, if it is to take the advantage of contracts, it must take the burden also. To allow it possession is difficult, for possession is matter of fact; still after hesitation the Roman lawyers made this concession. An action based upon unjust enrichment may lie against it; but it must not be charged with delict. To attempt to punish it is both absurd and unjust, though the State may dissolve a noxious group in an administrative way. Being but a fiction of the law, its personality must have its commencement in some authoritative act, some declaration of the State's will. Finally, it may continue to exist though it no longer has even one member.

For the last three centuries and more Englishmen have been repeating some of the canonical phrases, but Dr Gierke would probably say that we have never taken them much to heart. We are likely therefore to overlook some points in the Savignian theory which seem serious to those who have not raised convenient inconsequence to the level of an intellectual virtue. In particular, having made 'the corporation itself' a mindless being that can do no act, we must not think of the organized group of corporators as an 'agent' appointed by a somewhat inert 'principal.' Were the corporation 'itself' capable of appointing an agent, there would be no apparent reason why 'itself' should not do many other acts. Savigny is far more skilful. It is not in agency but in guardianship of the Roman kind that he finds the

---

[1] Germans distinguish between the Subject and the Object of a right. If Styles owns a horse, Styles is the Subject and the horse the Object of the right. Then if we ascribe the ownership of the horse to the Crown, we make the Crown a Subject; and then we can speak of the Crown's Subjectivity. And so in political theory, if we ascribe Sovereignty to the Crown or the Parliament or the People, we make the Crown, Parliament or People the Subject of Sovereignty. The reader of the following pages may be asked to remember this not inconvenient usage.

correct analogy. Those who wish to make fun of the theory say that it fills the legal world with hopeless idiots and their State-appointed curators; but, if we mean logic, we must be careful to see that our 'corporation itself'—that *Ding an sich* which some-how or another lies beyond the phenomenal group of corporators[1] —does no act, speaks no word, thinks no thought, appoints no agent. Also we may observe, and in history this is important, that this theory might play into the hands of a Prince or princeling inclined to paternal despotism. Really and truly the property of a corporation—for example a city or university—belongs to no real person or persons, and over the doings of guardians and curators the State should exercise, no mere jurisdiction, but administrative control. Of 'natural rights' there can here be no talk, for 'artificial persons' can have no natural rights. Furthermore, the strict con-finement of the *persona ficta* within the sphere of Private Law may escape notice in a country where (to use foreign terms) 'publicistic' matter has been wont to assume 'private-rightly' form in a fashion that some would call shamefully medieval but others enviably Germanic. The Savignian corporation is no 'subject' for 'liberties and franchises' or 'rights of self-government.' Really and 'pub-licistically' it can hardly be other than a wheel in the State's machinery, though for the purposes of Property Law a personifi-cation of this wheel is found to be convenient. Lastly, some popular thoughts about 'body' and 'members' must needs go overboard. The guardian is no 'member' of his ward; and how even by way of fiction could a figment be composed of real men? We had better leave body and members to the vulgar.

Savigny wrote on the eve of a great upheaval. A movement in which England played a prominent and honourable part was thrusting the joint-stock company to the very forefront of those facts whence a theory of corporations must draw its sustenance. Whatever may be said of municipal and other communes, of universities and colleges and churches, the modern joint-stock company plainly resents any endeavour to 'construe' it as a piece of the State's mechanism, though we may profitably remember that

---

[1] Pollock, Contract, ed. 6, p. 108: 'If it is allowable to illustrate one fiction by another, we may say that the artificial person is a fictitious substance conceived as supporting legal attributes.' But this happy phrase is not by itself an adequate expression of Sir F. Pollock's view. See the context.

early and exemplary specimens, notably the Bank of England and the East India Company, were closely related to the State.   Moreover, the modern joint-stock company, if it is an *universitas*, is exceedingly like a *societas*, a partnership, a *Gesellschaft*, and this resemblance seemed to threaten one of the securest results of legal science.   There were a few phrases in the Digest capable of perplexing the first glossators, but in clear words Innocent IV. had apprehended the distinction : the *universitas* is a person ; the *societas* is only another name, a collective name, for the *socii*[1]. Since then jurisprudence had kept or endeavoured to keep the two in very different boxes, in spite of the efforts of Natural Law to break down the partition.   In a system of *Pandektenrecht* the *universitas* appeared on an early page under the rubric ' Law of Persons,' while the *societas* was far away, probably in another volume, for a Partnership is a kind of Contract and Contract is a kind of Obligation.   Here, however, was a being whose very name of *Aktiengesellschaft* strongly suggested partnership, and yet the German legislators who had designed its mould had almost certainly meant that it should exhibit personality or legal 'subjectivity,' though they had not said this in so many words.   Was it *universitas*, or *societas*, or neither, or both ?   Could a mean term be found between unity and plurality ?   What was, what could be, the 'juristic nature' of a shareholder's 'share,' as we call it in England ?   Was it any conceivable form of co-ownership, any 'real' right in the company's lands and goods ?   Could it, on the other hand, be reduced to the mere benefit of a contract between the shareholder and the artificial person ?   Ideal walls were rocking and material interests were at stake.   Was it, for example, decent of the Prussian government to tax first the income of the company and then the dividends of the shareholders and yet disclaim all thought of double taxation[2] ?

Pausing here for a moment, we may notice that an Englishman

[1] Gierke, Genossenschaftsrecht, III. 285.

[2] Dernburg, Pandekten, ed. 5, I. 146.   The German lawyer has had a good many different types of association to consider, such as the *Gesellschaft des bürgerlichen Rechtes*, the *offene Handelsgesellschaft*, the *Kommanditgesellschaft*, the *Kommanditgesellschaft auf Aktien*, and the *Aktiengesellschaft ;* and, so I understand, the legislature had not explicitly told him which, if any, of these types were to display personality.   So a large room was left for rival ' constructions.'

will miss a point in the history of political theory unless he knows that in a strictly legal context the Roman *societas*, the French *société*, and the German *Gesellschaft* should be rendered by the English *partnership* and by no other word. Also he should know that, just as the English lawyer maintains that our English 'firm' is a mere collective name for the partners and displays no 'artificial personality,' so also he will be taught in Germany that the Roman *societas* and the German *Gesellschaft* are not 'juristic persons.' Now-a-days it will perhaps be added that the German *Gesellschaft* —and the same would be said of the English partnership—shews a tendency to develop towards corporate organization, from which tendency the extremely 'individualistic' *societas* of the Romans was wholly free[1]. That is a small matter; but it is a great matter that before the end of the Middle Ages the Roman word for partnership was assuming a vastly wide meaning and, under the patronage of Ciceronian comparisons[2], was entering the field of politics. 'Human Society' should be the partnership of mankind; 'Civil Society' should be the partnership of citizens; 'the Origin of Civil Society' should be a Social Contract or contract of partnership. If Rousseau writes of *le Contrat Social* and Pothier of *le Contrat de Société*, there should be, and there is, a link between their dissimilar books, and a German can say that both discussed the *Gesellschaftsvertrag*, the one with passion, the other with erudition. Here then we face one of the historical problems that Dr Gierke raises. How came it about that political theory, which went to the lawyers for most of its ideas, borrowed the contract of partnership rather than the apparently far more appropriate act of incorporation? In brief the answer is that the current doctrine of corporations, the classical and Innocentian doctrine, stood beneath the level of philosophic thought. A merely fictitious personality, created by the State and shut up within the limits of Private Law, was not what the philosopher wanted when he went about to construct the State itself.

And then political philosophy reacted upon legal theory. When the State itself had become a merely collective unit—a sum of presently existing individuals bound together by the operation of their own wills—it was not likely that any other group would seem capable of withstanding similar analysis. Where philosophy and

[1] Dernburg, loc. cit. [2] See below, p. 187.

jurisprudence met in such systems of Natural Law as were fashionable in the eighteenth century, the *universitas* was lowered to the rank of the *societas*, or (but this was the same process) the *societas* was raised to the rank of the *universitas*[1]. Both alike exhibited a certain unity in plurality; both alike might be called 'moral persons'; but in the one case as in the other this personality was to be thought of as a mere labour-saving device, like stenography or the mathematician's symbols. What we may call the Bracket Theory or Expansible Symbol Theory of the Corporation really stands in sharp contrast with the Fiction Theory as Savigny conceived it, though sometimes English writers seem to be speaking of the one and thinking of the other. The existing corporators, who in the one scheme are mere guardians for a somewhat that the State has instituted, become in the other scheme the real 'subjects' of those rights and duties that are ascribed to the corporation, though legal art usually keeps these 'subjects' enclosed within a bracket. However, despite this tendency of a 'natural' jurisprudence—a tendency which seems to have left an abiding mark in the legal terminology of Scotland—the Romanists of Germany had been holding fast the doctrine that the *universitas* is, while the *societas* is not, a person, when the joint-stock company, a new power in the theoretic as in the economic world, began to give trouble. That the *Aktiengesellschaft* was a corporation was generally admitted; but of all corporations a joint-stock company is that which seems to offer itself most kindly to the individualistic analyst. When all is said and done, and all due praise has been awarded to the inventors of a beautiful logarithm, are not these shareholders, these men of flesh and blood, the real and only sustainers of the company's rights and duties? So great a Romanist as Ihering[2] trod this 'individualistic' or 'collectivistic' path, and in America where law schools flourish, where supreme courts are many and the need for theory is more urgent than it is in England, highly interesting attempts have been made to dispel the Fiction, or rather to open the Bracket and find therein nothing but contract-bound men[3]. Contract, that greediest of legal categories,

---

[1] Gierke, Johannes Althusius, 103.

[2] See especially Geist des röm. Rechts, vol. III., p. 343.

[3] Dissatisfaction with the Fiction—or, as Americans sometimes say, with 'the Entity'—is expressed in some well-known text-books, e.g., Taylor, Law of Private Corporations, § 60; Morawetz, Law of Private Corporations, ch. I.

which once wanted to devour the State, resents being told that it cannot painlessly digest even a joint-stock company. Maine's famous sentence about Contract and Status might indeed be boldly questioned by anyone who remembered that, at least for the philologian, the Roman Status became that modern State, *État, Staat* which refused to be explained by Contract into a mere 'Civil Society.' Few words have had histories more adventurous than that of the word which is the *State* of public and the *estate* of our private law, and which admirably illustrates the interdependence that exists between all parts of a healthily growing body of jurisprudence. Still, though the analytic powers of Contract are by no means what they once seemed to be, many will think them equal to the task of expanding what they might call the Corporation Symbol.

It was in a Germany that was full of new ideas and new hopes that a theory was launched which styled itself 'the German *Genossenschaftstheorie.*' Even the hastiest sketch of its environment, if it notices the appearance of the joint-stock company, should give one word to the persistence in Germany of agrarian communities with world-old histories, to the intricate problems that their dissolution presented, and to the current complaint that Roman law had no equitable solution for these questions and had done scant justice to the peasant. Nor should the triumphs of biological science be forgotten. A name was wanted which would unite many groups of men, simple and complex, modern and archaic; and *Genossenschaft* was chosen. The English translator must carefully avoid Partnership; perhaps in our modern usage Company has become too specific and technical; Society also is dangerous; Fellowship with its slight flavour of an old England may be our least inadequate word. Beginning with Beseler's criticism of Savigny, the theory gradually took shape, especially in Dr Gierke's hands, and a great deal of thought, learning and controversy collected round it. Battles had to be fought in many fields. The new theory was to be philosophically true, scientifically sound, morally righteous, legally implicit in codes and decisions, practically convenient, historically destined, genuinely German, and perhaps exclusively Germanistic[1]. No, it seems to say, whatever

[1] However, some Romanists of repute have asserted their right to adopt and have adopted this theory. See in particular Regelsberger, Pandekten, vol. I. p. 289 ff. See also Dernburg, Pandekten, § 59.

the Roman *universitas* may have been—and Dr Gierke is for pinning the Roman jurists to Savignianism—our German Fellowship is no fiction, no symbol, no piece of the State's machinery, no collective name for individuals, but a living organism and a real person, with body and members and a will of its own. Itself can will, itself can act; it wills and acts by the men who are its organs as a man wills and acts by brain, mouth and hand. It is not a fictitious person; it is a *Gesammtperson*, and its will is a *Gesammtwille*; it is a group-person, and its will is a group-will[1].

This theory, which we might call Realism, may seem to carry its head among the clouds, though no higher perhaps than the Fiction Theory; but a serious effort has been made to give it feet that walk upon the earth. In one long book[2] Dr Gierke has in great detail argued his case throughout the whole domain of practicable modern law, contending, not indeed that all German 'authority' (as an English lawyer would say) is on his side, but that he has the support of a highly respectable body of authority, express and implied, and that legislatures and tribunals fall into self-contradiction or plain injustice when they allow themselves to be governed by other theories. Nothing could be more concrete than the argument, and, though it will sometimes shew an affection for 'the German middle age' and a distrust of ancient Rome, it claims distinctively modern virtues: for instance, that of giving of the shareholder's 'share' the only lawyerly explanation that will stand severe strain. Then in another book our author has been telling the history of German Fellowship Law[3].

Let us try to imagine—we are not likely to see—a book with some such title as English Fellowship Law, which in the first place

---

[1] The works of Dr Gierke which deal with this matter are (1) Das deutsche Genossenschaftsrecht, whereof three volumes were published in 1868, 1873, and 1881; (2) Die Genossenschaftstheorie und die deutsche Rechtsprechung, 1887; (3) The first volume of Deutsches Privatrecht, 1895, which contains a more succinct and more recent statement; (4) The monograph on Johannes Althusius, 1880, which should be well known to all students of political theory. Those who would rather begin their study of the realistic theory in French than in German may be sent to A. Mestre, Les Personnes Morales, 1899. French lawyers have been conservative, and Savignianism was in harmony with the spirit of the Codes; nevertheless the doctrine of the real group-will is finding disciples. The only English statement that I have seen of this theory is by Ernst Freund, The Legal Nature of Corporations, University Press, Chicago, 1897.

[2] This is the Genossenschaftstheorie of 1887.

[3] This is the Genossenschaftsrecht of 1868—73—81.

described the structure of the groups in which men of English race have stood from the days when the revengeful kindred was pursuing the blood feud to the days when the one-man-company is issuing debentures, when parliamentary assemblies stand three deep above Canadian and Australian soil and 'Trusts and Corporations' is the name of a question that vexes the great Republic of the West. Within these bounds lie churches, and even the medieval church, one and catholic, religious houses, mendicant orders, non-conforming bodies, a presbyterian system, universities old and new, the village community which Germanists revealed to us, the manor in its growth and decay, the township, the New England town, the counties and hundreds, the chartered boroughs, the gild in all its manifold varieties, the inns of court, the merchant adventurers, the militant 'companies' of English condottieri who returning home help to make the word 'company' popular among us, the trading companies, the companies that become colonies, the companies that make war, the friendly societies, the trade unions, the clubs, the group that meets at Lloyd's Coffee-house, the group that becomes the Stock Exchange, and so on even to the one-man-company, the Standard Oil Trust and the South Australian statutes for communistic villages. The English historian would have a wealth of group-life to survey richer even than that which has come under Dr Gierke's eye, though he would not have to tell of the peculiarly interesting civic group which hardly knows whether it is a municipal corporation or a sovereign republic. And then we imagine our historian turning to inquire how Englishmen have conceived their groups: by what thoughts they have striven to distinguish and to reconcile the manyness of the members and the oneness of the body. The borough of the later middle ages he might well regard with Dr Gierke as a central node in the long story. Into it and out from it run most of the great threads of development, economic and theoretical. The borough stretches one hand back to the village community and the other forward to freely formed companies of all sorts and kinds. And this Dr Gierke sets before us as the point at which the unity of the group is first abstracted by thought and law from the plurality, so that 'the borough' can stand out in contrast to the sum of existing burgesses as another person, but still as a person in whom they are organized and embodied.

To his medieval Germans Dr Gierke attributes sound and wholesome thoughts, and in particular a deep sense of the organic character of all permanent groups great and small. Not that, according to him, their thoughts were sharply defined: indeed he has incurred the dissent of some of his fellow Germanists by refusing to carry back to the remotest time the distinction between co-ownership and corporate ownership. In deeply interesting chapters he has described the differentiating process which gives us these two ideas. That process was prospering in the German towns when the catastrophe occurred. When German law was called upon to meet the alien intruder, it had reached 'the stage of abstraction,' but not 'the stage of reflection.' It had its *Körperschaftsbegriff*, but no *Korporationstheorie*. It could co-ordinate Man and Community as equally real persons of different kinds; but it had never turned round to ask itself what it was doing. And so down it went before the disciplined enemy: before the theory which Italian legists and decretists had been drilling.

Then in another volume we have the history of this theory. We should misrepresent our author if, without qualification, we spoke of Italian science as the enemy. All technical merits were on its side; it was a model for consequent thinking. Still, if it did good, it did harm. Its sacred texts were the law of an unassociative people. Roman jurisprudence, starting with a strict severance of *ius publicum* from *ius privatum*, had found its highest development in 'an absolutistic public law and an individualistic private law.' Titius and the State, these the Roman lawyers understood, and out of them and a little fiction the legal universe could be constructed. The theory of corporations which derives from this source may run (and this is perhaps its straightest course) into princely absolutism, or it may take a turn towards mere collectivism (which in this context is another name for individualism); but for the thought of the living group it can find no place; it is condemned to be 'atomistic' and 'mechanical.' For the modern German 'Fellowship Theory' remained the task of recovering and revivifying 'the organic idea' and giving to it a scientific form.

It is not easy for an Englishman to throw his heart or even his mind into such matters as these, and therefore it may not be easy for some readers of this book at once to catch the point of

all Dr Gierke's remarks about the personality of States and Corporations. If we asked why this is so, the answer would be a long
story which has never yet been duly told. However, its main
theme can be indicated by one short phrase which is at this
moment a focus of American politics: namely, 'Corporations and
Trusts.' That puts the tale into three words. For the last
four centuries Englishmen have been able to say, 'Allow us our
Trusts, and the law and theory of corporations may indeed be
important, but it will not prevent us from forming and maintaining
permanent groups of the most various kinds: groups that, behind
a screen of trustees, will live happily enough, even from century
to century, glorying in their unincorporatedness. If Pope Innocent
and Roman forces guard the front stairs, we shall walk up the
back.' From the age when, among countless other unchartered
fellowships, the Inns of Court were taking shape, to the age, when
monopolizing trusts set America ablaze, our law of corporations
has only been a part of our *Genossenschaftsrecht*, and not perhaps
the most important part[1]. We will mention but one example.
If we speak the speech of daily life, we shall say that in this
country for some time past a large amount of wealth has 'belonged' to religious 'bodies' other than the established church,
and we should have thought our religious liberty shamefully imperfect had our law prevented this arrangement. But until very
lately our 'corporation concept' has not stood at the disposal of
Nonconformity, and even now little use is made of it in this
quarter: for our 'trust concept' has been so serviceable. Behind
the screen of trustees and concealed from the direct scrutiny of
legal theories, all manner of groups can flourish: Lincoln's Inn
or Lloyd's[2] or the Stock Exchange or the Jockey Club, a whole
presbyterian system, or even the Church of Rome with the Pope
at its head. But, if we are to visit a land where Roman law has

---

[1] See the Stat. of (1531—2) 23 Hen. VIII., c. 10 : lands are already being held to the
use of unincorporated 'guilds, fraternities, comminalities, companies or brotherheads,'
and this on so large a scale that King Henry, as supreme landlord, must interfere.
Happily the lawyers of a later time antedated by a few years King Henry's dislike
of 'superstition,' and therefore could give to this repressive statute a scope far narrower
than that which its royal author assuredly intended. The important case is *Porter's
Case*, 1 Coke's Reports, 22 b.

[2] At length incorporated in 1871: see F. Martin, History of Lloyd's, pp. 356—7, a
highly interesting book.

been 'received,' we must leave this great loose 'trust concept' at the Custom House, and must not for a moment suppose that a meagre *fideicommissum* will serve in its stead.   Then we shall understand how vitally important to a nation—socially, politically, religiously important—its Theory of Corporations might be.

If it be our task legally to construct and maintain comfortable homes wherein organic groups can live and enjoy whatever 'liberty of association' the Prince will concede to them, a little, but only a little, can be done by means of the Romanist's co-ownership (*condominium*, *Miteigentum*) and the Romanist's partnership (*societas*, *Gesellschaft*).   They are, so we are taught, intensely individualistic categories: even more individualistic than are the parallel categories of English law, for there is no 'jointness' (*Gesammthandtschaft*) in them.   If then our Prince keeps the *universitas*, the corporate form, safe under lock and key, our task is that of building without mortar.   But to keep the *universitas* safe under lock and key was just what the received theory enabled the Prince to do.   His right to suppress *collegia illicita* was supplemented by the metaphysical doctrine that, from the very nature of the case, 'artificial personality' must needs be the creature of sovereign power.   At this point a decisive word was said by Innocent IV.   One outspoken legist reckoned as the fifty-ninth of the sixty-seven prerogatives of the Emperor that he, and only he, makes fictions: 'Solus princeps fingit quod in rei veritate non est[1].'   Thus 'the Fiction Theory' leads us into what is known to our neighbours as 'the Concession Theory.'   The corporation is, and must be, the creature of the State.   Into its nostrils the State must breathe the breath of a fictitious life, for otherwise it would be no animated body but individualistic dust.

Long ago English lawyers received the Concession Theory from the canonists.   Bred in the free fellowship of unchartered Inns, they were the very men to swallow it whole.   Blackstone could even boast that the law of England went beyond 'the civil law' in its strict adhesion to this theory[2]; and he was right, for the civilians of his day generally admitted that, though in principle the State's consent to the erection of a corporation was absolutely necessary, still there were Roman texts which might be deemed

[1] Lucas de Penna, cited by Gierke, Genossenschaftsrecht, III. 371.
[2] Comment. I. 472.

to have given that consent in advance and in general terms for the benefit of corporations of certain innocuous kinds. But then, what for the civilians was a question of life and death was often in England a question of mere convenience and expense, so wide was that blessed back stair. The trust deed might be long; the lawyer's bill might be longer; new trustees would be wanted from time to time; and now and again an awkward obstacle would require ingenious evasion; but the organized group could live and prosper, and be all the more autonomous because it fell under no solemn legal rubric. Lawyers could even say that the common law reckoned it a crime for men 'to presume to act as a corporation'; but as those lawyers were members of the Inns of Court, we should hardly need other proof—there is plenty to be had—that the commission of this crime (if crime it were) was both very difficult and wholly needless[1]. Finally it became apparent that, unless statute law stood in the way, even a large company trading with a joint-stock, with vendible shares and a handsome measure of 'limited liability' could be constructed by means of a trust deed without any incorporation[2].

Nowhere has the Concession Theory been proclaimed more loudly, more frequently, more absolutely, than in America; nowhere has more lip-service been done to the Fieschi. Ignorant men on board the 'Mayflower' may have thought that, in the presence of God and of one another, they could covenant and combine themselves together into 'a civil body politic[3].' Their descendants know better. A classical definition has taught that 'a Corporation is a Franchise,' and a franchise is a portion of the State's power in the hands of a subject[4]. A Sovereign People

---

[1] Lindley, Company Law, Bk. I., ch. 5, sect. I. In the curious case of *Lloyd* v. *Loaring*, 6 Ves. 773, Lord Eldon had before him a lodge of Freemasons which had made an imprudent display of what a Realist would call its corporate character. His lordship's indignation was checked by the thought that 'Mr Worseley's silver cup' belonged to 'the Middle Temple.'

[2] The directors are bound to give notice to every one who gives credit that he has nothing to look to beyond the subscribed fund, and that no person will be personally liable to him. As to these 'attempts to limit liability,' see Lindley, Company Law, Bk. II., ch. 6, sec. 2.

[3] The Mayflower Compact can be found, among other places, in Macdonald, Select Charters, p. 33.

[4] Kent, Comment. Lect. 33: 'A corporation is a franchise possessed by one or more individuals, who subsist as a body politic under a special denomination, and are vested,

has loved to deck itself in the purple of the Byzantine Basileus and the triple crown of the Roman Pontiff. But the picture has another side. Those 'Trusts' that convulsed America were assuredly organized bodies which acted as units, and if ever a *Gesammtwille* was displayed in this world, assuredly they displayed it: but some of them were not corporations[1]. A reader of American trust deeds may well find himself asking what, beyond a few highly technical advantages, an incorporating act could bestow. No doubt, if the State mutters some mystical words there takes place in the insensible substance of the group, some change of which lawyers must say all that a Roman or Romanesque orthodoxy exacts; but to the lay eyes of debtors and creditors, brokers and jobbers, all sensible accidents seem much what they were. Already in 1694 in the stock and share lists that John Houghton was publishing the current prices of 'actions' in unincorporated bodies were placed alongside the prices of the stocks of chartered corporations[2]. Certainly it will be curious, but it will not be inexplicable, if when the Concession Theory has perished in other lands it still lurks and lingers in England or among men of English race. Probably our foreign critics would not suffer us to say that it does us no harm; but they would confess that the harm which it does is neither very grave nor very obvious. A certain half-heartedness in our treatment of unincorporate groups, whose personality we will not frankly recognize while we make fairly adequate provision for their continuous life, is the offence against jurisprudence with which we might most fairly be charged, and it is an offence which tends to disappear now that groups of many kinds, cricket clubs, religious societies, scientific societies, and so forth, are slowly taking advantage of that offer of legal corporateness which has been open to them for nearly forty years[3] and are discovering that it is well to be regarded as persons.

We can therefore imagine a German Realist bringing to bear

---

by the policy of the law, with the capacity of perpetual succession, and of acting in several respects, however numerous the association may be, as a single individual.'

[1] Of late—so we understand on this side of the sea—some of the largest combinations of capitalists have taken corporate form under the laws of New Jersey.

[2] Houghton, A Collection for the Improvement of Trade. See especially No. 98 ff. where the author gives an account of joint-stock enterprise.

[3] Companies Act, 1862, sec. 6.

upon English law some such criticism as the following :—'There is much in your history that we can envy, much in your free and easy formation of groups that we can admire. That great 'trust concept' of yours stood you in good stead when the days were evil: when your Hobbes, for example, was instituting an un-savoury comparison between corporations and ascarides[1], when your Archbishop Laud (an absolutist if ever there was one) brought Corporation Theory to smash a Puritan Trust[2], and two years afterwards his friend Bishop Montague was bold enough to call the king's attention to the shamelessly unincorporate character of Lincoln's Inn[3]. And your thoroughly un-Roman 'trust concept' is interesting to us. We have seen the like of it in very ancient Lombard charters[4]; and, by the way, it was Georg Beseler who suggested to the present Chief Justice of Massachusetts the quarter in which the origin of your trusts might be found[5]. Also the connexion between trust and group takes back our thoughts all the way to the Lex Salica where the *trustis* is a group of comrades. Then, again, we can well understand that English lawyers were concerned to deny, at least in words, the personality of what you call an 'unincorporate body'—a term which seems to us to make for truth, but also for self-contradiction. An open breach with Innocentian orthodoxy and cosmopolitan enlightenment seemed impossible, and so you maintained that the unincorporate body could, as we should say, be 'construed' as a mere sum of in-dividuals bound only by co-ownership and agreement. But you must excuse us for doubting whether you have pressed this theory to its logical conclusion. For example, we feel bound to ask whether, when a man is elected to one of your clubs (and you have been great makers of clubs), the existing members execute an assignment to him of a share in the club-house and its furniture,

---

[1] Leviathan, II. 29 (Works, ed. Molesworth, vol. III., p. 321): 'like worms in the entrails of a natural man.'

[2] For this case of the Feoffees of Impropriations, see Gardiner, Hist. of England, ann. 1633, vol. VII., 258.

[3] Black Book of Lincoln's Inn, vol. II., p. 333, ann. 1635.

[4] Schultze, Die Lombardische Treuhand, Breslau, 1895.

[5] O. W. Holmes, Law Quart. Rev. I. 163: 'The feoffee to uses of the early English law corresponds point by point to the Salman of the early German law as described by Beseler fifty years ago.'

M.   *c*

and whether, when he resigns, he executes a release to the continuing members. If that be not so, and we fancy that it is not,
election to, and resignation of, membership in 'unincorporate
bodies' should appear somewhat prominently in your books
among the modes in which rights are acquired and lost, and then
it would be plain enough that, beside a *Korporationstheorie* of
Italian origin, you have a *Körperschaftsbegriff* of your own: an
idea of a 'bodiliness' which is not the effect of the State's fiat.
Then why, we should like to know, did your legislature lately
impose a tax on the property of 'unincorporate bodies' as well
as on that of corporate bodies? When the property of individuals
and of corporations was already taxed, was there still property
that escaped taxation[1]? And what can your legislature mean
when it says that in Acts of Parliament (unless a contrary in-
tention appears) the word 'person' is to include 'any body of
persons corporate or unincorporate[2]'? If once we are allowed
to see personality wherever we see bodiliness, the victory of
Realism is secure, though an old superstition may die very hard.
Some day the historian may have to tell you that the really
fictitious fiction of English law was, not that its corporation was
a person, but that its unincorporate body was no person, or (as
you so suggestively say) was nobody. There are many other
questions that we should like to ask of you. Why, for instance,
are free-born and commercially-minded Englishmen prohibited by
statute from trading in large partnerships[3]? Is it not because your
good sense and experience have taught you that, do what you will
and say what you will, the large trading group will assuredly
display, as it does in America, the phenomena of corporateness
and therefore ought to stand under the law for corporations? And
do you not think that some part at least of the appalling mess—
forgive us—the appalling mess that you made of your local
government was due to a bad and foreign theory which, coupling
corporateness with princely 'privilege,' refused to recognize and
foster into vigour the bodiliness that was immanent in every

---

[1] Customs and Inland Revenue Act, 1885, sec. 11: 'Whereas certain property, by
reason of the same belonging to or being vested in bodies corporate or unincorporate,
escapes liability to probate, legacy, or succession duty.'

[2] Interpretation Act, 1889, sec. 19.

[3] Companies Act, 1862, sec. 4.

English township, in every rural *Gemeinde*? Even our theory-ridden Romanists were not guilty of that fatal blunder which you are now endeavouring tardily to repair by the invention of Parish Councils and from which some of your less pedantic kinsmen in the colonies kept themselves free when they suffered 'the New England town' to develop its inherent corporateness[1].'

To say these few words of our own law has seemed advisable in order that foreign controversies over the nature and origin of a corporation's or a State's personality may be the better understood. We may spend one moment more in observing that the English Trust, nurtured though it was within the priviest recesses of Private Law, and educated, if we may so say, in a private school, has played a famous part on the public, the world-wide, and world-historic stage. When by one title and another a ruler-ship over millions of men in the Indies had come to the hands of an English Fellowship, this corporation aggregate was (somewhat unwillingly) compelled by Acts of Parliament to hold this precious thing, this 'object of rights,' this rulership, upon trust for a so-called corporation sole, namely, the British Crown[2]. If at the present time our courts and lawgivers find it needless openly to declare that the colonies are, to use the old phrase, 'bodies corporate and politic in deed, fact and name,' this is because our hard-worked Crown is supposed to hold some property for or 'in right of' the Dominion of Canada and other property for or 'in right of' the Province of Ontario, and a court, after hearing the attorneys-general for these beneficiaries, these communities or commonwealths, will decide how much is held for one, and how much for another. Certainly we work our Trust hard and our Crown harder, and it seems possible that some new thoughts or some renovation of old thoughts about the personality of the organized group might shew us straighter ways to desirable and even necessary ends.

In the days when Queen Elizabeth was our 'Prince,' she did

---

[1] A case of 1497 (Year Book, Trin. 12 Hen. VII., f. 27, pl. 7) marks the beginning of an unhappy story. See Toulmin Smith, The Parish, ed. 2, p. 269.

[2] The theory finds explicit statement in the Act of 1833 (3 & 4 Will. IV., c. 85), preamble : 'And whereas it is expedient that the said territories now under the government of the said Company be continued under such government, but in trust for the Crown of the United Kingdom.'

not forbid her secretary to write in Latin *de Republica Anglorum*, or in English *of the Commonwealth of England*: Prince and Republic were not yet incompatibles. Events that happened in the next century outlawed some words that once were good and lawful, and forced us to make the most that we could of the 'Subject' (or subjectified Object) that lies in the Jewel House at the Tower. Much we could make of it, but not quite all that was needful. Not having always been a punctual payer, the Crown was not always a good borrower, and so our Statute Book taught us to say that the National Debt was owed, not by the Crown, but by 'the Publick'; and this Public looks much like a *Respublica* which, to spare the feelings of 'a certain great personage,' has dropped its first syllable[1]. Those who rely upon 'the faith of the Public' receive their annuities in due season, even if we have no neat theory about the relationship between that 'passive subject,' the Public, which owes them money, and that 'active subject,' the Crown, to which they pay their taxes. Possibly the Crown and the Public are reciprocally trustees for each other; possibly there is not much difference now-a-days between the Public, the State, and the Crown[2], for we have not appraised the full work of the Trust until we are quitting the province of jurisprudence to enter that of political or constitutional theory.

In the course of the eighteenth century it became a parliamentary commonplace that 'all political power is a trust'; and this is now so common a commonplace that we seldom think over it. But it was useful[3]. Applied to the kingly power it gently

---

[1] Already in 1697 (8 & 9 Will. III., c. 20, sec. 20) provision is made for 'the better restoring of the credit of the Nation.' There follow a good many financial transactions between 'the Publick' and the East India Company. For example in 1786 'the Publick stands indebted' to the Company in a sum of four millions and upwards. Stat. 26 Geo. III., c. 62.

[2] Pensions (Colonial Service) Act, 1887, sec. 8: 'The expressions "permanent civil service of the State," "permanent civil service of Her Majesty," and "permanent civil service of the Crown" are hereby declared to have the same meaning.'

[3] At the time when these words were being written one of Her Majesty's Principal Secretaries of State was 'operating' on a magnificent scale with our 'trust concept.' Her Majesty's Government, he was repeatedly saying, is (or are) a trustee (or trustees) for 'the whole Empire.' Already in Locke's Essay on Civil Government (e.g. secs. 142, 149) a good deal is said of trust and breach of trust. As the beneficiary (cestui que trust) who seeks the enforcement of a trust is not necessarily or even normally the trustor or creator of the trust, the introduction of talk about trusts into such work as Locke's serves to conceal some of the weak points in the contractual theory of Government.

relaxed that royal chord in our polity which had been racked
to the snapping point by Divine right and State religion. Much
easier and much more English was it to make the king a trustee
for his people than to call him officer, official, functionary, or even
first magistrate. The suggestion of a duty, enforceable indeed,
but rather as a matter of 'good conscience' than as a matter of
'strict law' was still possible; the supposition that God was the
author of the trust was not excluded, and the idea of trust was
extremely elastic. For of trusts we know many, ranging from
those which confer the widest discretionary powers to those which
are the nudest of nude rights and the driest of legal estates.
Much has happened within and behind that thought of the king's
trusteeship: even a civil death of 'personal government,' an
euthanasia of monarchy. And now in the year 1900 the banished
Commonwealth, purged of regicidal guilt, comes back to us from
Australia and is inlawed by Act of Parliament. Wonderful
conjuring tricks with a crown or a basket (*fiscus*) may yet be
played by deft lawyers, especially by such as are familiar with
trusts for 'unincorporate bodies'; but we may doubt whether
they will much longer be able to suppress from legal records the
thought that was in Bracton's mind when he spoke of the *universitas regni*[1]. 'The crown,' said Coke, 'is an hieroglyphic of
the laws[2].' Such hieroglyphics, personified dignities, abstract
rulerships, subjectified crowns and baskets are (so the realistic
historian would tell us) the natural outcome of a theory which
allows a real personality and a real will only to Jameses and
Charleses and other specimens of the zoological genus *homo* and
yet is compelled to find some expression, however clumsy, for
the continuous life of the State. Names, he might add, we will
not quarrel over. Call it Crown, if you please, in your Statute
Book, and Empire in your newspapers; only do not think, or
even pretend to think, of this mighty being as hieroglyphic or as
persona ficta or as collective name.

In Germany (for we must return) the Concession Theory has
fallen from its high estate; the Romanists are deserting it[3]; it
is yielding before the influence of laws similar to, though less

[1] Bracton, f. 171 b.   [2] *Calvin's Case*, 7 Rep. 11 b.
[3] Windscheid, Pandekten, § 60; Dernburg, Pandekten, § 63; Regelsberger, Pandekten, § 78. See also Mestre, Les Personnes Morales, 197 ff.

splendidly courageous than, our Act of 1862, that 'Magna Carta of co-operative enterprise[1]' which placed corporate form and legal personality within easy reach of 'any seven or more persons associated for any lawful purpose.' It has become difficult to maintain that the State makes corporations in any other sense than that in which the State makes marriages when it declares that people who want to marry can do so by going, and cannot do so without going, to church or registry. The age of corporations created by way of 'privilege' is passing away. The constitutions of some American States prohibit the legislatures from calling corporations into being except by means of general laws[2], and among ourselves the name 'Chartered' has now-a-days a highly specific sense. What is more, many foreign lawyers are coming to the conclusion that in these days of free association, if a group behaves as a corporation, the courts are well-nigh compelled to treat it as such, at least in retrospect. It has purposely, let us say, or negligently omitted the act of registration by which it would have obtained an unquestionable legal personality. Meanwhile it has been doing business in the guise of a corporation, and others have done business with it under the belief that it was what it seemed to be. It is strongly urged that in such cases injustice will be done unless corporateness is treated as matter of fact, and American courts have made large strides in this direction[3]. It seems seriously questionable whether a permanently organized group, for example a trade union, which has property held for it by trustees, should be suffered to escape liability for what would generally be called 'its' unlawful acts and commands by the technical plea that 'it' has no existence 'in the eye of the law[4].' Spectacles are to be had in Germany which, so it is said, enable the law to see personality wherever there is bodiliness, and a time seems at hand when the idea of 'particular creation' will be as antiquated in Corporation Law as it is in Zoology. Whether we like it or no, the Concession Theory has notice to quit, and may carry the whole Fiction Theory with it.

[1] Palmer, Company Law, p. 1.

[2] Morawetz, Private Corporations, § 9 ff.; Dillon, Municipal Corporations, § 45.

[3] For the treatment of these 'de facto corporations' see Taylor, Private Corporations, § 145 ff.; Morawetz, § 735 ff.

[4] This was written some months before Mr Justice Farwell issued an injunction against a Trade Union (*Times*, 6 Sept. 1900). Of this matter we are likely to hear more.

The delicts, or torts and crimes, of corporations have naturally been one burning point of the prolonged debate. To serious minds there is something repulsive in the attribution of fraud or the like to the mindless *persona ficta*. The law would set a bad example if its fictions were fraudulent. But despite some fairly clear words in the Digest, and despite the high authority of the great Innocentius, the practice of holding communities liable for delict was, so Dr Gierke says, far too deeply rooted in the Germanic world to be eradicated. Even Savigny could not permanently prevail when the day of railway collisions had come. And so in England we may see the speculative doubt obtruding itself from time to time, but only to be smothered under the weight of accumulating precedents, while out in America the old sword of *Quo warranto*, forged for the recovery of royal rights from feudal barons, is descending upon the heads of joint-stock companies with monopolizing tendencies. When an American judge wields that sword and dissolves a corporation, he is performing no such act of discretionary administration as Savigny would have permitted; he uses the language of penal justice; he may even say that he passes sentence of death, and will expend moral indignation on the culprit that stands before him[1].

It is worthy of remark, however, that in this region Englishmen have been able to slur a question which elsewhere assumes great importance: namely, whether a corporation 'itself' can do unlawful, or indeed any acts. We have been helped over a difficulty by the extremely wide rule of employers' liability which prevails among us and towards which some of our neighbours have cast wistful eyes. A servant of Styles acting within the scope of his employment does a wrong; we hold Styles liable. We substitute a corporation for Styles, and then this corporation is liable. This being so, we can say that 'of course' the corporation would be liable if the wrongful act were done or commanded by its directorate or by its members in general meeting. It matters little whether we affirm or deny that in this case the act would be that of the corporation 'itself,' for if it were not this, it could still be represented as the act of an agent or servant done within

[1] For example see the solemn words of Finch, J. in *People* v. *North River Sugar Refining Co.*, 1890 ; Jer. Smith, Select Cases on Private Corporations, II. 944.

the scope of his employment. Whether that picture of the assembled members or directors as agents or servants of an Un-knowable Somewhat, which cannot have appointed or selected them, is a life-like picture we need hardly ask: the conclusion is foregone. Such is our happy state. But where Roman law has been received the primary rule is that a master has not to answer for acts that he has not commanded, at all events if he has shewn no negligence in his choice of a servant. If then the directorate of a company has done wrong, for example has published a libel, much may depend on the manner in which the case is envisaged. If we say that the corporation itself has acted by its organs, as a man acts by brain and hand, then the corporation is liable; but the result may be very different if we reduce the directors to the level of servants or agents. Those therefore who have been striving for the 'organic idea' have not been fighting for a mere phrase; and now the term 'Organ' stands in the Civil Code of Germany. That is no small triumph of Realism[1].

That the theory of the Group Person and the Group Will has a long struggle before it if it is ever to dominate the jurisprudence of the world would be admitted even by its champions. We have just been touching the confines of a region in which lies the stronghold of an opposing force. That ancient saying—its sub-stance is as old as Johannes Andreae—which bids the body politic fear no pains in another world represents profound beliefs. Not-withstanding all that we may say of 'national sins' and 'the national conscience' and the like, a tacit inference is drawn from immunity (real or supposed) to impeccability, and, until they are convinced that corporations and States can sin, many people will refuse to admit that a corporation or State is a thoroughly real person with a real will. We cannot wait for eschatology to say its last word, but even in quarters where jurisprudence is more at its ease there are many contestable points of which we must not speak. However, the general character of the debate is worthy of observation. The Realist's cause would be described by those who are forwarding it as an endeavour to give scientific precision and legal operation to thoughts which are in all modern minds and which are always displaying themselves especially in the political

[1] Bürgerliches Gesetzbuch, § 32. The term has for some time past been used in German laws and by German courts. Gierke, Genossenschaftstheorie, p. 614.

field. We might be told to read the leading article in to-day's paper and observe the ideas with which the writer 'operates': the will of the nation, the mind of the legislature, the settled policy of one State, the ambitious designs of another: the praise and blame that are awarded to group-units of all sorts and kinds. We might be asked to count the lines that our journalist can write without talking of organization. We might be asked to look at our age's criticism of the political theories and political projects of its immediate predecessor and to weigh those charges of abstract individualism, atomism and macadamization that are currently made. We might be asked whether the British Empire has not yet revolted against a Sovereign that was merely Many (a Sovereign Number as Austin said) and in no sense really One, and whether 'the People' that sues and prosecutes in American courts is a collective name for some living men and a name whose meaning changes at every minute. We might be referred to modern philosophers: to the social tissue of one and the general will, which is the real will, of another. Then perhaps we might fairly be charged with entertaining a deep suspicion that all this is metaphor: apt perhaps and useful, but essentially like the personification of the ocean and the ship, the storm and the stormy petrel. But we, the Realist would say, mean business with our Group Person, and severe legal logic. We take him into the law courts and markets and say that he stands the wear and tear of forensic and commercial life. If we see him as the State in an exalted sphere where his form might be mistaken for a cloud of rhetoric or mysticism, we see him also in humble quarters, and there we can apprehend and examine and even vivisect him. For example, we are obliged to ask precise questions concerning the inferior limit of group-life. Where does it disappear? That is no easy question, for the German Partnership goes near to disengaging a group-will from the several wills of the several partners; but on the whole we hold, and can give detailed reasons for holding, that in this quarter the line falls between our partnership and our joint-stock company.

By those who have neither leisure nor inclination to understand competing theories of German partnerships, German companies and German communes, it may none the less be allowed that theories of the State and theories of the Corporation must be closely connected. The individualism which dissolves the company into its component shareholders is not likely to stop at that exploit, and the State's possession of a real will is insecure if no other groups may have wills of their own.   Hence the value of a theory which at all events endeavours to cover the whole ground. To say more would be to say much more; and enough, it is hoped, has been said to enable a reader of the following pages to understand the place that they hold in an historical and doctrinal exposition of 'German Fellowship Right.'   We have, it must be supposed, made a brief survey of the history from first to last of German groups; then we have turned back to explore the thoughts that were implicit in the Group Law of medieval Germany; then, having reached the eve of the Reception, we have investigated the genesis and adventures of that learned theory of Corporations which is about to cross the Alps; we have been among Greek philosophers, Roman lawyers, Christian fathers, and have spent a long time in Italy with the canonists and legists.   We are now on the point of returning to the Germany of the sixteenth century to watch the Reception of this theory and the good and ill that follow, when Dr Gierke interpolates the following brief, but surely valuable, account of the political (or rather 'publicistic') theories of the Middle Age: theories which, as he remarks, have numerous points of contact with the main theme of his book.

The reader need not fear that he will here encounter much that he could call technical jurisprudence.   Indeed so much as has been said in this Introduction touching Corporation Law and German Fellowships has been intended to explain rather the context than the text of an excerpted chapter.   It will be seen, however, that while Dr Gierke is careful of those matters to which any historian of political theory would attend—for instance, the growth of definitely monarchical and definitely democratic doctrines—an acute accent, which some English readers might not have anticipated, falls upon the manner in which States, rulers and peoples were conceived or pictured when theorists made them the 'subjects' of powers, rights and duties.   The failure of medieval theorists to grasp the personality of the State appears as a central defect whence in later times evil consequences are likely to issue.   It will be seen that the stream of political theory when it debouches from the defile of the Middle Age into the sun-lit plain is flowing in a direction which, albeit destined and explicable, is not regarded by our author as ultimate. However much the river may be gaining in strength and depth and lucidity as it sweeps onwards towards the Leviathan and the Contrat Social, its fated course runs for some centuries away from organization and towards mechanical construction, away from biology and towards dynamics, away from corporateness and towards contractual obligation, away (it may be added) from Germanic lands and towards the Eternal City. It will be gathered also that the set of thoughts about Law and Sovereignty into which Englishmen were lectured by John Austin appears to Dr Gierke as a past stage. For him Sovereignty is an attribute, not of some part of the State, but of the *Gesammtperson*, the whole organized community. For him it is as impossible to make the State logically prior to Law (*Recht*) as to make Law logically prior to the State, since each exists in, for and by the other. Of these doctrines nothing must here be said, only let us remember that if the *Rechtsstaatsidee*, much discussed in Germany, seems to us unfamiliar and obscure, that may be because we have no practical experience of a *Polizeistaat* or *Beamtenstaat*. Some friendly critics would say that in the past we could afford to accept speciously logical but brittle theories because we knew that they would never be subjected to serious strains. Some would warn us that in the future the less we say about a supralegal, suprajural plenitude of power concentrated in a single point at Westminster— concentrated in one single organ of an increasingly complex commonwealth—the better for that commonwealth may be the days that are coming.

III.

The task of translating into English the work of a German lawyer can never be perfectly straightforward. To take the most obvious instance, his *Recht* is never quite our *Right* or quite our *Law*. I have tried to avoid terms which are not current in England. For this reason I have often written *political* when I would gladly have written *publicistic*. On the other hand I could not represent our author's theory without using the term *Subject* in the manner in which it is used by German jurists and publicists[1]. For *nature-rightly* an apology may be due, but there was a pressing

---

[1] See above p. xx., note 1.

need for some such adjective. A doctrine may be *naturrechtlich*, though it is not a doctrine of Natural Law nor even a doctrine about Natural Law, and a long periphrasis would probably say more or less than Dr Gierke intended[1]. It will be seen that in his historical scheme a large part is played by the contrast between genuinely medieval thought and 'antique-modern' ideas. These are ideas which proceeding from Classical Antiquity are becoming modern in their transit through the Middle Ages, but not without entering into combination with medieval elements. I could call them by no other name than that which Dr Gierke has given to them : they must be 'antique-modern.' I would not if I could induce the reader to forget that he has before him the work not only of a German jurist but of a leader among Germanists.

Some of the treatises to which Dr Gierke refers in his notes have been re-edited since his book was published (1881). The main event of this kind is, so I believe, the publication in the Monumenta Germaniae of the numerous pamphlets which were evoked by the struggle over the Investitures and which set before us the papal and imperial theories of Public Law in the first stage of their formation[2]. I have thought it best to repeat Dr Gierke's references as I found them and not to attempt the perilous task of substituting others. Among the new materials is the highly interesting and astonishingly anti-papal treatise of an anonymous canon of York, apparently of Norman birth, who about the year 1100 was warmly taking our king's side in the dispute about Investitures and was writing sentences that Marsiglio and Wyclif would not have disowned. But of him we may read in Böhmer's valuable and easily accessible history of Church and State in England and Normandy[3]. A few notes about some English publicists I might have been tempted to add, had I not made this translation in a land where

---

[1] When, for example, Dr Brunner (v. Holtzendorff, Encyklopädie, ed. 5, p. 347) mentioned 'die naturrechtlichen Theorien Benthams und Austins über den radikalen Beruf des Gesetzgebers' he was not accusing Bentham and Austin of believing in what they would have consented to call Natural Law. Austin's projected science of General Jurisprudence which was to bring to light 'necessary' principles (p. 1108) would apparently have been very like a system of *Naturrecht*.

[2] Libelli de lite imperatorum et pontificum, 3 vols., 1891—2—7. See Fisher, The Medieval Empire, II. 57.

[3] Böhmer, Kirche und Staat in England und in der Normandie, Leipzig, 1899, p. 177 ff.

books of any kind are very rare. Some references to Richard Fitz Ralph, to the Song of Lewes, to Sir John Fortescue and the English law-books might have been inserted. But the works of Mr Poole[1], Mr Kingsford[2] and Mr Plummer[3] are likely to be in the hands of every English student of medieval politics; to John of Salisbury and William of Ockham—who belong rather to the World-State than to England—Dr Gierke seems to have done ample justice; I know of little, if anything, that would tend to impair the validity of his generalizations[4]; and my endeavour has been to obtain for him the hearing to which he is justly entitled. I hope that I may induce some students of medieval and modern history, law and political theory to make themselves acquainted with his books[5].

[1] A large part of the treatise of Fitz Ralph (Armachanus) is to be found in Mr R. L. Poole's edition of Joh. Wycliffe, De dominio divino, Wyclif Society, 1890. See also Mr Poole's Illustrations of the History of Medieval Thought, 1884.

[2] Kingsford, The Song of Lewes, 1890.

[3] Plummer, Fortescue's Governance of England, 1885. An English reader will hardly need to be told that Dr Creighton's History of the Papacy will introduce him to the practical aims and projects of some of the medieval publicists. Mr Jenks's Law and Politics in the Middle Ages (1898) will also deserve his attention.

[4] In England the idea of a World-State which is governed by the Emperor appears chiefly in the much modified form of a notion that somehow or another the king of England either is an Emperor or will do instead of an Emperor. Henry I. was Gloriosus Caesar Henricus: Leg. Hen. Prim. pref. Bracton, f. 5 b; Bracton and Azo (Seld. Soc.), p. 57. Rishanger, Chron. et Ann. (Rolls Ser.), p. 255 : Speech of the bishop of Byblos : dominus Rex hic censetur imperator. Rot. Parl. III. 343: Richard II. is 'entier Emperour de son Roialme.' On the other side stands that strange book the Mirror of Justices (Seld. Soc.), pp. xxxiv., 195.

[5] Dr Gierke's notes are foot-notes. I thought that I should consult the tastes of English readers by placing them at the end of the book. The marginal catch-words are mine, but the summary of the argument is Dr Gierke's. I owe my thanks for many valuable suggestions to Mr J. N. Figgis whose essays on the Divine Right of Kings (1896) and on Politics at the Council of Constance (Trans. Roy. Hist. Soc. N. S. XIII. 103) will be known to students. Last year, being sent from England, I was encouraged to undertake this translation by Professor Henry Sidgwick. What encouragement was like when it came from him his pupils are now sorrowfully remembering.

ANALYTICAL SUMMARY.

I. *The Evolution of Political Theory.*

Development of a Political Theory (p. 1). It becomes a Philosophy of State and Law (1). Cooperation of the various Sciences (1). Unity and generality of the doctrine beneath all controversies (2). Combination into a system of elements which came from various quarters (2). The various methods mutually complete each other (3). Theologico-philosophical Speculation, political pamphleteering, and professional Jurisprudence (3). The Medieval Theory of State and Society is a stream which flows in a single bed (3). Relation of Medieval to Antique-Modern Thought (3). The system of the Medieval Spirit (4). Reception of the antique ideas of State and Law (4). Genesis of the specifically modern ideas (4). Growth of an antique-modern kernel in the shell of the medieval system (4). Stages in the work of dissolution and reconstruction (5). Relation of Political Theory to the Romano-Canonical Theory of Corporations (6).

II. *Macrocosm and Microcosm.*

The Political Thought of the Middle Age starts from the Whole but attributes intrinsic value to every partial whole down to the individual (7). Hence its theocratic and spiritualistic traits (7). Idea of the divinely-willed Harmony of the Universe (7). The Universe as Macrocosm and every partial whole as Microcosm (8). The first principles of the Doctrine of Human Society must be borrowed from the idea of the divinely-organized Universe (8).

III. *Unity in Church and State.*

The Principle of Unity (9). It is the constitutive principle of the Universe (9). Therefore it must be valid in every Partial Whole (9). Unity as the source and goal of Plurality (9). The *Ordinatio ad unum* an all-pervading principle (9). Application thereof to Human Society (9). Wider and narrower social units (10).

The postulate of an external unity of All Mankind (10). Mankind as a mystical body, *Ecclesia universalis, Respublica generis humani* (10). The divinely appointed severance of this body into two Orders of Life, the Spiritual and the Temporal (10). Each of these Orders a separate external realm (11). This dualism cannot be final, but must find recon ciliation in some higher unity (11).

The clerical party sees the solution in the Sovereignty of the Spiritual Power (11). The Principle of Unity is the philosophic foundation of the hierarchical theory which is developed from the time of Gregory VII. onward (11). The Church is the true Cosmopolis (11). The Pope is its earthly Head (12). The divinely appointed separation of the two Powers extends only to their use (12). The Temporal Power possesses a divine sanction and mandate only through the mediation of the Church (12). Unholy origin of the State (12). It needs hallowing by ecclesi astical authority (13). 'Institutio' of the Realm by the Priesthood (13) The Temporal Order remains a subservient part of the Ecclesiastical Order and a means for ecclesiastical ends (13). *Leges* and *Canones* (13). Duty of obeying the Church (13). Worldly Rulership as ecclesiastical office (13). Papal claims to Overlordship above the Emperor and other independent wielders of worldly power (13). The Theory of the Two Swords (13) The Pope has *utrumque gladium* but demises the use of the Temporal Sword (14). Application of the feudal idea (14). The Temporal Sword to be wielded in the service and at the instance of the Church (14). The Pope's right of supervision by virtue of the Spiritual Sword (14). Right and duty of the Pope in certain cases to make a direct use of the Temporal Sword (14). *Translatio imperii* (14). Institution of Emperors and Kings (14). Guardianship of the Realm when it is vacant or the Ruler is neglectful (15). Jurisdiction over Emperors and Kings, Protection of Peoples against Tyranny, Deposition of Rulers and Liberation of Subjects (15). All these claims are the direct outcome of *ius divinum* (15). Positive Law cannot derogate from them (15).

The champions of the State but very rarely deduce a Sovereignty of State over Church from the Principle of Unity (16). Reminiscences of an older condition of affairs (16). Ockham (16). Marsilius of Padua (16). In general the doctrine of two co-ordinate Powers each with a divinely appointed sphere is maintained (16). Battle for the independence of Temporal Law (16). And for the maxim *Imperium immediate a Deo* (17). Particular claims of the Church Party resisted (17). Concession of an equal Sovereignty and Independence to the Spiritual Sword (17). Superior rank allowed to the Church (17). Twofold attempt to resolve the duality in a higher unity (17). Christ's invisible Headship a sufficient presentment of Unity (17). An internal Unity of the two Orders of Life resulting from their intimate connexion and mutual support (17). Reciprocal completion of the two Powers in the production of a single Life (17). Curious theory of a law of necessity permitting one of the two Powers to assume functions that are not its own (18).

The Principle of Unity within Church and State respectively (18). In the Church (18). The Church as a single visible Polity (19). Reaction against the tendency to make a State of the Church (19). Unity in the Temporal Sphere (19). Necessity and divine origin of the World-State (19). The *imperium mundi* of the Romano-German Emperor (20). Controversy as to possible exemptions from the Empire (20). Universality of the Empire denied in principle (20).

The visible Unity postulated in Church and State does not extend beyond those matters which lie within the purpose that is common to All Mankind (20). Organically Articulated Structure of Human Society (21). The units that mediate between the Community of Mankind and the Individual (21). Attempt to establish general schemes of these intermediate units: village, city, kingdom etc. (21). Appearance of a centralizing tendency in Church and State which is opposed to this federalistic system (21).

IV. *The Idea of Organization.*

Comparison of Mankind and every smaller group to a body informed by a soul (22). Mankind as a *Corpus Mysticum* (22). Heads of this Body (22). Church and State as soul and body (22). Inferences drawn from this picture resisted (23). Nicholas of Cues on the Body of Mankind (23). The ecclesiastical or temporal group as a *Corpus mysticum* (24). The *Corpus morale et politicum* of Engelbert of Volkersdorf (24).

The comparison descending to particulars (24). Anthropomorphic conceits of John of Salisbury (24). Of Aquinas and others in relation to the Church (25). Ptolemy of Lucca (25). Aegidius Colonna (25). Engelbert of Volkersdorf (26). Marsilius of Padua (26). Ockham (27). Later writers (27). Nicholas of Cues (27).

Derivation of other ideas from the fundamental idea of the Social Organism (27). Idea of Membership (27). Differentiation and grouping of members (28). Idea of Mediate Articulation (28). Idea of Organization (28). Idea of Function (28). Idea of an Organ (28). Idea of the governing part as the Living Principle (28). Idea of the natural growth of social bodies is suppressed by the idea of Creation (29).

As in Antiquity, so in the Middle Age, the idea of Organization fails to issue in the legal concept of the Personality of the unified Whole (29). Just for this reason it can conceal, but cannot hinder, the progress of the atomistic and mechanical mode of constructing the State (30).

V. *The Idea of Monarchy.*

God as Monarch of the Universe and therefore of the spiritual and temporal Community of Mankind (30). As an Institution, all Rulership proceeds from God (30). But from Him proceed also the office and mandate of every particular wielder of earthly power (31). All power immediately or mediately demised by God (31). Since every Partial Whole should be like the Universal Whole, a monarchical constitution of Church and State seems self-evident (31). The medieval Publicist's preference for Monarchy (31). Divine institution of Monarchy in the Church (32). Divine institution of Monarchy in the Empire (32). In every smaller body Monarchy is normal (32). Dissolution of these thoughts under the influence of Antiquity (32). Relative rightfulness of Republican Constitutions (32). Attacks on the divine origin of Monarchy in Church and State (33). Preference for Republics among the Humanists (33). Rejection of inferences favourable to Monarchy that are drawn from the Principle of Unity (33).

The Doctrine of the Monarch's position (33). The genuinely Medieval Doctrine, in which the Germanic idea of Lordship lives on but is deepened by Christianity, sees in every Lordship an Office proceeding from God (33). Exaltation of the Ruler's person (33). But energetic development of the official character of Rulership (34). Reciprocal Rights and Duties of Ruler and Community (34). All duty of obedience conditioned by the rightfulness of the command (35). The Doctrine of Active Resistance (35). Development of the idea of the Ruler's Sovereignty beside that of the Ruler's Office (35). The *plenitudo potestatis* of the Pope (36). Struggle between this notion and that of *potestas limitata* (36). The *plenitudo potestatis* of the Emperor (36). Opposition (36). Starting points of a doctrine limiting monarchical rights (37).

VI. *The Idea of Popular Sovereignty.*

The medieval notion of the active and aboriginal Rights of the Community (37). Conflict over the quality and scope of these Rights (37). Original influence of the Germanic idea of Fellowship (37). Transmutation under the influence of antique elements (37). Issue in the direction of Popular Sovereignty (38). Combinations of People's Sovereignty with Ruler's Sovereignty (38).

1. In the Temporal Sphere: Rights of the Community (38). The People's Will the source of Lordship (38). Doctrine of the State of Nature (38). Appeal to the Corpus Iuris Civilis to prove that the highest earthly power proceeds from the Will of the People (39). Legal origin of all subjection in the voluntary and contractual submission of the Community (39). Escheat of the Imperium to the People (40). Claims of the Roman townsfolk (41). Rejection of those claims by Leopold of Bebenburg (41). Cooperation of the People in the transfer of the Empire from the Greeks to the Germans (41). Guardianship of the vacant Empire (42). Right of the People to choose its Head (42). The pure Elective Principle preferable to the institution of Hereditary Dignities (42). Legal foundation and legal nature of the electoral rights of the Prince Electors (42).

Rights of the Community as against a legitimately instituted Ruler (43). Controversy among the Glossators as to the significance of the *translatio imperii* by the *populus* to the *princeps* (43). Theory of an out-and-out conveyance (43). Theory of a mere *concessio* (43). Extension of this controversy to the general case of Prince and People (43).

The champions of Ruler's Sovereignty (43). Derivation of Absolute Monarchy from an Abdication of the Community (43). But even on this side a continuing right of the People as against the Ruler is conceded (44). Contractual relationship between Ruler and People (44). A right of active participation in the life of the State conceded to the People (44). Acts prejudicial to the Community's Rights require the consent of the Community (44). Cooperation of the People in Legislation and Government (44). Deposition of the Ruler in a case of necessity (45).

The champions of an intermediate theory (45). Limited Monarchy (45). The Mixed Constitution (45).

The champions of the People's Sovereignty (45). They also maintain a contractual relationship between People and Ruler and so concede an independent right of ruling to the Ruler (45). But they declare the People to be the true Sovereign: 'populus maior principe' (45). Consequences touching Legislative Power (45). Deposition and punishment of the Ruler who neglects his duties (46). Popular Sovereignty in Leopold of Bebenburg (46). The system of Marsilius of Padua (46). The system of Nicholas of Cues (47). Similar doctrines in cent. xv. (48).

2. Development of analogous thoughts about the Church and their significance in political theory (49). Survival of the idea of a right of the ecclesiastical Community even within the Doctrine of an Absolute

VII. *The Idea of Representation.*

reserves the exercise of true rights of Sovereignty for a primary Assembly (66). Limited representative functions of collegiate bodies (66). Leopold of Bebenburg on the Prince Electors (66). The Cardinals (66). Beginnings of the doctrine that the Representatives of the People act representatively when, and only when, they act as a Corporate Whole (67).

VIII. *The Idea of Personality.*

Personality of Church and State (67). The idea does not receive at the hands of the Publicists the development that might have been expected (68). The professional Jurists work with this idea, but employ only a 'fictitious' personality developed within the province of Private Law (68). Hence a tendency which increasingly prevails until our own day (68). Church and State as juristic persons for the Jurists (69). Baldus on the State's Personality (69). No application of the notion of Personality by the Publicists when they discuss the 'Subject' in which State-Power resides (70). Disruption of the State-Person into two 'Subjects' embodied respectively in Ruler and People (70). The Ruler's Personality (71). The Community as a 'Subject' of rights and duties (71). The concept of the People tends to take the 'individual-collective' shape (72). In the Church (72). In the State (72). Influence of this on the theory of Representation (72). Germs of the later theories of Natural Right (73).

IX. *The Relation of the State to Law.*

The ancient Germanic conception of a Reign of Law yields before the influence of Antiquity (73). The Idea of the State becomes independent of the Idea of Law (73). Howbeit, genuinely Medieval Thought holds fast the independence of the Idea of Law (74). Solution of the problem by a distinction between Positive and Natural Law (74).

The Medieval Doctrine of Natural Law (74). The *lex naturalis* before and above all earthly power (75). The *ius naturale* strictly so called (75). The *ius divinum* (75). The *ius gentium* (76). Limitation of the principle (76).

The Medieval Doctrine of Positive Law (76). The *ius civile* as product, instrument and sphere of human power (77). Exaltation of the Ruler above the Law (77). Resistance to this on the part of the advocates of the People's Sovereignty (78). But they contend for a Popular Assembly which is similarly before and above all Positive Law (78).

Application of these principles to the Rights given respectively by the

X. *The Beginnings of the Modern State.*

The fundamental notions of Public Law (92). The Idea of Sovereignty (93). Formulation thereof in the Middle Age (93). But not then exalted to its modern height (93). Still it necessarily induces a concentration of all State Power at a single point (94). The concentrated State Power begins to claim an equal and equally immediate control over all individuals (94). Tendency towards a dissolution of all intermediate Communities (94). Development of the notion of the State as The (exclusive) Community (94).

Reservation of equal or superior rights of the Church (94). But already Medieval Theory is preparing an absorption of Church in State (94). The Church is pure State Institution for Marsilius of Padua (95). Particular consequences of the same principle drawn by other writers (95).

The Medieval Idea of the Empire shattered by the Modern Idea of the State (95). Reception of the Aristotelian definition of the State (96). Inconsequence of Philosophers who adopt it (96). Inconsequence of Jurists (96). Gradual emergence in philosophic doctrine of the State's exclusive character (97). Aid derived from the legist's concept of an *universitas superiorem non recognoscens* (97). External Sovereignty becomes the characteristic mark of the State (97). Above there is no room for a World-State and below there are only communes and corporations (97).

The concentration of all State Life at a single point did not necessarily imply a concentration at that point of all Communal Life (97). Idea of the Organic Articulation of Communities within the State (98). Still on the whole, even in the Middle Age, the prevailing tendency of Theory is towards such an exaltation of the State's Sovereignty as would make the State the only representative of Communal Life (98). In this direction Philosophy precedes Jurisprudence with giant strides (98). Theoretic dissolution of the independent lordship-rights of Germanic origin (99). Treatment by Philosophy of Germanic fellowship-rights (99). Natural Law outlaws the Corporation (100).

SUBJECT MATTER OF THE NOTES[1].

[1] The titles given to the notes proceed from the translator.

LIST OF AUTHORITIES.

I. The Medieval Publicists.

Century XI.

1. Petrus Damiani (born about 990, died 1072). Opera : ed. Migne, Patrologiae Cursus Completus, Tom. 145. [See also Libelli de Lite (Mon. Germ.) I., p. 15 ff.]

2. Gregory VII. (pope 1073—1085). Registrum ; a collection of his letters compiled, according to Jaffé, by himself ; together with such letters as have otherwise become known ; edited by Jaffé, Bibliotheca rerum Germanicarum, II. (Monumenta Gregoriana, Berol. 1865) ; also in Migne, Tom. 148.

3. Henry IV. (reign. 1053—1106). Laws and Proclamations in Monumenta Germaniae, Leges II., p. 14 sq.

4. Petrus Crassus Cardinalis. Complaint against Gregory VII. on behalf of the Synod at Brixen on 25 June 1080 : in Sudendorf, Registrum, Jenae, 1849, I., pp. 22—50 ; compared with the edition in Ficker, Forschungen, IV., pp. 106—124. [See Libelli de Lite (Mon. Germ.) I. 432 ff.]

5. Wenrich of Trier. Epistola ad Gregorium VII. Papam, d. a. 1083 ; in Martene, Thesaurus Novorum Anecdotorum, I., pp. 214—230. [See Libelli de Lite (Mon. Germ.) I., p. 280 ff.]

6. Manegold of Lautenbach. Tract against Wenrich, written 1085 (comp. P. Ewald, in Forsch. zur Deut. Gesch., vol. 16, pp. 383—5) ; extracts in Floto, Heinrich IV., vol. II., pp. 299—303, and information in v. Giesebrecht, Magister Manegold v. Lautenbach, Sitzungsberichte der Bair. Akad. 1868, II., pp. 297—326. [See Libelli de Lite (Mon. Germ.) I., p. 301 ff.]

7. Wido Episcopus Ferrariensis. De scismate Hildebrandi ; composed in 1086 (according to the most recent investigation : K. Panzer, Wido v. Ferrara de scismate Hildebrandi, Leipz. 1880) ; ed. Wilmans in Mon. Germ. Scriptores XII., pp. 148—179. [See Libelli de Lite (Mon. Germ.) I., p. 529 ff.]

8. Walram Episcopus Naumburgensis. De unitate ecclesiae conservandae; composed 1093; in Schard, De iurisdictione auctoritate et praeeminentia imperiali ac potestate ecclesiastica, Basil. 1566, pp. 1—126. [See Libelli de Lite (Mon. Germ.) II., p. 285 ff.]

9. Letter of the Schismatical Cardinals against the Decree of P. Gregory VII. an. 1095; in Sudendorf, loc. cit. II., nr. 34, pp. 45—90.

10. Deusdedit Cardinalis (d. 1099). Contra invasores et simoniacos et reliquos schismaticos; in Mai, Nova P. P. Bibl. VII., pars ult., pp. 77—111 (only a very imperfect extract in Migne, loc. cit., Tom. 150, pp. 1569—72). [See Libelli de Lite (Mon. Germ.) II., p. 292 ff.]

11. Goffredus abbas Vindocinensis (d. 1132). Opera omnia; in Migne, loc. cit., Tom. 157. [See Libelli de Lite (Mon. Germ.) II., p. 676.]

12. S. Anselmus Cantuariensis archiepiscopus (1033—1109). Opera omnia; in Migne, loc. cit., Tom. 158—9.

13. Ivo Carnotensis episcopus (d. 1115). Opera omnia; in Migne, loc. cit., Tom. 161—2; the Epistolae in Tom. 162. [See Libelli de Lite (Mon. Germ.) II., p. 640 ff.]

Century XII.

14. Sigebert of Gembloux. Writings in defence of the Church of Lüttich against Paschal II., d. a. 1103; in Jaffé, Bibl. rer. Germ. v. 201 ff.; also in Schard, loc. cit., pp. 127—141. [See Libelli de Lite (Mon. Germ.) II., 436 ff.]

15. Tractatus de investitura episcoporum per imperatores facienda; a. 1109; in Schard, loc. cit., pp. 711—17 and Kunstman in Tüb. Theol. Quartalschrift for 1837: ascribed to Walram by Schard; ascribed to the diocese of Lüttich by Bernheim, Forsch. zur Deut. Gesch., vol. 16, pp. 281—95. [See Libelli de Lite (Mon. Germ.) II., p. 495 ff.]

16. Hugo Floriacensis. Tractatus de regia et sacerdotali dignitate; written between 1100 and 1106; in Stephani Baluzii Miscellaneorum liber quartus, Paris, 1683, pp. 9—68. [See Libelli de Lite (Mon. Germ.) II., 465.]

17. Honorius Augustodunensis (d. soon after 1152). Summa gloria de Apostolico et Augusto sive de praecellentia sacerdotii prae regno; in Migne, Tom. 172, pp. 1257—1270. [See Libelli de Lite (Mon. Germ.) III., p. 29 ff.]

18. Hugo de S. Victore (d. 1141). Opera omnia; in Migne, loc. cit., Tom. 175—7.

19. S. Bernhardus abbas Clarevallensis (1091—1153). Opera omnia; in Migne, loc. cit., Tom. 182—6 (Nov. ed. Paris. 1879): especially the Epistolae (Tom. 182, p. 67 sq.); those to the Emperor Lothar and King Conrad, also in Goldast, Monarchia Romani Imperii, Hanov. 1612, II., p. 66 sq.; and the Tract De consideratione libri v. ad Eugenium III. Papam, l. c., Tom. 186, p. 727 sq. (in Goldast, l. c., p. 68 sq.).

20. Gerhohus Reicherspergensis (1093—1169). Opera omnia; in Migne, l. c., Tom. 193—4. [See Libelli de Lite (Mon. Germ.) III., p. 131 ff.]

21. S. Thomas Cantuariensis archiepiscopus (Thomas Becket, 1116—1170). Opera omnia; in Migne, l. c., Tom. 190.

22. Johannes Saresberiensis (1120—1180). Opera omnia; in Migne, Tom. 199; therein the Epistolae, p. 1 sq., the Polycraticus, ann. 1159, p. 385 sq.; for the latter the edition used was Polycraticus sive de nugis curialium et vestigiis philosophorum libri octo, Lugd. Bat. 1639.

23. Frederick I. (reign. 1152—1190). Laws and Proclamations in Monumenta Germaniae, Leges II., p. 89 sq. and Boehmer, Regesta Imperii; Information in Wibald and Otto of Freisingen.

24. Wibald of Stablo and Corvey. Epistolae; in Jaffé, Monumenta Corbeiensia, Berol. 1864.

25. Writings of the Arnoldists, 1152, in Wibald's Book of Concepta, in Jaffé, l. c.

26. Otto Frisingensis (b. not before 1111, d. 1158). Chronicon; composed between 1143—6; in Monumenta Germaniae, Scriptores, xx., p. 131 sq.—Gesta Friderici (to 1156) with the continuation by Ragewin (to 1160) ib., p. 351 sq.

27. Alexander III. (pope 1159—1181). Opera; in Migne, l. c., Tom. 200.

28. Petrus Blesensis (d. 1200). Opera omnia; in Migne, l. c., Tom. 207.

29. Petrus Blesensis iunior (nephew of the above). Opusculum de distinctionibus sive Speculum iuris canonici, ed. Reimarus, Berol. 1837; written about 1180.

30. Innocent III. (pope 1198—1216). Opera; in Migne, l. c., Tom. 214—7; therein the collection of his letters (vols. 214—6) and the Registrum super negotiis Romani Imperii (vol. 216, p. 995 sq.).

31. Philip of Swabia (1198—1208) and Otto IV. (1198—1218) in Monumenta Germaniae, Leges II., p. 201 sq.

Century XIII.

32. Frederick II. (1211—1250), in Monumenta Germaniae, Leges II.,
    p. 223 sq.; in P. Huillard-Bréholles, Historia diplomatica
    Friderici II., Paris, 1859 sq.; and in Petrus de Vineis.

33. Petrus de Vineis (Chancellor of Frederick II.). Epistolae; Basil,
    1566. Compare P. Huillard-Bréholles, Vie et correspondance
    de Pierre de la Vigne, Paris, 1865.

34. Eike von Repgow in the Sachsenspiegel (between 1224 and 1235),
    ed. Homeyer, 3rd ed. 1861.

35. German Poets of the time of the Hohenstaufen; the passages
    collected by Höfler, Kaiserthum u. Papstthum, Prag, 1862, p.
    105 ff.

36. Gregory IX. (pope 1227—1243). Decretals in the Corpus iuris
    canonici; and Letters in Raynald, Annal. eccl., vol. XIII.

37. Innocent IV. (pope 1243—1254). Decretals in the Corpus iuris
    canonici; and Letters in Raynald, l. c.

38. Alexander Halensis (d. 1245). Summa theologica; Col. 1622.

39. S. Thomas Aquinas (d. 1274). Opera omnia; ed. Antverp. 1612 and
    Parm. 1852—72.—Summa Theologiae; ed. Migne, Paris, 1864;
    ed. Antv. vols. X.—XII.; ed. Parm. vols. I.—IV.—Summa de veritate
    fidei contra gentiles; ed. Uccellius, Romae, 1878; ed. Antv. vol. IX.;
    ed. Parm. vol. V.—In quattuor libros Sententiarum magistri Petri
    Lombardi Comment.; ed. Antv. vols. VI.—VII.; ed. Parm. vols.
    VI.—VII.—Quaestiones disputatae and Quodlibetanae s. Placita;
    ed. Antv. vol. VIII.; ed. Parm. vols. VIII.—IX.—Expositio on the
    Psalms; ed. Antv. vol. XIII.—Commentarius in Epistolas omnes
    Pauli; ed. Ant. XVI.—Commentary on the Ethics of Aristotle;
    ed. Antv. vol. V.; ed. Parm. vol. XXI.—Commentary on the Politics
    of Aristotle; ed. Antv. vol. V.; ed. Parm. vol. XXI., p. 366 sq.
    (our citation of pages refers to this edition).—Opuscula omnia
    theologica et moralia, Paris, 1656; in ed. Antv. vol. XVII.; ed.
    Parm. vols. XV.—XVI.—In particular, Opusc. I contra errores
    Graecorum.—Opusc. 34, p. 534 sq. (or Opusc. 19) contra im-
    pugnantes religionem.—Opusc. 40, p. 843 sq. (or Opusc. 21) de
    regimine Iudaeorum ad Ducissam Brabantiae.—Opusc. 39, p.
    764 sq. (in ed. Antv. Opusc. 39, f. 160vo, in ed. Parm. vol. XVI.,
    p. 224 sq.) de regimine principum ad regem Cypri; unfinished,
    since only lib. I. and lib. II. c. I—4 come from him, and the
    continuation is by Ptolomaeus of Lucca.—See Baumann, die

Staatslehre des h. Thomas v. Aquino, Leipz. 1873. Nic. Thoemes, Commentatio literaria et critica de S. Thomae Aquinatis operibus ad ecclesiasticum, politicum, socialem statum 'reipublicae Christianae' pertinentibus deque eius doctrinae fundamentis atque praeceptis, Berol. 1874.

40. Vincentius Bellovacensis (d. 1274 or 1264). Speculum doctrinale, lib. VII.—XI.; ed. Duaci, 1624.

41. Schwabenspiegel (about 1275), ed. Lassberg, 1840.

42. Jordanus of Osnabrück, De praerogativa Romani imperii; written about 1281, probably in 1285; ed. by Waitz in the Abhandlungen der kön. Gesellschaft der Wiss. zu Göttingen, vol. 14, p. 43 ff.

43. Aegidius Romanus Colonna (1247—1315). De regimine principum libri III.; written after 1280; ed. per Simon. Bevilaquam, Venet. 1498.—De potestate ecclesiastica libri tres, from the description and analysis of its contents by F. X. Kraus, Oesterr. Vierteljahrsschrift für kathol. Theol., vol. I. (Wien, 1862), p. 11 ff.

44. Engelbert of Volkersdorf, Abbot of Admont (1250—1311). De regimine principum; written in all probability after 1290; ed. Jo. Georg. Theophil. Huffnagl, Ratisbonae, s. a.—De ortu, progressu et fine Romani imperii liber; probably between 1307 and 1310; ed. Basil. 1553.

45. Ptolomaeus of Lucca. De regimine principum; written after 1298; as a continuation of Thomas Aquinas, De regimine principum.

46. Dante Alighieri (1265—1321). De Monarchia libri tres; written about 1300 (according to Witte 1296—1299, according to Wegele not until 1311—1313); ed. altera per Carolum Witte, Vindobonae, 1874.

47. Boniface VIII. (pope 1294—1303). Decretals in the Corpus iuris canonici and letters in Raynald, l. c. vol. XIV.

48. Rudolf I. (1273—1291), Adolf (1292—1298) and Albert I. (1298—1308) in Monumenta Germaniae, Leges II., pp. 382 sq., 459 sq., 466 sq.

Century XIV.

49. Johannes Parisiensis (d. 1306). Tractatus de regia potestate et papali; written about 1303; ed. in Schard, l. c. pp. 142—224; in Goldast, l. c. II., p. 108 sq.

50. Disputatio inter militem et clericum super potestate praelatis ecclesiae atque principibus terrarum commissa; written about 1303, perhaps by Peter Dubois; ed. in Schard, l. c. pp. 677—687, Goldast, l. c. I. 13 sq.

51. Clement V. (pope 1305—1314), in Corpus iur. can. and in Raynald, l. c. vol. xv.

52. Henry VII. (1308—1313), in Monumenta Germaniae, Leges ii., p. 490 sq.

53. Guilelmus Durantis iunior (d. 1328). Tractatus de modo celebrandi concilii et corruptelis in ecclesia reformandis ; written between 1308 and 1311 ; in Tractatus universi iuris, Venet. 1584, xiii. 1, p. 154 sq.

54. Landulfus de Colonna. De translatione imperii; written 1310—1320; ed. Schard, l. c. pp. 284—297, Goldast, l. c. ii. 88 sq.

55. Lewis the Bavarian (1314—1348), in Boehmer, Regesta Imperii.

56. John XXII. (pope 1316—1334), in Corpus iur. can. and in Raynald, l. c.

57. Marsilius Patavinus of Maynardina (d. after 1342). Defensor pacis ; composed between 1324 and 1326 with the help of John of Jandun ; ed. s. l. 1622 ; also in Goldast, ii. 154—308.—Tractatus de translatione imperii ; written in 1325 or 1326 ; in Schard, l. c. pp. 224—237, Goldast, ii. 147—153.

58. Augustinus Triumphus de Ancona (1243—1328). Summa de potestate ecclesiastica ; written after 1324 (according to Riezler, but according to Friedberg about 1320) ; ed. Romae, 1583.

59. Petrus Paludanus (Patriarch of Jerusalem). De causa immediata ecclesiasticae potestatis ; written about 1329 ; from citations in Raynald, l. c. ann. 1328, nr. 30—32 (vol. xv., p. 346 sq.) and Bellarmin, De scriptoribus ecclesiasticis, p. 271.

60. Peter Bertrand (Bishop of Autun, afterwards Cardinal). De iurisdictione ecclesiastica et politica ; written 1329 ; ed. Goldast, l. c. ii. 1261—1283.

61. Guilelmus Occam (ob. 1347). Opus nonaginta dierum ; written soon after 1330 ; ed. Goldast, l. c. ii. 993—1236.—Compendium errorum Papae Johannis XXII. ; written 1335—1338 ; ed. Goldast, ii. 957—976.—Octo quaestiones ; written 1339—1342 ; ed. Goldast, ii. 314—391.—Dialogus ; written in 1342 or 1343, but Pars ii. already in 1333 or 1334 ; ed. Goldast, ii. 398—957.

62. Michael de Cesena. Letters of 1331, 1333 and undated (but probably also 1333), in Goldast, ii. 1236, 1238, 1244.—Other writings relating to the Minorite Quarrel, ib. pp. 1291—1344.

63. Alvarius Pelagius. De planctu ecclesiae ; according to ii. art. 93 in fine, begun in 1330 and finished in 1332 at Avignon, but according to its last words revised a first time in 1335 at Algarbia in Portugal and a second time in 1340 at Compostella ; ed. Lugd. 1617.

64. Documents relating to the Unions at Lahnstein and Rense in 1338, in

Ficker, zur Gesch. des Kurvereins von Rense, Sitzungsber. der k. k. Akad. der Wiss., vol. XI. (1853), Beilagen, p. 699 ff.

65. Excerpta ex libro Nicolai Minoritae de controversia paupertatis Christi, in Boehmer, Fontes IV. 588—608.—Therein Articuli de iuribus imperii et praelatorum ac principum, ad quos pertinet imperatoris electio, et de iure domini Ludovici IV. imperatoris, of 1338, p. 592 sq.—Tractate of 1338, p. 598 sq.—Opinions of Bonagratia of Bergamo, 1338, p. 606 sq.

66. Definition of the rights pertaining to Elect Emperors and Kings according to the laws and customs of the Empire; ann. 1338; in Ficker, l. c. nr. 6, p. 709 ff.

67. Informatio de nullitate processuum papae Johannis contra Ludov. Bavar., 1338, in Goldast, I. 18—21.

68. Lupold of Bebenburg (d. 1363). De iure regni et imperii; written between 1338 and 1340; ed. princeps s. t. ‘Lupoldus de iuribus et translatione Imperii’ Arg. 1508, and ed. in Schard, l. c. pp. 328—409.—Libellus de zelo catholicae fidei veterum principum Germanorum; ed. Schard, l. c. pp. 410—465.—Ritmaticum querulosum et lamentosum dictamen de modernis cursibus et defectibus regni ac imperii Romanorum; ed. Boehmer, Fontes, I. 479 sq.

69. Konrad of Megenberg (circ. 1309—1374). Oeconomica; written 1352 —1362; the dedicatory epistle and abstract of contents in Struve, Act. lit. Jenae 1706, Fasc. IV. 81—91.—Tractatus de translatione imperii, 1354 or 1355, and Treatise against Ockham from the same time; extracts given by Höfler, Aus Avignon, Prag, 1868, p. 26 ff.

70. Johann von Buch. Gloss on the Sachsenspiegel; ed. used being those by Zobel, Leipz. 1525, and by Gärtner, Leipz. 1732.

71. The Town-Clerk (Stadtschreiber) Johannes, in the Brünner Schöffenbuch; second half of cent. XIV.; ed. Rösler, die Stadtrecht v. Brünn, Prag, 1852.

72. Petrarca (1304—1374). Epistolae de iuribus imperii Romani; circ. 1350—70; ed. Goldast, II. pp. 1345 (l. 1445)—1465.

73. Quaestio in utramque partem disputata de potestate regia et pontificali; dedicated to Charles V. [of France], written probably about 1364—1380, and according to Riezler perhaps by Raoul de Presles; in Goldast, II. 95 sq. (French translation I. 39 sq.).

74. Somnium Viridarii; written in 1376 or 1377, probably by Philippe de Mazières; in Goldast, I. 58—229.

75. Johannes Wycliffe (1324—1387). Trialogus et supplementum Trialogi; ed. Oxon. 1869.—The twenty-four Articles condemned by the Synod of London in 1382.—Compare Lechner, Johann v. Wiclif, Leipz. 1873 (the Articles, I. p. 669 ff.).

76. Ubertus de Lampugnano. Utrum omnes Christiani subsunt Romano Imperio; lecture delivered in 1380; in Zeitschr. für geschichtliche Rechtswissenschaft, II. 246—256.

77. Henricus de Langenstein dictus de Hassia (1325—1397). Consilium pacis de unione ac reformatione ecclesiae; written in 1381; in Joh. Gerson, Opera omnia, Antverp. 1706, II. p. 809 sq.—See also O. Hartwig, Henricus de Langenstein dictus de Hassia, Marb. 1857.

78. Konrad v. Gelnhausen. Tractatus de congregando concilio tempore schismatis, in Martene, Thesaurus anecdot. II., pp. 1200—1226.

79. Mathaeus de Cracovia (d. 1410). De squaloribus Romanae curiae, in Walch, Monumenta medii aevi, I. 1, pp. 1—100.—Epistola Universitatis Parisiensis ad Regem Francorum d. a. 1394.—Memorandum of 1396.—Resolution of the National Synod at Paris of 1398.—Speeches and writings of Simon Cramaud, Pierre Plaoul, Aegidius de Campis de Rothomago and Pierre du Mont de St Michel; as given by Hübler, die Constanzer Reformation und die Konkordate von 1418, Leipz. 1867, p. 360 ff., also in Schwab, Joh. Gerson, Würzburg, 1858.—Also Consultatio de recusanda obedientia Petro de Luna, circ. 1399, in Martene, l. c. II. 1189 sq.—Appellatio interposita per Leodienses a papa post subtractionem obedientiae per eos sibi factam, a. 1400, ib. 1250 sq.—Letter of Simon Cramaud d. a. 1400, ib. 1230 sq.

80. Tractatus de aetatibus ecclesiae; from the time of the Great Schism; in Goldast, I. 30 sq.

Century XV.

81. Franciscus de Zabarellis. Tractatus de schismate; written circ. 1406; in Schard, pp. 688—711.

82. Conclusiones per studium Bononiense a. 1409, in Martene, Ampl. Collect. VIII. 894.

83. Octo conclusiones per plures doctores in Ital. part. approb., in Gerson, Op. II. p. 110 sq.

84. Petrus de Alliaco (1350—1425). Treatises and Speeches in the matter of the Schism, in Gerson, Op. I. p. 489 sq. and II. p. 867 sq., also Propositiones, ib. II. p. 112; Tractatus de ecclesiastica potestate, a. 1416, in v. d. Hardt, Conc. Const. VI. 6, p. 15 sq.—See also Tschackert, Peter von Ailli, Gotha, 1877.

85 Johannes Gerson (1363—1429). Opera omnia, Antverp. 1706.—Therein the 'Schismatica' in Tom. II.; in particular, Protestatio

super statu ecclesiae, p. 2; Sententia de modo habendi se tempore schismate, p. 3; De schismate tollendo, p. 76; Trilogus in materia schismatis, p. 83; Tractatus de unitate ecclesiastica, p. 113; Propositio, p. 123; Sermones, pp. 131 and 141; De auferibilitate Papae ab ecclesia, p. 209; De potestate ecclesiae et origine iuris et legum (1415), p. 225; Propositio in Conc. Const. p. 271; Quomodo et an liceat in causis fidei a Papa appellare, p. 303.—Also some few matters in Tom. III. (Opera moralia) and IV. (Opera exegetica et miscellanea).—See also J. B. Schwab, Johannes Gerson, Professor der Theologie und Kanzler der Universität Paris, Würzburg, 1858.

86. Johannes Hus (1373—1415). Determinatio de ablatione temporalium a clericis, a. 1410; in Goldast, I. 232 sq.—See also Lechner, Johann v. Wiclif, vol. II.

87. Johannes Breviscoxa. De fide et ecclesia, Romano pontifice et concilio generali; in Gerson, Op. II. p. 805 sq.

88. Andreas of Randuf. De modis uniendi ac reformandi ecclesiam in concilio universali; written circ. 1410; in Gerson, Op. II. 161 sq.

89. Theodoricus de Niem. De schismate; written in the reign of Rupert; ed. Basil, 1566.—Privilegia et iura imperii circa investituras episcopatuum et abbatiarum, written 1410—1419; in Schard, pp. 785—859.—De difficultate reformationis ecclesiae; in von der Hardt, l. c. 1. 6, p. 255.—De necessitate reformationis ecclesiae, ib. 1. 7, p. 277.

90. Nilus archiepiscopus Thessalonicus. De primatu Papae Romani; written in all likelihood about 1438 (not about 1360 as is supposed by Riezler and O. Lorenz who have followed in this a mistake made by Goldast which he himself corrected in the Diss. de autor.); in Goldast, I. 30—39.

91. Nicolaus of Cues (1401—1464). Opera omnia, Basil. 1565. The treatise De concordantia catholica (to which our references are made unless the contrary is stated), written 1431—3 and presented to the Council of Basel, is found ib. 692 sq. and in Schard, pp. 465—676.—A treatise De auctoritate praesidendi in concilio generali, in Düx, Der deutsche Kardinal Nikolaus v. Kusa, Regensb. 1847, I., pp. 475—491.—See also Stumpf, Die polit. Ideen des Nicolaus v. Cues, Köln, 1865; Scharpff, Nicolaus v. Cusa als Reformator in Kirche, Reich und Philosophie, Tüb. 1871.

92. Laurentius Valla. De falso credita et ementita Constantini donatione; written 1439; in Schard, pp. 734—780.

93. Gregory of Heimburg (d. 1472). Admonitio de iniustis usurpationibus paparum Romanorum; written about 1441; in Goldast, I. 557—563.—Controversial writings concerning the affair of Brixen,

1460—1461, ib. II. 1576—1595.—Apologia contra detractiones et blasphemias Theodori Laelii, ib. II. 1604 sq.—Invectiva in Nicolaum Cusanum, ib. 1622—1631.—See also Clemens Brockhaus, Gregor v. Heimburg, Leipz. 1861.

94. Theodoricus Laelius episcopus Feltrensis. Replica pro Pio Papa II. et sede Romana ; in Goldast, II. 1595—1604.

95. Aeneas Sylvius Piccolomini (1405—1464, from 1458 Pope Pius II.). De ortu et auctoritate imperii Romani ; written in 1446 ; in Schard, pp. 314—328.—See also Voigt, Enea Silvio de' Piccolomini, 3 vols., Berlin, 1856 ff.

96. Petrus de Monte (1442—1457 Bishop of Brixen). De potestate Romani pontificis et generalis concilii s. de primatu, Tract. univ. iuris, XIII. 1, p. 144 sq.

97. Johannes a Turrecremata (d. 1468). Summa de ecclesia, Venet. 1561.—De pontificis maximi conciliique auctoritate, Venet. 1563 ; under the title De potestate papae et concilii generalis tractatus notabilis, ed. Friedrich, Oenoponti, 1871.

98. Antonius de Rosellis (d. 1466). Monarchia s. de potestate imperatoris et papae ; in Goldast, I. 252—556.

99. Petrus de Andlo. De imperio Romano-Germanico ; written in 1460 ; ed. Marquardus Freher, Norimb. 1657.

100. Franciscus Patricius Senensis Pontifex Cajetanus (d. 1494). De institutione reipublicae libri IX.; ed. Arg. 1595.—De regno et regis institutione libri IX.; addressed to King Alphonso of Aragon and Calabria ; ed. Arg. 1594.

101. Klagspiegel ; ed. Strasb. 1527 ; appeared at Schwäbisch-Hall near the beginning of cent. xv., according to Stintzing, Geschichte der populären Litteratur des römisch-kanonischen Rechts in Deutschland, Leipz. 1867, p. 353 ff., and Geschichte der deutschen Rechtswissenschaft, Münch. u. Leipz., I. p. 43.

102. Ulrich Tengler. Laienspiegel ; appeared in 1509 ; ed. Strasb. 1527.

103. Thomas de Vio Cajetanus (1469—1534). De auctoritate papae et concilii utraque invicem comparata ; written in 1511 ; in his Opuscula omnia, Antv. 1612, I. 1.

104. Jacobus Almainus (d. 1515). Expositio circa decisiones Magistri G. Occam super potestate summi Pontificis ; written in 1512; in Gerson, Op. II., p. 1013 sq. and (as Expositio de suprema potestate ecclesiastica et laica) in Goldast, I. 588—647.—De dominio naturali civili et ecclesiastico ; in Gerson, Op. II., p. 961 sq.—De auctoritate Ecclesiae et Conciliorum generalium, adv. Thomam de Vio Cajetanum ; ib. 1013 sq.

II. LEGISTS[1].

105. Glossa Ordinaria, compiled by Accursius (1182—1258): in the edition of the Corpus Iuris Civilis, Venetiis apud Juntas 1606, compared with earlier editions. [Irnerius (circ. 1100) is the founder of the school; Bulgarus, Martinus, Jacobus, Hugo are 'the four doctors.']

106. Placentinus (d. 1192). De varietate actionum (before 1180), Mog. 1530.

107. Jacobus de Arena (last mentioned in 1296). Commentarii in universum ius civile, ed. Lugd. 1541.

108. Andreas de Isernia (Neapolitan, b. circ. 1220, d. 1316). Super usibus feudorum, ed. Lugd. 1561.

109. Oldradus de Ponte (de Laude) (first mentioned 1302, d. 1335). Consilia, ed. Francof. 1576.

110. Jacobus Buttrigarius (b. circ. 1274, d. 1348). Lectura in Digestum Vetus, ed. Romae, 1606.

111. Cinus (Guittoncino Sinibaldi) (b. 1270, d. 1336). Lectura super Codicem, ed. Francof. 1578.—Lectura super Digestum Vetus, in eadem editione.

112. Albericus de Rosciate (d. 1354). Commentarii, ed. Lugd. 1545.—Dictionarium, ed. Venet. 1573.

113. Bartolus de Sassoferrato (b. 1314, d. 1357). Commentarii—Consilia—Quaestiones—Tractatus. All from the edition of his works, Basil. 1562.

114. Baldus de Ubaldis (1327—1400). Commentarii on the various parts of the Corpus Iuris, ed. Venet. 1572—3.—Commentarius in usus feudorum, written in 1391, ed. Lugd. 1566.—Commentariolum super pace Constantiae, in eadem editione.—Consilia, ed. Venet. 1575.

115. Bartholomaeus de Saliceto (d. 1412). Commentarius super Codice; finished in 1400; ed. Venet. 1503.

116. Christoforus de Castellione (1345—1425). Consilia, ed. Venet. 1560.

117. Raphael Fulgosius (1367—1427). Consilia posthuma, Ambergae, 1607.

---

[1] On pp. 186, 238, 351 and 416 Dr Gierke gives long lists of legists and canonists. We here select only such writers as are referred to in the chapter that is here translated.

118. Johannes de Imola (d. 1436). Commentarius on the Infortiatum and Digestum Novum, ed. Lugd. 1549.
119. Ludovicus de Ponte Romanus (1409—1439). Commentarii, ed. Francof. 1577.—Consilia, ed. Lugd. 1548.
120. Paulus de Castro, Castrensis (d. 1441). Commentarii on Digests and Code, ed. Lugd. 1585.
121. Johannes Christophorus Parcus (Portius, Porcius) (from 1434 professor at Pavia). Commentarius in Institutiones, ed. Basil. 1548.
122. Tartagnus, Alexander de Imola de Tartagnis (1424 or 1423—1477). Commentarii on the three Digests and the Code, ed. Francof. 1610.—Consilia, ed. Aug. Taur. 1575 (with additions by Marcus Antonius and Natta).
123. Johannes de Platea (of Bologna, cent. xv.). Super Institutionibus, ed. Lugd. 1539.—Super tribus ultimis libris Codicis, ed. Lugd. 1528.
124. Paris de Puteo (1413—1493). Tractatus de Syndicatu, ed. Francof. 1608 (also in Tr. U. J. vii. 127).
125. Johannes Bertachinus (d. 1497). Repertorium iuris, Lugd. 1521.
126. Jason de Mayno (1435—1519). Commentarii on the three Digests and the Code, ed. Aug. Taur. 1576.—Consilia, ed. Francof. 1611.
127. Paulus Picus a Monte Pico (pupil of Jason, professor at Pavia, end of cent. xv.). Opera, ed. Francof. 1575.
128. Johannes Crottus (of Casale, professor at Bologna, Pavia and Pisa, circ. 1500). Consilia, ed. Venet. 1576.
129. Franciscus Marcus (member of the Parlement of Dauphiné). Decisiones Delphinenses, ed. Francof. 1624.
130. Franciscus Curtius junior (d. 1533). Consilia, ed Spirae, 1604.
131. Philippus Decius (1454—1536 or 1537). Commentarii in Digestum vetus et Codicem, ed. Lugd. 1559.—De regulis iuris, ed. Col. 1584.—Consilia, ed. Venet. 1570.
132. Martinus de Caratis Laudensis. Lectura super feudis, ed. Basil. 1564.—De fisco, Tr. U. J. xii. 2.—De represaliis, ib. xii. 279.

III. Canonists.

133. Glossa Ordinaria on the Decretum Gratiani : compiled by Johannes Teutonicus (d. about 1220): editions used Lugd. 1512 and Argent. p. Henr. Eggesteyn, 1471.
134. Innocentius IV., Sinibaldus Fliscus (d. 1254). Apparatus (Com-

mentaria) in libros quinque decretalium, ed. Francof. 1570 : finished soon after the Council of Lyons (1245).

135. Bernardus Compostellanus iunior. Lectura on the Decretals (1245—1260, unfinished), ed. Paris, 1516.

136. Hostiensis, Henricus de Segusia Cardinalis Ostiensis (d. 1271). Summa aurea super titulis decretalium, ed. Basil. 1573 ; written after 1250.

137. Glossa ordinaria on the Liber Extra, compiled by Bernhardus Parmensis de Botone (d. 1263); finished shortly before his death ; ed. Lugd. 1509 and Basil. 1482.

138. Guilelmus Durantis, 'Speculator' (1237—1296). Speculum iudiciale; first finished in 1272, revised before 1287 ; ed. Basil. 1574 and Francof. 1612.

139. Glossa ordinaria on the Liber Sextus (1304 or 1305) and the Clementines (1326) by Johannes Andreae.

140. Johannes Andreae Mugellanus (1270—1348). Novella in Decretales Gregorii IX. ; in I. et II. libr. ed. Venet. 1612 ; super III. libr. ed. Venet. 1505 ; super IV. et V. libr. ed. Venet. 1505.

141. Idem. Novella super Sexto, ed. Lugd. 1527 ; written between 1334 and 1342.

142. Henricus Bouhic (Bohic) (b. 1310, d. after 1350). Distinctiones in libros quinque Decretalium, Lugd. 1520; written 1348.

143. Baldus de Ubaldis (1327—1400). Commentarius super tribus prioribus libris decretalium, Lugd. 1585.

144. Petrus de Ancharano (1330—1416). Lectura super sexto decretalium libro, Lugd. 1543.

145. Franciscus de Zabarellis Cardinalis (1335—1417). Commentaria in v. libros decretalium, Venet. 1602.—Lectura super Clementinis, Venet. 1497 ; written between 1391 and 1410.—Consilia, Venet. 1581.

146. Antonius de Butrio (1338—1408). Commentaria in v. libros decretalium, Venet. 1578.—Consilia, Lugd. 1541.

147. Dominicus de Sancto Geminiano (first half of cent. xv.). Lectura super decreto, Venet. 1504.—Lectura super libro sexto, Lugd. 1535.—Consilia et Responsa, Venet. 1581.

148. Johannes ab Imola (d. 1436). Commentarius super Clementinis, Lugd. 1551.

149. Prosdocimus de Comitibus (d. 1438). De differentiis legum et canonum, Tr. U. J. I. 190.

150. Panormitanus, Nicholaus de Tudeschis (Abbas Siculus, Abbas modernus) (d. 1453). Commentaria, Venet. 1605 (vols. I.—VII.).—Consilia et Quaestiones, in eadem ed. vol. VIII. ; the Quaestiones also in Selectae Quaestiones, Col. 1570, p. 303.

151.   Johannes de Anania (d. 1457). Commentarius super Decretalibus and super Sexto Decretalium, Lugd. 1553.

152.   Alexander Tartagnus ab Imola (1424—1477). Consilia, ed. Francof. 1610.

153.   Cardinalis Alexandrinus, Johannes Antonius de S. Gregorio (d. 1509). Commentaria super Decreto, Venet. 1500; written between 1483 and 1493.

154.   Philippus Franchus de Franchis (d. 1471). Lectura in Sextum Decretalium, Lugd. 1537.

155.   Dominicus Jacobatius Cardinalis (d. 1527). Tractatus de concilio, in Tr. U. J. XIII. 1, pp. 190—398.

156.   Hieronymus Zanettinus (d. 1493). Contrarietates seu diversitates inter ius civile et canonicum, in Tr. U. J. I. p. 197.

157.   Benedictus Capra (d. 1470). Regulae et Tractatus, Venet. 1568.— Consilia, Lugd. 1556.

158.   Ludovicus Bologninus (1447—1508). Consilia: along with those of Benedictus Capra, Lugd. 1556.

159.   Felinus Sandaeus (1444—1503). Opera, Lugd. 1540 (Lectura in decretales).

160.   Philippus Decius (1454—1536 or 1537). Super Decretalibus, Lugd. 1551.

IV.   Modern Books.

161.   Förster, Quid de reipublicae vi ac natura medio aevo doctum sit, Vratisl. 1847.

162.   Förster, Die Staatslehre des Mittelalters, Allg. Monatschr. für Wiss. u. Litt. 1853, pp. 832 ff. and 922 ff.

163.   Friedberg, Die mittelalterlichen Lehren über das Verhältniss von Kirche und Staat, Zeitschr. für Kirchenrecht, vol. 8, p. 69 ff.

164.   Friedberg, Die Grenzen zwischen Staat und Kirche, Tübingen, 1872.

165.   Friedberg, Die mittelalterlichen Lehren über das Verhältniss von Staat und Kirche, Leipz. 1874.

166.   Höfler, Kaiserthum und Papstthum, Prag, 1862.

167.   Döllinger, Die Papstfabeln des Mittelalters, München, 1863.

168.   Hübler, Die Constanzer Reformation und die Konkordate von 1418, Leipz. 1867.

169.   Schulte, Die Stellung der Koncilien, Päpste und Bischöfe vom historischen und kanonischen Standpunkte, 1871.

170. Hergenröther, Katholische Kirche und christlicher Staat, Freiburg i. B. 1872.

171. S. Riezler, Die literarischen Widersacher der Päpste zur Zeit Ludwigs des Baiers, Leipz. 1874.

172. F. v. Bezold, Die Lehre von der Volkssouveränetät während des Mittelalters, Hist. Zeitschr. vol. 36 (1876), p. 340 ff.

173. W. Molitor, Die Dekretale Per Venerabilem von Innocenz III. und ihre Stellung im öffentlichen Recht der Kirche, Münster, 1876.

174. O. Lorenz, Deutschlands Geschichtsquellen im Mittelalter seit der Mitte des dreizehnten Jahrhunderts, ed. 2, Berl. 1876, II. p. 288 ff.

175. W. v. Giesebrecht, Geschichte der deutschen Kaiserzeit, vol. III.

176. Raumer, Geschichte der Hohenstauffen und ihrer Zeit, vol. VI.

177. Wessenberg, Die grossen Kirchenversammlungen des 15 u. 16 Jahrh., Konstanz, 1845 ff.

178. Hefele, Konciliengeschichte, vols. I.—IV. in ed. 2.

179. Ficker, Forschungen zur Reichs- u. Rechtsgeschichte Italiens, Innsbruck, 1868—1874.

INDEX TO LIST OF AUTHORITIES[1].

[1] This Index may help a reader to pass from Dr Gierke's notes to the above List of Authorities.

POLITICAL THEORIES OF THE MIDDLE AGE.

I. *The Evolution of Political Theory.*

THE development by Legists and Canonists of a Theory of Corporations came into contact at many points with the efforts of the Medieval Spirit rationally to comprehend Church and State in their entirety, and therefore scientifically to conceive the nature of all Human Society. For the first beginnings of this movement we may look as far back as the great Quarrel over the Right of Investiture, but not until the thirteenth century did it issue in a definite Theory of Public Law. From that time onwards the doctrines of the Publicists, doctrines which were being steadily elaborated and unfolded, became no mere doctrines of Public Law, but were also the exponents of an independent Philosophy of State and Law such as had not previously existed. And just because this was so, they introduced a quite new force into the history of legal ideas.

This result was due to the co-operation of various sciences. Theology and Scholastic Philosophy, Political History and practical arguments touching the questions of the day, here encountered both each other and professional Jurisprudence in one and the same field. Their starting-points, their goals, their equipments might be different; still here as elsewhere Medieval Science preserved a high degree of unity and generality. In the first place, though a war of opinions over the great questions of Public Law might be loudly raging, still all men shared one common concept of the Universe, the supreme premises being regarded by medieval minds as no discoveries to be made by man, but as the divinely revealed substratum of all human science. Secondly, men readily borrowed on all sides whatever they needed, so that there was an always increasing store of intellectual treasure amassed by co-operative labour and common to all.

Diversity of materials.

In this manner elements that derived from the most diverse sources were fused into a system. Holy Writ and the expositions thereof, Patristic Lore and more especially the *Civitas Dei* of Augustine, these furnished the medieval Doctrine of Society with its specifically Christian traits. Genuinely Germanic ideas flowed into it from the tales of medieval historians and from the popular thought which those tales had influenced. The resuscitation of the Political Philosophy of the Antique World, and above all the exaltation of the Politics of Aristotle to the position of an irrefragable canon, had from the first dictated at least the scientific form of the whole doctrine. And then to all that was obtained from these various sources Jurisprudence added the enormous mass of legal matter that was enshrined in Roman and Canon Law, and, to a smaller degree, in the ordinances of the medieval Emperors, for Jurisprudence regarded what these texts had to say of Church and State, as being not merely the positive statutes of some one age, but rules of eternal validity flowing from the very nature of things.

Then again, in the method of handling this wealth Diverse methods. of material the tendencies of the different sciences supplemented each other. The deepest speculative penetration falls to the share of the theologian and philosopher; the keenest practical appreciation of newly-won ideas falls to the share of politicians with an eye on the question of the hour; still Jurisprudence, albeit with some hesitation, yielded to the impulses that were thus given. Conversely, it was professional Jurisprudence which by its assiduously detailed work brought the aerial scheme of thought into combination with the actual public life of great and small societies, and by so doing both started a science of Positive Public Law[1] and provided the philosopher and the speculative politician with a series of legal concepts serviceable for the construction of a system. More-over, at this point the other writers adhered as closely as was possible to the Legists, Canonists, and Feudists, and by so doing began to give to their abstractions and their postulates a stable formulated shape and a more solid basis among realities.

Thus, notwithstanding the diversity of its sources Unity of the move-ment. and its confluents, the Medieval Doctrine of State and Society flowed along one single bed. Within that bed were commotions that shook the world. But all this conflict between opinions, ecclesiastical and secular, absolutistic and democratic, only accelerated the speed of a current which as a whole swept onwards in but one direction.

Beneath this movement, however, there was an Medieval and Antique-Modern Thought. internal contest, which in the history of ideas was of more importance than all the external differences be-tween partizans: namely, the contest between Properly Medieval and 'Antique-Modern' Thought.

Throughout the Middle Age and even for a while Medieval Thought.

longer, the outward framework of all Political Doctrine consisted of the grandiose but narrow system of
thoughts that had been reared by the Medieval Spirit.
It was a system of thoughts which culminated in the
idea of a Community which God Himself had constituted and which comprised All Mankind.   This
system may be expounded, as it is by Dante, in all its
purity and all its fulness, or it may become the shadow
of a shade; but rudely to burst its bars asunder is an
exploit which is but now and again attempted by some
bold innovator.

Antique-
Modern
Thought.
   None the less, this Political Doctrine, even when
it was endeavouring contentedly to live within the
world of medieval thoughts, had from the first borne
into that world the seeds of dissolution.   To the cradle
of Political Theory the Ancient World brought gifts :
an antique concept of The State, an antique concept
of Law.   Of necessity these would work a work of
destruction upon the medieval mode of thought.   As
a matter of fact the old system began internally to
dissolve.   The several elements that were thus set
free began to combine with the antique ideas, and from
these combinations new mental products issued.   So
much of Medieval Thought as was in this wise completely fused with the Antique Tradition came down
with that Tradition into the Modern World, and became the specifically modern factor in the scheme of
Natural Law.   All the more irreparable was the downfall of the Medieval System.

Advance
of An-
tique-
Modern
Thought.
   If from the point at which we have placed ourselves we survey the Political Doctrine of the Middle
Age, we see within the medieval husk an 'antique-
modern' kernel.   Always waxing, it draws away all
vital nutriment from the shell, and in the end that shell
is broken.   Thus the history of the Political Theories

of the Middle Age is at one and the same time a history of the theoretical formulation of the System of Medieval Society and the history of the erection of that newer edifice which was built upon a foundation of Natural Law. As might be expected, we may see great differences between the different writers and manifold fluctuations. Still, if we look at the whole movement, there is a steady advance all along the line. We may say that the first forces to tread the road that leads away from the Middle Age are the champions of Papal Absolutism, though to a first glance they seem so genuinely medieval. Then the study of Roman Law and the arguments for Imperial Absolutism with which it supplies the Hohenstaufen really march in the same direction. New forces were marshalled by the scholastic students of the Aristotelian Philosophy, and even Thomas of Aquino unconsciously laboured in a work of destruction and innovation. A new and powerful impulse was given by the literary strife that broke forth in France and Germany when the fourteenth century was young : strife over the relation between Church and State, in the course whereof many of the ideas of the Reformation, and even many of the ideas of the French Revolution were proclaimed, though in scholastic garb, by such men as Marsilius of Padua and William of Ockham. Then along very various routes the writers of the Conciliar Age forwarded, whether they liked it or no, the victorious advance of the Antique-Modern forces. Finally in the fifteenth century Humanism broke with even the forms of the Middle Age and, in its desire to restore the purely classical, seemed for a while to be threatening those medieval elements without the retention of which the Modern World could not have been what it is. The drift towards Antiquity

pure and undefiled, whether it takes with Aeneas
Sylvius the turn to absolutism or with Patricius of
Siena the turn to republicanism, did as a matter of
fact wholly repulse for a season the Germanic notions
of State and Law.   Yet was the medieval tradition
held by the many, and on the other hand the thoughts
of the German Reformation were being prepared.
Revolutionary thoughts they were, but harmonious in
their innermost characteristics with the work of the
Germanic Spirit.   Isolated, it is true, and in the shape
that he gave it fruitless, appears the effort of Nicholas
of Cues.   The genius of his powerful mind endeavoured
to unify two ages, and, as it were, to bring to a new
birth and to modern vigour the medieval system of
ideas.   But fundamental Germanic thoughts which lay
in that system lived on, doing a mighty work both
among the political ideas of the Reformation and also
in the construction of the 'nature-rightly' Doctrine of
the State.

Influence
of Cor-
poration
Law upon
Political
Theory.
As to the relation between the development of
Political Theory and that Doctrine of Corporations
upon which Legists and Decretists had laboured, we
shall see that it was just this lore of Corporations
which furnished Political Theory with genuinely legal
elements.   Not only were the Jurists themselves
acquiring a Theory of Church and State which, at
least in part, was obtained by a direct application of
the ideas and rules of Corporation Law to the largest
and highest Communities, but the Philosophers and
Speculative Politicians, though they might hold that
a mere corporation was unworthy of their attention,
borrowed from this quarter a wealth of ideas and rules
that could be employed in the scientific construction of
Church and State.

Conversely, Political Theory necessarily reacted

upon the Doctrine of Corporations. For one thing, the latter was from the very first, and as a matter of course called upon to represent the fundamental thought of the world-embracing Medieval Spirit touching the highest and widest of all Communities. And, on the other hand, every advance of the 'antique-modern' idea of The State was a preparation for the negative and destructive influence which modern modes of thought have brought to bear upon the medieval lore of corporations. *Influence of Political Theory upon Corporation Law*

Having thus indicated the main tendencies and combinations that will deserve our attention, we may now more closely examine those leading thoughts which find a theoretical formulation in the Political Doctrine of the Middle Age.

II. *Macrocosm and Microcosm.*

Political Thought when it is genuinely medieval starts from the Whole, but ascribes an intrinsic value to every Partial Whole down to and including the Individual. If it holds out one hand to Antique Thought when it sets the Whole before the Parts, and the other hand to the Modern Theories of Natural Law when it proclaims the intrinsic and aboriginal rights of the Individual, its peculiar characteristic is that it sees the Universe as one articulated Whole and every Being—whether a Joint-Being (Community) or a Single-Being—as both a Part and a Whole: a Part determined by the final cause of the Universe, and a Whole with a final cause of its own. *Medieval Thought and the Universe*

This is the origin of those theocratic and spiritual-istic traits which are manifested by the Medieval Doctrine of Society. On the one side, every ordering of a human community must appear as a component *The idea of Theo-cracy.*

part of that ordering of the world which exists because God exists, and every earthly group must appear as an organic member of that *Civitas Dei*, that God-State, which comprehends the heavens and the earth. Then, on the other hand, the eternal and other-worldly aim and object of every individual man must, in a directer or an indirecter fashion, determine the aim and object of every group into which he enters.

The Divine Harmony.

But as there must of necessity be connexion between the various groups, and as all of them must be connected with the divinely ordered Universe, we come by the further notion of a divinely instituted Harmony which pervades the Universal Whole and every part thereof. To every Being is assigned its place in that Whole, and to every link between Beings corresponds a divine decree. But since the World is One Organism, animated by One Spirit, fashioned by One Ordinance, the self-same principles that appear in the structure of the World will appear once more in the structure of its every Part. Therefore every particular Being, in so far as it is a Whole, is a diminished copy of the World; it is a *Microcosmus* or *Minor Mundus* in which the *Macrocosmus* is mirrored. In the fullest measure this is true of every human individual; but it holds good also of every human community and of human society in general. Thus the Theory of Human Society must accept the divinely created organization of the Universe as a prototype of the first principles which govern the construction of human communities[2].

III. *Unity in Church and State.*

Now the Constitutive Principle of the Universe is The principle of Unity.
in the first place Unity. God, the absolutely One, is
before and above all the World's Plurality, and is the
one source and one goal of every Being. Divine
Reason as an Ordinance for the Universe (*lex aeterna*)
permeates all apparent plurality. Divine Will is ever
and always active in the uniform government of the
World, and is directing all that is manifold to one
only end.

Therefore wherever there is to be a Particular or The Unity of Mankind.
Partial Whole with some separate aim and object
subordinated to the aim and object of the Universe,
the Principle of Unity (*principium unitatis*) must once
more hold good. Everywhere the One comes before
the Many. All Manyness has its origin in Oneness
(*omnis multitudo derivatur ab uno*) and to Oneness it
returns (*ad unum reducitur*). Therefore all Order
consists in the subordination of Plurality to Unity
(*ordinatio ad unum*), and never and nowhere can a
purpose that is common to Many be effectual unless
the One rules over the Many and directs the Many to
the goal. So is it among the heavenly spheres ; so in
the harmony of the heavenly bodies, which find their
Unity in the *primum mobile*. So is it in every living
organism. Here the Soul is the aboriginal principle,
while Reason among the powers of the Soul and the
Heart among the bodily organs are the representatives
of Unity. So is it in the Whole of inanimate nature,
for there we shall find no compound substance in
which there is not some one element which determines
the nature of the Whole. Not otherwise can it be in
the Social Order of Mankind[2]. Here also every

Plurality which has a common aim and object must in relation to that aim and object find source and norm and goal in a ruling Unity, while, on the other hand, every of those Parts which constitute the Whole, must, in so far as that Part itself is a Whole with a final cause of its own, itself appear as a self-determining Unit[4]. Unity is the root of All, and therefore of all social existence[5].

Mankind as one Community. Then in the Middle Age these thoughts at once issue in the postulate of an External, Visible Community comprehending All Mankind. In the Universal Whole, Mankind is one Partial Whole with a final cause of its own, which is distinct from the final causes of Individuals and from those of other Communities[6]. Therefore in all centuries of the Middle Age Christendom, which in destiny is identical with Mankind, is set before us as a single, universal Community, founded and governed by God Himself. Mankind is one 'mystical body'; it is one single and internally connected 'people' or 'folk'; it is an all embracing corporation (*universitas*), which constitutes that Universal Realm, spiritual and temporal, which may be called the Universal Church (*ecclesia universalis*), or, with equal propriety, the Commonwealth of the Human Race (*respublica generis humani*). Therefore that it may attain its one purpose, it needs One Law (*lex*) and One Government (*unicus principatus*)[7].

Separation of Church and State. Then however, along with this idea of a single Community comprehensive of Mankind, the severance of this Community between two organized Orders of Life, the spiritual and the temporal, is accepted by the Middle Age as an eternal counsel of God. In century after century an unchangeable decree of Divine Law seems to have commanded that, corresponding to the doubleness of man's nature and destiny, there must be two separate Orders, one of which should fulfil man's temporal and worldly destiny, while the other should make preparation here on earth for the eternal hereafter. And each of these Orders necessarily appears as an externally separated Realm, dominated by its own particular Law, specially represented by a single Folk or People and governed by a single Government[8].

The conflict between this Duplicity and the requisite Unity becomes the starting-point for speculative discussions of the relation between Church and State. The Medieval Spirit steadily refuses to accept the Dualism as final. In some higher Unity reconciliation must be found. This was indubitable ; but over the nature of the reconciling process the great parties of the Middle Age fell a-fighting. *Duality of Church and State reducible to Unity.*

The ecclesiastical party found a solution of the problem in the Sovereignty of the Spiritual Power. Always more plainly the Principle of Unity begins to appear as the philosophical groundwork of that theory which, from the days of Gregory VII onwards, was demanding—now with more and now with less rigour —that all political arrangements should be regarded as part and parcel of the ecclesiastical organization. The 'argumentum unitatis' becomes the key-stone of all those other arguments, biblical, historical, legal, which support the papal power over temporal affairs[9]. If Mankind be only one, and if there can be but one State that comprises all Mankind, that State can be no other than the Church that God Himself has founded, and all temporal lordship can be valid only in so far as it is part and parcel of the Church. Therefore the Church, being the one true State, has received by a mandate from God the plenitude of all spiritual and temporal powers, they being integral parts *The High Church Theory: Sovereignty of the Church.*

of One Might[10]. The Head of this all-embracing State is Christ. But, as the Unity of Mankind is to be realized already in this world, His celestial kingship must have a terrestrial presentment[11]. As Christ's Vice-Regent, the earthly Head of the Church is the one and only Head of all Mankind. The Pope is the wielder of what is in principle an Empire (*principatus*) over the Community of Mortals. He is their Priest and their King; their spiritual and temporal Monarch; their Law-giver and Judge in all causes supreme[12].

The Pope's temporal power.

If the papal party none the less held fast the doctrine that a separation of Ecclesiastical and Temporal Powers was commanded by God, it explained that the principle of separation was applicable merely to the mode in which those powers were to be exercised[13]. The bearer of the supreme plenitude of power in Christendom is forbidden by divine law to wield the temporal sword with his own hand. Only the worthier portion of Ecclesiastical Might is reserved for the Priesthood, while the worldly portion is committed to less worthy hands[14]. It must be confessed therefore that God has willed the separation of the *Regnum* from the *Sacerdotium*, and therefore has willed the existence of the Secular State : the worldly magistrature is ordained of God[15]. Still it is only by the mediation of the Church that the Temporal Power possesses a divine sanction and mandate. The State in its concrete form is of earthly and not, like the Church, of heavenly origin. In so far as the State existed before the Church and exists outside the Church, it is the outcome of a human nature that was impaired by the Fall of Man. It was founded, under divine sufferance, by some act of violence, or else was extorted from God for some sinful purpose. Of itself it has no power to raise itself above the insufficiency of a piece of human

handiwork[16]. In order therefore to purge away the
stain of its origin and to acquire the divine sanction as
a legitimate part of that Human Society which God
has willed, the State needs to be hallowed by the
authority of the Church. In this sense therefore it is
from the Church that the Temporal Power receives its
true being, and it is from the Church that Kaiser and
Kings receive their right to rule[17]. And all along the
Temporal Government when it has been constituted
remains a subservient part of the Ecclesiastical Order.
It is a mean or instrument of the single and eternal
purpose of the Church. In the last resort it is an
Ecclesiastical Institution[18]. For this reason all human
laws (*leges*) find their boundaries set and their spheres
of competence assigned to them by the law spiritual
(*canones*)[19]. For this reason the Temporal Power is
subject to and should obey the Spiritual[20]. For this
reason the offices of Kaiser, King, and Prince are
ecclesiastical offices[21].

From these fundamental principles flowed with The Pope
logical necessity the claims to Over-Lordship which has both
the Pope, as bearer of the sovereign *Sacerdotium*, swords.
urged against the Emperor as bearer of the *Imperium*,
and also against all other independent wielders of
worldly might. That the Emperor, and likewise all
other Rulers, derive their offices but mediately from
God, and immediately from the Church's Head, who
in this matter as in other matters acts as God's Vice-
Regent—this became the general theory of the Church.
It was in this sense that the allegory of the Two Swords
was expounded by the ecclesiastical party. Both
Swords have been given by God to Peter and through
him to the Popes, who are to retain the spiritual sword,
while the temporal they deliver to others. This
delivery, however, will confer, not free ownership, but

the right of an ecclesiastical office-holder. As before the delivery, so afterwards, the Pope has *utrumque gladium*. He has both Powers *habitu*, though only the Spiritual Power *actu*. The true ownership (*dominium*) of both swords is his, and what he concedes in the temporal sword is merely some right of independent user, which is characterized as *usus immediatus*, or perhaps as *dominium utile*[22]. In the medium of feudal law the papal right in the Temporal Power appears as neither more nor less than a feudal lordship. The Emperor assumes the place of the highest of papal vassals, and the oath that at his coronation he swears to the Pope can be regarded as a true *homagium*[23]. In any case the Emperor and every other worldly Ruler are in duty bound to use in the service and under the direction of the Church the sword that has been entrusted to them[24]. It is not merely that the Pope by virtue of his spiritual sword may by spiritual means supervise, direct and correct all acts of rulership[25]. Much rather must we hold that, though in the general course of affairs he ought to refrain from any immediate intermeddling with temporal matters, and to respect the legitimately acquired rights of rulers[26], he is none the less entitled and bound to exercise a direct control of temporalities whenever there is occasion and reasonable cause for his intervention (*casualiter et ex rationabili causa*)[27]. Therefore for good cause may he withdraw and confer the *Imperium* from and upon peoples and individuals[28]: and indeed it was by his plenitude of power that the *Imperium* was withdrawn from the Greeks and bestowed upon the Germans (*translatio Imperii*)[29]. His is it to set Kaisers and Kings over the peoples, and the right so to do he uses whenever no other mode of instituting a ruler has been established or the established mode has shown its insufficiency[30]. In particular, if the Emperor is chosen by the Prince-Electors, this is a practice which rests solely upon a concession which the Pope has made and might for good cause revoke[31]. It is he that is and remains the true Imperial Elector. Therefore to him pertains the examination and confirmation of every election; upon him devolves the election whenever, according to the rules of Canon Law, a case of 'lapse' occurs; and it is by his act of unction and coronation that the Emperor Elect first acquires imperial rights[32]. In case of vacancy or if the temporal Ruler neglects his duties, the immediate guardianship of the Empire falls to the Pope[33]. And lastly, it is for him to judge and punish Emperors and Kings, to receive complaints against them, to shield the nations from their tyranny, to depose rulers who are neglectful of their duties, and to discharge their subjects from the oath of fealty[34].

All these claims appeared as logical consequences of a legal principle ordained by God Himself. The subsidiary arguments touching the Pope's right and title, arguments derived from history and positive law, had no self-sufficient validity, but were regarded as mere outward attestations and examples. Conversely, no title founded on Positive Law could derogate from the Divine Law of the Church. For this reason whatever was in the first instance said of the Emperor's subjection to the Pope could be analogically extended to every other temporal Ruler[35]. And thus in fact was derived immediately from the *Ius Divinum* an ideal Constitution comprehending all Mankind, a Constitution which by the universal Sovereignty of the Church thoroughly satisfied the postulate of Unity above Duality.

Very rarely in the Middle Age were the partizans

The Community of Mankind and the Sovereignty of the Church.

of the Secular State bold enough to attempt a con-
version of this theory to the interest of the Temporal
Power, or to deduce from the Principle of Unity a
Sovereignty of the State over the Church. It is true
that the earlier age in which the Church was more or
less completely subjected to the Empire was never
wholly forgotten[36]. Yet was the reminiscence of it
seldom used except as a purely defensive weapon.
Even Ockham will go no further than the hypothetical
assertion that if really and truly there must be just one
single State comprising all Mankind with just one
single Head upon Earth, then this Head must be the
Emperor, and the Church can be no more than a part
of his Realm[37]. Lonely in the Middle Age was Marsilius of Padua when he taught as a principle the
complete absorption of Church in State. He, like
others, deduced conclusions from the idea of Unity;
but then with him this idea assumed a thoroughly un-
medieval form. Already it was transmuting itself into
the 'antique-modern' idea of an all-comprehending
internal Unity of the State and was proclaiming in
advance those principles of the State's Absoluteness
which would only attain maturity in a then distant
future. To this we must return hereafter.

In general throughout the Middle Age the doctrine
of the State's partizans remained content with the older
teaching of the Church : namely, that Church and State
were two Co-ordinate Powers, that the Two Swords
were *potestates distinctae*, that *Sacerdotium* and *Imperium* were two independent spheres instituted by
God Himself[38]. This doctrine therefore claimed for
the Temporal Power an inherent authority not derived
from ecclesiastical canons[39]. In century after century
it fought a battle for the principle that the *Imperium*,
like the *Sacerdotium*, proceeds immediately from God

(*imperium a Deo*), and therefore depends from God and not from the Church (*imperium non dependet ab ecclesia*)[40]. Now with more and now with less vigour this doctrine contested the various claims that were urged on the Church's side against the Emperor and Temporal Power[41]. Still it conceded a like sovereignty and independence to the Spiritual Sword, and merely demanded that the Ecclesiastical Power should confine itself within the limit of genuinely spiritual affairs, the Church having been instituted and ordained by God as a purely Spiritual Realm[42]. Nay, this theory was almost always willing frankly to admit that, when compared with the State, the Church, having the sublimer aim, might rightly claim, not only a higher intrinsic value, but also a loftier external rank[43].

The writers, however, who took the State's side in the debate, they also were full of the idea of the organized Oneness of all Mankind, and could see in the Spiritual and Temporal Orders but two sides of the one Christian Commonwealth. So in a two-fold wise they endeavoured to reduce the contending principles to Unity. Sometimes they held that the external Unity of the Universal Realm finds an adequate presentment in that Celestial Head in which the Body of Mankind attains completion—a Head whence the two Powers flow and whither they return in confluence[44]. Sometimes they developed the thought that in the terrestrial sphere an internal Unity of the two Orders will suffice: such a Unity as results from internal connexion and mutual support. The *Sacerdotium* and the *Imperium*, each of these, taken by itself was but one vital Function of the social Body, and the fulness of Life was only attained by their 'harmonious concord' and by their mutually supplementing co-operation in the task that is set before

[margin note:] Unity and the two coordinate powers.

Mankind[45]. Hence were drawn, not only the conclusion that the State must be subject to the Church in Spirituals, and the Church to the State in Temporals[46], but also a remarkable and further reaching theory by virtue whereof each of the two powers can and must in case of necessity (*casualiter* and *per accidens*) assume, for the weal of the whole body, functions which in themselves are not its proper functions. By such a 'law of necessity' an explanation could be given of those historical occurrences which seemed to stand in contradiction to a system which severs the Two Swords, and from such a 'law of necessity' political consequences of a practical kind could be deduced. Since, when there is a vacancy in the office of supreme temporal Magistrate, it is for the Pope to judge even temporal matters, the *translatio imperii*, the decision of disputed elections to the Empire, nay, in some circumstances even the deposition of a Kaiser, might perhaps have fallen within the Pope's competence[47]. But the same legal principle required that in case of necessity the Temporal Head of Christendom should take the Church under his care, and either himself decide ecclesiastical controversies or else summon a General Council to heal the faults of the Church[48].

Unity within Church and State. Then when each of these two Orders is taken by itself we once more see the medieval Principle of Unity at work and constituting that Order as a single whole.

Visible Unity of the Church. From it there arises within the Church the idea of the divinely instituted, visible and external Unity of the Spiritual Realm. Throughout the whole Middle Age there reigned, almost without condition or qualification, the notion that the Oneness and Universality of the Church must manifest itself in a unity of law, constitution and supreme government[49], and also the

notion that by rights the whole of Mankind belongs to
the Ecclesiastical Society that is thus constituted[50].
Therefore it is quite common to see the Church
conceived as a 'State.' That the Principle of Oneness
demands of necessity an external Unity was but very
rarely doubted[51]. Very slowly was ground won by a
reaction which protested, not merely against the increasing worldliness of the Church, but also against
the whole idea of a 'Spiritual State.' It was reserved
for Wyclif and Hus decisively to demand that the
Church should be conceived in a more inward, less
external, fashion, as the Community of the Predestin-
ated, and so to prepare the way for that German
Reformation which at this very point broke thoroughly
away from the medieval Idea of Unity[52].

Similarly within the mundane sphere the Middle
Age deduced from the Principle of Oneness the
divinely ordained necessity of a one and only World-
State[53]. Theological, historical and juristic arguments
were adduced to prove that the world-wide Roman
Dominion was the final member in that series of
Universal Monarchies which was foreordained and
foretold by God, and that, despite many appearances
to the contrary, this Roman Dominion was legitimately
acquired and legitimately administered even in the
days of heathenry[54]. Then this Dominion was hallowed and confirmed by the birth, life and death of
Christ. It was transferred for a while to the Greeks
by Constantine, but finally with the approval of God
was conferred upon the Germans[55]. Therefore the
Romano-German Kaiser, as immediate successor in
title to the Caesars, was by divine and human law
possessed of the *Imperium Mundi*, by virtue whereof
all Peoples and Kings of the earth were subject unto
him[56]. Like the Roman Church, the Roman Realm

Unity of the temporal power. Imperialism.

2—2

was indestructible until the time when its downfall
would usher in the Judgment Day[57]. Consistent be-
lievers in this Imperial Idea drew the further conclusion
that *de iure*, as well as *de facto*, this Monarchy of
divine right was indestructible. Neither custom nor
privilege could effect any deliverance from its sway
that would have any sort of legal validity. Every
alienation, every partition, every other human act
which diminished this Empire, even though the act
were done by the Emperor's self, was *de iure* null and
void[58]. For a long while even doubters and opponents
would not directly call in question this Imperial Idea,
but would only maintain the legal validity of exceptions that were based upon privilege or prescription[59],
and there were many who expressly asserted that
exceptions of this kind did not impugn the idea of the
Realm Universal[60].

Imperial theory contested.
Nevertheless, as a matter of fact the principle of
the Universal State was assailed while as yet the
principle of the Universal Church was not in jeopardy.
Especially in France, we hear the doctrine that the
Oneness of all Mankind need not find expression in a
one and only State, but that on the contrary a Plurality
of States best corresponds to the nature of man and of
temporal power[61]. Thus at this point also medieval
theory develops modern ideas, the process of development being in harmony with the growth of National
States in the world of fact.

Theory of partial groups. Federal-istic structure.
If, however, medieval thought, whenever it was
purely medieval, postulated the visible Unity of Mankind in Church and Empire, it regarded this Unity as
prevailing only up to those limits within which Unity
is demanded by the Oneness of the aim or object of
Mankind. Therefore the Unity was neither absolute
nor exclusive, but appeared as the vaulted dome of an

organically articulated structure of human society. In Church and Empire the Total Body is a manifold and graduated system of Partial Bodies, each of which, though itself a Whole, necessarily demands connexion with the larger Whole[62]. It has a final cause of its own, and consists of Parts which it procreates and dominates, and which in their turn are Wholes[63]. Between the highest Universality or 'All-Community' and the absolute Unity of the individual man, we find a series of intermediating units, in each of which lesser and lower units are comprised and combined. Medieval theory endeavoured to establish a definite scheme descriptive of this articulation, and the graduated hierarchy of the Church served as a model for a parallel system of temporal groups. When it comes to particulars, there will be differences between different schemes ; but it is common to see five organic groups placed above the individual and the family : namely village, city, province, nation or kingdom, empire : but sometimes several of these grades will be regarded as one[64].

But as time goes on we see that just this federalistic construction of the Social Whole was more and more exposed to attacks which proceeded from a centralizing tendency. This we may see happening first in the ecclesiastical and then in the temporal sphere. The 'antique-modern' concept of the State-Unit as an absolute and exclusive concentration of all group-life gradually took shape inside the medieval doctrine, and then, at first unconsciously but afterwards consciously, began to burst in pieces the edifice of medieval thought. Hereafter we shall return to this process of disintegration ; for the moment we will continue to pursue the leading ideas of the medieval publicists.

Federalistic and centralizing tendencies.

IV. *The Idea of Organization.*

Society as Organism.

Medieval Thought proceeded from the idea of a single Whole. Therefore an organic construction of Human Society was as familiar to it as a mechanical and atomistic construction was originally alien. Under the influence of biblical allegories and the models set by Greek and Roman writers, the comparison of Mankind at large and every smaller group to an animate body was universally adopted and pressed. This led at an early time to some anthropomorphic conceits and fallacies which do not rise above the level of pictorial presentment[65], but also to some fruitful thinking which had a future before it[66].

Mankind as one Organism.

In the first place, Mankind in its Totality was conceived as an Organism. According to the allegory that was found in the profound words of the Apostle— an allegory which dominated all spheres of thought— Mankind constituted a Mystical Body, whereof the Head was Christ[67]. It was just from this principle that the theorists of the ecclesiastical party deduced the proposition that upon earth the Vicar of Christ represents the one and only Head of this Mystical Body, for, were the Emperor an additional Head, we should have before us a two-headed monster, an *animal biceps*[68]. Starting from the same pictorial concept, the theorists of the imperial party inferred the necessity of a Temporal Head of Christendom[69], since there must needs be a separate Head for each of those two Organisms which together constitute the one Body[70]. The ultimate Unity of this Body, they argued, was preserved by the existence of its Heavenly Head, for, though it be true that the body mystical, like the body natural, cannot end in two heads, still there is exactly this difference between the two cases, namely, that in the mystical body under its one Supreme Head there may be parts which themselves are complete bodies, each with a head of its own[71].

Moreover, from of old, behind the conception of Mankind as Organism, lay the desire that State and Church should complete each other and unite with each other into a one and only life. At this point ecclesiastical theorists could make profit of the old comparison which likens the Realm to the body and the Priesthood to the soul. A basis might thus be easily acquired for all their assertions touching the subjection of State to Church[72]. Their opponents sometimes tried to substitute one picture for another[73], but sometimes were content with resisting inferences. The latter course was taken, for example, by Nicholas of Cues when he drew his magnificent portrait of Organized Mankind. For him the *Ecclesia* is the *Corpus Mysticum*. Its Spirit is God and His Sacramental Dispensation. Its Soul is the Priesthood, and All the Faithful are its Body. But the Ghostly Life and the Corporal are, according to Nicholas, separately constituted and organized under the Unity of the Spirit, so that there are two Orders of Life with co-ordinate and equal rights. But as each Order is merely a side of the great Organism, they must unite in harmonious concord, and must permeate each other throughout the whole and in every part. As the soul, despite its unity, operates in every member as well as in the total body (*est tota in toto et in qualibet parte*), and has the body for its necessary correlate, so there should be between the Spiritual and Temporal Hierarchies an inseverable connexion and an unbroken interaction which must display itself in every part and also throughout the whole. To every temporal member of this Body of Mankind corresponds some spiritual office which represents the Soul in this member. [*Thus the Papacy will be Soul in the brain; the Patriarchate will be Soul in the ears and eyes; the Archiepiscopate, Soul in the arms, the Episcopate, Soul in the fingers, the Curacy, Soul in the feet, while Kaiser, Kings and Dukes, Markgrafs, Grafs, 'Rectores' and the simple laity are the corresponding members of the 'corporal hierarchy[74].']

Bodies moral and politic. Like Mankind as a whole, so, not only the Universal Church and the Universal Empire, but also every Particular Church and every Particular State, and indeed every permanent human group is compared to a natural body (*corpus naturale et organicum*). It is thought of and spoken of as a Mystical Body. Contrasting it with a Body Natural, Engelbert of Volkersdorf [1250—1311] already uses the term 'Body Moral and Politic[75].'

Anthropomorphism. At a still early time some men, anticipating modern errors, spun out this comparison into superficial and insipid detail. John of Salisbury made the first attempt to find some member of the natural body which would correspond to each portion of the State[76]. He professedly relied upon an otherwise unknown Epistle to Trajan, falsely attributed to Plutarch, but remarked that he had taken thence not his phrases but only the general idea[77]. Later writers followed him, but with many variations in minor matters[78]. The most elaborate comparison comes from Nicholas of Cues, who for this purpose brought into play all the medical knowledge of his time[79].

Deductions from the idea of the body politic. Still even in the Middle Age there were not wanting endeavours to employ the analogy of the Animated Body in a less superficial manner, and in such wise that the idea of Organization would be more

* In the original this passage stands in a footnote.—*Transl.*

or less liberated from its anthropomorphic trappings. Already John of Salisbury deduced thence the propositions—indisputable in themselves—that a well ordered Constitution consists in the proper apportionment of functions to members and in the apt condition, strength and composition of each and every member;—that all members must in their functions supplement and support each other, never losing sight of the weal of the others, and feeling pain in the harm that is done to another;—that the true *unitas* of the Body of the State rests on the just *cohaerentia* of the members among themselves and with their head [80]. Thomas Aquinas, Alvarius Pelagius and many others applied the doctrine in its traditional and mystical vestments to the structure and unity of the Church [81]. Ptolomaeus of Lucca pursued the thought that the life of the State is based upon a harmony analogous to that harmony of organic forces (*vires organicae*) which obtains in the Body Natural, and that in the one case as in the other it is Reason, which, being the ruler of all inferior forces, brings them into correlation and perfects their unity [82]. Aegidius Colonna, who constantly employs the picture of the Body Natural, leads off with the following statement:—'For as we see that the body of an animal consists of connected and co-ordinated members, so every realm and every group (*congregatio*) consists of divers persons connected and co-ordinated for some one end.' Consequently he distinguishes the 'commutative justice' which regulates the relations between the members and furthers their equipoise, their reparation and their mutual influence, from the 'distributive justice,' which proceeding outwards from some one point, such as is the heart in the body, distributes and communicates in due proportion vital force and movement to the several members [83]. Engelbert of Volkersdorf based his whole exposition of the external and internal goods of the well-ordered State upon the supposition of a thorough-going analogy between State and Individual; the Individual as Part and the State as Whole are governed by like laws and benefited by like virtues and qualities[84]. In an original and spirited fashion Marsilius of Padua, who founded his doctrine of the State upon the proposition ' civitas est velut animata seu animalis natura quaedam,' carried out the comparison of a well-ordered State to an ' animal bene dispositum'; only in the case of the animal the constitutive principle is mere natural force, while in the case of the State it is the force of human reason, and therefore the life of the organism is governed in the one case by the Law of Nature and in the other by the Law of Reason. So he compared even in detail the Reason which fashions the State with the Nature which shapes organisms. In both instances a Plurality of proportionately adjusted Parts is ordered into a Whole in such a way that they communicate to each other and to the Whole the results of their operations (componitur ex quibusdam proportionatis partibus invicem ordinatis suaque opera sibi mutuo communicantibus et ad totum). When the union is at its best, when it is *optima dispositio,* the consequence in the Body Natural is health, and in the State it is *tranquillitas.* And, as in a healthy body every part is perfectly fulfilling its own proper functions (perfecte facere operationes convenientes naturae suae), so the *tranquillitas* of the State results in the perfect performance of all functions by those parts of the State to which, in accordance with Reason and constitutional allotment, such functions are respectively appropriate (unaquaeque suarum partium facere perfecte operationes convenientes sibi secundum rationem et suam institutionem) [85]. (Ockham, who in many contexts treated the State as an organism, deduced, in a manner that was his own, the principle that in case of need one organ can supply the place of another, and so the State may in some cases exercise ecclesiastical and the Church temporal functions [86]. Manifold employment was found for this analogy between State and Body Natural by Dante, John of Paris, Gerson, d'Ailly, Peter of Andlau and other writers of the fourteenth and fifteenth centuries. This mode of thought, however, attained its most splendid development in Nicholas of Cusa's system of Cosmic Harmony. He endeavours to present to our eyes a harmonious equipoise between, on the one hand, the separate vital spheres of all the particular social organisms—be they large or small—and, on the other hand, the higher and wider spheres of combined activity proper to those superior organisms which the inferior engender by their coalition.

Then from the fundamental idea of the Social Organism, the Middle Age deduced a series of other ideas. In the first place, the notion of Membership was developed to portray the positions filled by individual men in the various ecclesiastical and political groups. It is remarked, on the one side, that the Member is but part of a Whole, that the Whole is independent of the changes in its parts, that in case of collision the welfare of the Member must be sacrificed to that of the Body; and, on the other side, that the Whole only lives and comes to light in the Members, that every Member is of value to the Whole, and that even a justifiable amputation of a Member, however insignificant, is always a regrettable operation which gives pain to the Whole [87]. Then again, from the notion of an Organism, whose being involves a union

Ideas of Membership, Differentiation, Function, and the like.

of like with unlike, was derived the necessity of differences in rank, profession and estate, so that the
individuals, who were the elements in ecclesiastical
and political Bodies, were conceived, not as arithmetically equal units, but as socially grouped and
differentiated from each other [88].   Moreover, from the
picture of the human body was obtained the notion of
a Mediate Articulation, by virtue whereof smaller
groups stood in graduated order between the supreme
Unit and the Individual [89].   In particular, the necessity
of this arrangement was upheld against the centralizing
efforts of the Popes which tended to break through the
organic structure of the Church [90].   Furthermore, the
constitutional order which combined the Parts into a
Whole was regarded as an Organization which imitated
the processes of Nature.   The task therefore that was
set before it was that of so ordering the parts, that, as
Marsilius of Padua says, every of them might perfectly
and undisturbedly act upon all the rest and so form a
Whole, or, as Ptolemy of Lucca opines, the lower
forces should be set in motion and controlled by the
higher, and all by the highest force [91].   Naturally therefore the idea of a Function (*operatio, actus, officium*) of
the Whole Body [92] seemed appropriate to every case of
social activity, and the member which performs the
function appeared as an Organ [93].   Lastly, from the
nature of an Organism was inferred the absolute
necessity of some Single Force, which as *summum
movens*, vivifies, controls and regulates all inferior
forces.   Thus we come to the proposition that every
Social Body needs a Governing Part (*pars principans*)
which can be pictured as its Head or its Heart or its
Soul [94].   Often from the comparison of Ruler to Head
the inference was at once drawn that Nature demanded
Monarchy, since there could be but one head [95]: nay,

not unfrequently the inference that, were it not for connexion with a rightful Head, the whole Body and every member thereof would be altogether lifeless[96]. Other writers however expressly rejected these fallacies, urging that, despite all resemblance, there are differences between Natural Bodies and Mystical[97].

The comparison appears once more when medieval theory deals with the Origin of ecclesiastical and political groups. However, in accordance with its general view of the Universe, it could not find the constitutive principle of the group in a natural process of Growth, but in every case had recourse to the idea of Creation. Therefore, on the one hand, a divine act of Creation appeared as the ultimate source of all social grouping, in such sort that the divine influence either (as was beyond doubt the case of the Church) directly fashioned and animated the Mystical Body, or else less directly effected the union of Parts in Whole by virtue of some natural and instinctive impulse. On the other hand, a creative act performed by man is supposed, more or less explicitly by most of the theorists, for to produce the State in conformity with the type of organization which Nature supplies is in their eyes the work of human Reason[98]. In elaborate detail Marsilius of Padua endeavoured to explain how the Reason which is immanent in every Community engenders the Social Organism by a conscious imitation of the life-making forces of Nature[99]. *Growth and Creation of Social Organisms.*

Howbeit, though at all these points an energetic expression was found for the thought that human groups are organic, nevertheless medieval doctrine paused here without attaining that ultimate resting place where it would have been able to formulate this thought in the terms of jurisprudence. As in Antiquity, so also in the Middle Age, the idea of Organic Society *Theory fails to conceive Church and State as persons.*

failed to issue in the legal idea of Personality—the single Personality of the group—and yet it is only when this process has taken place that the idea which is before us becomes of service in legal science. Therefore it is that medieval doctrine, despite all the analogies that it drew from organic life, might indeed occasionally conceal, but could not permanently hinder, the progress of a mode of thought which regards the State as a mechanism constructed of atoms. Indeed that mode of thought lay in the womb of the medieval theory. But of that, hereafter.

V. *The Idea of Monarchy.*

Medieval preference for a Monarchy.

We must now turn to that idea of Monarchy which governed all truly medieval theory and was intimately connected with those fundamental notions which we have been portraying. Through all the work of medieval publicists there runs a remarkably active drift towards Monarchy ; and here we see a sharp contrast between antique and medieval thinking.

God as Monarch.

The Middle Age regards the Universe itself as a single Realm and God as its Monarch. God therefore is the true Monarch, the one Head and motive principle of that ecclesiastical and political society which comprises all Mankind[100]. All earthly Lordship is a limited representation of the divine Lordship of the World. Human Lordship proceeds from, is controlled by, and issues in, divine Lordship. Therefore as permanent Institutions, the ecclesiastical and temporal ' Powers that be ' are ordained of God. If at one moment the champions of the Church were inclined to contest the truth of this principle when applied to the temporal Power, still, as time went on, even extreme partizans were once more willing to concede the divine

origin—at least the mediately divine origin—of the
State [101], while on the immediately divine origin of the
State great stress was laid by the advocates of secular
Government [102].   Furthermore, the office and authority
of every particular wielder of Lordship flow from God.
Immediately or mediately He is the lender of all
power, using as His tools the Electors or other con-
stituents of the Ruler.   Immediately from God derives
the office of His ecclesiastical Vicar [103].   The like, so
said imperialists, is true of the Kaiser who is God's
temporal Vicar [104], while their opponents here introduced the mediating action of the Church, but just for
that reason expressly declared that the imperial office
and all other lordships were loans from God [105].   And
so too, not only the sovereign right of the independent
ruler, but every magisterial function may be mediately
traced to Him, for all powers that are sub-demised by
superior rulers can in the last resort be regarded
as emanations from the divine Government of the
World [106].

But since, as already said, every Partial Whole
must be like unto the Universal Whole, the Monarchical
Constitution of ecclesiastical and political groups needed
no further proof.   Almost with one voice, the medieval
publicists declared a monarchical to be the best form of
Constitution.   They thought that they found, not only
in the Universe at large, but throughout animate and
inanimate Nature, a monarchical order, and thence
they drew the conclusion that this order is the best
also for Church and State.   Attempts were made to
strengthen this conclusion by historical and practical
arguments; but in the main it rests on philosophical
reasoning as to the essence of all human Communities.
In this context all arguments descend from the principle that the essence of the Social Organism lies in

Divine Right of Monarchs.

Unity, that this Unity must be represented in a Governing Part, and that this object can be best attained if that Governing Part be in itself a Unit (*per se unum*) and consequently a single individual [107]. Dante gave yet deeper import and sharper form to this thought when he argued that the unifying principle of Bodies Politic is Will, and that, for the purpose of presenting a Unity of Wills (*unitas in voluntatibus*) the governing and regulating Will of some one man (*voluntas una et regulatrix*) is plainly the aptest mean [108].

Monarchy in Church and State. From this preferability of Monarchy it followed that in the Church, whose constitution was founded directly by God, Monarchical Government existed *iure divino*, for God could will for His Church none but the best of constitutions [109]. In like fashion the doctrine which taught that the Empire also was willed by God led to the assertion of a divine institution of the Kaiser's universal Monarchy [110]. Similarly in every Body which is a Member of the Church or Empire, and consequently in every human group, a monarchical appeared to the Middle Age as the normal form of government [111]. The current legal doctrine of corporations was wont either tacitly to assume that every corporation would have,—or even expressly to assert that it must have,—a monarchical head.

Comparison of forms of government. But here once more a germ of disintegration was introduced into Medieval Theory by the references that it made to Antiquity. Those who in their proof of the excellence of Monarchy appealed to Aristotle would also borrow from him the doctrine of Republican Constitutions, their forms, conditions, advantages [112]. But the divine right of Monarchy was threatened so soon as comparisons of this kind were instituted. In truth we begin often to hear the opinion that no one form of government is more divine than another, that the advantages of Monarchy are relative, not absolute, and that there may be times and circumstances in which Republican Constitutions would deserve preference[113]. In particular, whenever the Kaiser's *imperium mundi* is disputed, an attack is made upon the foundation of the medieval ideal of Monarchy, and utterance may be given even to the opinion that the State which comprehends all Mankind may perchance be conceived as an Aristocracy: an Aristocracy of Sovereigns[114]. Even in the ecclesiastical region the divinity and necessity of Monarchy did not escape all doubts[115]. And then in the books of the humanists we often encounter an outspoken preference for antique, republican forms[116]. Already in the fourteenth century there were decisive assertions that the *argumentum unitatis* gives no unconditional judgment for Monarchy, since the *unitas principatus* is possible and necessary in a Republic[117]. In this context it became usual to represent the ruling Assembly of a Republic as a composite Man, and, in the antique manner, it could be contrasted with the mass of the ruled[118], so that the Monarchical State and the Republican could be brought under one and the same rubric.

So again, as regards the Monarch's position in the State there was a mixture of and a struggle between medieval and antique-modern thought. The Monarch's position.

The genuinely medieval lore saw in every Lordship a personal office derived from God.   Despite all references to the Antique, what we have here is plainly the Germanic idea of Lordship, but that idea had received a new profundity from Christianity.

So there was, on the one hand, a tendency to exalt the person of the Ruler.   In his own proper person he was thought of as the wielder of an authority that Apotheosis of the Monarch.

came to him from without and from above. He was
set over and against that body whereof the leadership
had been entrusted to him. He had a sphere of
powers which was all his own. He was raised above
and beyond the Community[119]. The Universal Whole
being taken as type, the relation of Monarch to State
was compared with that of God to World. Nay, even
a quasi-divinity could be ascribed to him, as to the
Vice-Gerent of God[120]. The lengths that the Pope's
supporters could go in this direction are well known[121];
and their opponents lagged not behind when Kaiser
and Kings were to be extolled[122].

Monarchy
as Office.

None the less, however, the thought that Lordship
is Office found emphatic utterance. The relationship between Monarch and Community was steadily
conceived as a relationship which involved reciprocal
Rights and Duties. Both Monarch and Community
were 'subjects' of political rights and duties, and it
was only in the union of the two that the Organic
Whole consisted. Moreover, in the Community all
the individuals stood in legal relationships to the
Monarch: relationships which properly deserved to
be called legal and which were of a bilateral kind.
Lordship therefore was never mere right; primarily
it was duty; it was a divine, but for that very reason
an all the more onerous, calling; it was a public
office; a service rendered to the whole body[123]. Rulers
are instituted for the sake of Peoples, not Peoples for
the sake of Rulers[124]. Therefore the power of a Ruler
is, not absolute, but limited by appointed bounds.
His task is to further the common weal, peace and
justice, the utmost freedom for all[125]. In every
breach of these duties and every transgression of the
bounds that they set, legitimate Lordship degenerates
into Tyranny[126]. Therefore the doctrine of the uncon-

ditioned duty of obedience was wholly foreign to the
Middle Age. Far rather every duty of obedience was
conditioned by the rightfulness of the command. That
every individual must obey God rather than any
earthly superior appeared as an absolutely indisputable
truth[127]. If, however, already at an early time, some
writers went no further in limiting the obedience due
from subjects than this point—a point to which Holy
Scripture itself would carry them—and, in opposition
to the claims of the Tyrant, allowed only the right and
duty of a martyr's 'passive resistance[128],' still the
purely medieval doctrine went much further. For
one thing, it taught that every command which exceeded the limits of the Ruler's authority was for his
subjects a mere nullity and obliged none to obedience[129]. And then again, it proclaimed the right of
resistance, and even armed resistance, against the compulsory enforcement of any unrighteous and tyrannical
measure—such enforcement being regarded as an act
of bare violence. Nay more, it taught (though some
men with an enlightened sense of law might always
deny this) that tyrannicide is justifiable or at least
excusable[130].

But alongside of this medieval idea of the Ruler's
Office, there appeared already in the twelfth century
the germ of a doctrine of Sovereignty which in its
monarchical form exalts the one and only Ruler to an
absolute plenitude of power. The content of this
plenitude needed no explanation, its substance was
inalienable, impartible and proof against prescription,
and all subordinate power was a mere delegation from
it. However, during the Middle Age the idea of
Monarchical Sovereignty remained, even for its boldest
champions, bound up with the idea of Office. Nor was
this all, for its appearance soon awakened a growing

The idea of Sovereign-ty.

opposition, which, always setting a stronger accent on the rights of the Community, finally issued in the doctrine of Popular Sovereignty.

Sovereign-
ty of the
Pope.

It was within the Church that the idea of Monarchical Omnicompetence first began to appear. It appeared in the shape of a *plenitudo potestatis* attributed to the Pope[131]. And yet just at this point even the extremest theories were unable utterly to abolish the notion of an Office instituted for the service of the Whole Body or to free the supreme power from every limitation[132]. Moreover, in antagonism to this explication of ecclesiastical Monarchy, there set in a swelling movement which not only denied to the Pope any power in temporal affairs, but would allow him, even in spiritual affairs, no more than a *potestas limitata*, and, in so doing, laid emphatic stress on the official character of Monarchy[133]. Gradually also the doctrines of Conditioned Obedience, of a right of resistance against Tyranny, of a right of revolution conferred by necessity were imported into the domain of ecclesiastical polity[134].

Sovereign-
ty of the
Emperor.

In the temporal sphere also the idea of Monarchy tended to assume an absolute form when in the days of the Hohenstaufen the Jurists began to claim for the Kaiser the *plenitudo potestatis* of a Roman Caesar, and soon the complete power of an Emperor was treated as the very type of all Monarchy. Still in the Middle Age absolutistic theory invariably recognized that the Monarchy which it extolled to Sovereignty was subject to duties and limitations[135], and (what is more important) there steadily survived an opposite doctrine which, holding fast the notion that Monarchy is Office, would concede to the Emperor and other princes only a *potestas limitata* and a right conditioned by the fulfilment of duty[136].

The element of Limitation which was thus imma- nent in the medieval idea of Monarchy began to receive theoretical development in the doctrine of the rights of the Community. To this we now must turn. Here- after we shall have to observe that the Middle Age set legal boundaries to State-Power of every sort, and it is matter of course that the Monarch is restricted within these, even if all the Powers of the State are united in his person.

VI. *The Idea of Popular Sovereignty.*

It is a distinctive trait of medieval doctrine that within every human group it decisively recognizes an aboriginal and active Right of the group taken as Whole. As to the quality and extent of this Right, there was strife among parties. For all that, however, we may also see plainly enough the contrast between the once prevalent and strictly medieval conception and that antique-modern manner of thought which was steadily developing itself. Clearly in the first instance what lies before us is the Germanic idea of a Fellowship (*die germanische Genossenschaftsidee*). Just as in the actual life of this age, within and without the groups constituted by lord and men, there might be found what we may call 'fellowshiply' grouping, so also, along with the Germanic idea of Lordship, the Germanic idea of Fellowship forces its way into the domain of learned theory. But antique elements were at work in this quarter also. In part their introduction was due to the Romano-Canonical doctrine of Corpo- rations, whence the publicists were wont to borrow, and in part to the influence of the Political Law and Political Philosophy of the ancient world. Gradually they transmuted the medieval lore of the Right of Communities until it bore the form of the modern doctrine of Popular Sovereignty. As, however, even in the Middle Age the thought of Popular Sovereignty was connected in manifold wise with the thought of the Ruler's Sovereignty, there was here a foundation on which the most diverse constitutional systems of an abstract kind could be erected : systems which might range from an Absolutism grounded on the alienation of power by the people, through Constitutional Monarchy, to Popular Sovereignty of the Republican sort.

Popular sovereignty in the State.

1. It was in the province of Temporal Power that the Right of the Community first assumed a doctrinal form.

The will of the people and the State of Nature.

An ancient and generally entertained opinion regarded the Will of the People as the Source of Temporal Power. A friendly meeting took place between this traditional opinion and that Patristic Doctrine of the State of Nature which the Church was propagating. That doctrine taught that at one time under the Law of God and the Law of Nature community of goods, liberty and equality prevailed among mankind. It followed that Lordship made its first appearance as a consequence of the Fall of Man[137]. It followed also that the authority of Rulers was grounded on human ordinance. Then, during the Strife over the Investitures, the Church could draw from these premisses the conclusion that this humanly instituted Temporal Power must be subject to that Priesthood of which God Himself was the direct and immediate Founder. The defenders of the State were content to resist this ecclesiastical reasoning without deserting the old ground. In contrast to theories which would insist more or less emphatically on the usurpatory and illegitimate origin of Temporal Lordship, there was developed a doctrine which taught that the State had a rightful beginning in a Contract of Subjection to which the People was party[138]. Many reminiscences of events in the history of Germanic Law came to the help of this theory, as also the contractual form which agreements between Princes and Estates had given to many of those rights and duties which fell within the sphere of Public Law. Still it was also supposed that a successful appeal could be made both to Holy Writ, which told (II. Reg., v. 3) of a contract made at Hebron between David and the People of Israel, and also to a principle, proclaimed by the Jurists, which told that, according to the *ius gentium*, every free People may set a *Superior* over itself[139]. Then, on the other hand, efforts were made to demonstrate that the human origin thus discovered for the State was not incompatible with the divine origin and divine right of Monarchy, since the People was but an instrument in the hands of God[140], and indeed received from His influence the spiritual power of engendering the Ruler's Office[141].

The victory of this manner of thinking was largely due to the decisive fact that just in relation to the very highest of all earthly Powers, the Jurists could find in the *Corpus Iuris* a text which seemed expressly to indicate the Will of the People as the source of Ruler-ship. Ever since the days of the Glossators [the twelfth century] the universally accepted doctrine was that an act of alienation performed by the People in the *Lex Regia* was for Positive Law the basis of the modern, as well as of the ancient, Empire[142]. *Controversy over the Lex Regia.*

For this cause it was all the easier to generalize this truth concerning the highest of all temporal Com-munities, until it appeared as a principle grounded in Divine and Natural Law. Indeed that the legal title *Voluntary subjection the source of rightful power.*

to all Rulership lies in the voluntary and contractual submission of the Ruled could therefore be propounded as a philosophic axiom[143]. True, that concrete cases might demand the admission that the Power of the State had its origin or extension in violent conquest or successful usurpation. Still in such cases, so it was said, an *ex post facto* legitimation by the express or tacit consent of the People was indispensable if the Ruler was to have a good title to Rulership. It was in this wise that men sought to explain the existence *de iure* of the Roman Empire, notwithstanding the violence which had been employed in its making, for they could say that the requisite *subiectio voluntaria* could be found in the tacit consent of the Nations[144]. William of Ockham and Antonius Rosellus go even as far as an express constitution of this World-Monarchy by the vote of the majority of the Nations, and they refer to the doctrine of Corporations to prove that in such a case the vote of the majority is conclusive, since, on the one hand, the whole of Mankind, if regard be had to that original community of goods which is prescribed by the Law of Nature, may be treated as a single college and corporation (*unum collegium et corpus*), and, on the other hand, the establishment of the Universal Monarchy was, in the words of Ockham, an act of necessity, or else in the words of Rosellus, an act which was done *pro bono communi*[145].

Reversion of power to the People. If then the *Imperium* proceeded from the People, the inference might be drawn that it would escheat or revert to the People whenever no rightful Emperor existed. The Church, it is true, avoided this conclusion by the supposition that, since the advent of Christ, the rights of the People had passed to Him and from Him to Peter and Peter's successors. On the other hand, the opponents of papal claims made manifold use of the idea of Escheat or Reversion. The older Jurists were indeed so much entangled in the network of the ancient texts that in their eyes the 'subject' of those rights which they ascribed to the *populus Romanus* in relation to the *Imperium* was the population of the town of Rome as it existed in their own day. About the middle of the twelfth century the followers of Arnold of Brescia made a serious attempt to claim for the city a right to bestow the vacated Empire[146]. Leopold von Babenberg was the first forcibly to protest against this identification of the Roman townsfolk with the sovereign *populus Romanus.* The Roman burghers, he says, have nowadays no more right than has *quicunque alius populus Romano imperio subiectus*; and when rights of sovereignty in the Empire are in question, the term *populus Romanus* must be understood to mean the whole People that is subject to the Roman *Imperium*[147].

A first application of this idea of the Escheat to the People of a forfeited or otherwise vacant Rulership was made when the opponents of the Popes had to explain the so-called *translatio imperii* : that is, the transfer of the Empire from the Greeks to the Germans. The Greek Emperor, so it was said, forfeited his right, and thereupon the Roman people once more acquired power to dispose of the Empire. Therefore the *consensus populi,* which is mentioned on the occasion of Charles the Great's coronation, was the true act of transfer, and the Pope merely declared and executed the Will of the People[148]. Leopold von Babenberg, however, refuses to recognize this power of the Roman citizens, who at that time, so he says, neither possessed the Lordship of the World nor represented the People of the World. So at this point he has recourse to the authority of the Pope, who by virtue of necessity—necessity in fact, not necessity in

The translation of the Empire.

law—had to occupy the vacant seat of the highest of temporal judges[149].

Guardian-
ship of the
vacant
Empire.

In like manner many writers claimed for the People a guardianship over the Empire or the State, pending a vacancy of the throne[150].

Election of
the Ruler.

In particular, however, from this same way of thinking was deduced the right of every People to choose a new Head in a case of necessity : provided that no mode of appointment by a superior and no strict right of succession had been established. For all power was originally based upon Choice, and Divine and Natural Law declared that, as a matter of principle, it was for the Whole Body of the ruled to institute its Head[151]. True, that by a grant of Lordship to a whole family, or, it may be, by other means, an Hereditary Monarchy might be validly created[152]. None the less, the Elective Principle was preferable, being in fuller accord with Divine and Natural Law[153]. Therefore it is that the Elective Principle prevails in the Empire, which needs must have the best of constitutions, and in the Empire this principle has always been observed, albeit under different forms[154]. The People may itself exercise the right of Election, or may delegate that right to others. To such an act of delegation the opponents of the papal claims were wont to trace the rights of the princely Electors of Germany[155], while the Pope, so they said, had acted in this matter as one of the People, or, at the most, as the People's mandatory[156]. Also it was argued that, as the electing Princes performed the election as representatives of the whole People of the Realm, their act had all the effect of an election directly made by the People, and, without any co-operation on the part of the Pope, immediately conferred upon the Elect the full rights of an Emperor[157].

Then as to the rights that the Community could

assert against its Ruler when once he had been legiti- Relation of
mately instituted, there were wide differences of opinion. Ruler to People.
The conflict of theories appears already in all its sharpness so soon as the Glossators have begun to controvert
each other over that *translatio imperii* from *populus* to
princeps, which was mentioned in the classical text.
Some of them declared that there had been a definitive
alienation, whereby the People renounced its power for
good and all, and that therefore the People, when once
subjected to the Emperor, had no legislative power and
could never resume what it had alienated[158].   Others
saw the *translatio* as a mere *concessio*, whereby an office
and a *usus* (right of user) were conveyed, while the
substance of the *Imperium* still remained in the Roman
People.   Thence they argued that the People is above
the Emperor (*populus maior imperatore*), can at the
present day make laws, and is entitled to resume the
imperial power[159].   The controversy that was thus begun
within the field of Roman law, extended itself, until in a
more general fashion the relation between Prince and
People was brought into debate.   Out of the debate
there issued diametrically opposite systems.

For those who adopted the first of these explana- The
tions of the *translatio* [that, namely, which told of 'an system of Ruler's
out and out conveyance'] it was easy to erect a system Sovereign.
of Absolute Monarchy upon the original Sovereignty
of the People.   In this sense even the Hohenstaufen
could acknowledge the derivation of Lordship from the
Popular Will[160], and in fact many lawyers were at pains
to deduce from that Abdication of the People which
was implied in the Institution of a Ruler, a Right of
the Monarch which should be as absolute as they could
make it.

Still even the advocates of 'Ruler's-Sovereignty,' The
when once they had grounded this upon a Contract of Sovereign Ruler and the People.

Subjection, were unable to avoid the recognition of a right against the Ruler which still perdured in the Body of the People. Even they were compelled to regard the legal relationship between Ruler and Ruled as being in all respects a contractual relationship between the Body of the People—which Body could be treated as a corporation (*universitas*)—and its Head, so that the People had a strict right corresponding to the duty incumbent upon the Sovereign. Furthermore, throughout the Middle Age even the partizans of Monarchy were wont to concede to the Community an active right of participation in the life of the State. Political Institutions being what they everywhere were, some such concession was almost unavoidable. There was unanimity in the doctrine that the consent of the Whole Community was requisite for the validation of any acts of the Ruler which were prejudicial to the rights of the Whole, and among such acts were reckoned submission to another lord, alienation or partition of the lordship, and indeed any renunciation of the essential rights of a lord[161]. It was just from this uncontested principle that Leopold von Bebenberg concluded that any act done by an Emperor which could be deemed to imply the recognition of the Pope's claim to examine and confirm imperial elections, or which could be deemed to have effected any sort of subjection of the Empire to the Church, was powerless to alienate the rights of the Empire and its Princes and Peoples without their concurrence[162]. Also men explained that, though as matter of pure law this was not necessary, still a general custom required that the Monarch should of his own free will bind himself not to make laws or do other important acts of rulership without the consent of the Whole Body or its representatives[163]. Not unfrequently the opinion was expressed that even the right of deposing the Ruler in a case of necessity could be conceded to the People without any surrender of the maxim '*Princeps maior populo*[164].'

Then there was a mediating tendency which sought to combine the idea of the Ruler's Sovereignty with that of the People's Sovereignty. It co-ordinated Ruler and Community and ascribed the supreme power to both of them in union. Those who occupied this position rejected Pure Monarchy and held that Limited Kingship or a mixture of Monarchy, Aristocracy and Democracy was the best of Constitutions[165]. *The system of Divided Sovereignty.*

On the other hand, the second of the two explanations proposed by the Glossators [for the classical text touching the *Lex Regia*]—namely the doctrine that the People granted to the Monarch merely 'the use' of supreme power—issued, when it was consistently developed, in the system of pure Popular Sovereignty: a Sovereignty that remained in the People despite the institution of a Monarch. True, that even the advocates of this system held fast the thought—and the idea of a Contract with the Ruler favoured it—that the relation between People and Ruler was a bilateral legal relationship, which conferred upon the Ruler an independent right of Lordship, of which he could not be deprived so long as he was true to his pact. However, no matter what the form of government, the People was always the true Sovereign, and this was expressly stated by the maxim '*Populus maior principe*.' Hence was generally drawn the inference that the Community still retained a legislative power over the Prince and a permanent control over the exercise of the rights of Rulership[166]. But, in particular, the further inference was drawn that, if the Ruler neglected his duties, the People might sit in *The system of Popular Sovereignty.*

judgment upon him and depose him by right and doom[167]. Just this last consequence was very generally drawn, and a peculiar importance was attributed to it. Here might be found an explanation of those cases in which the Pope had, or might seem to have, deposed Emperors and Kings and absolved Nations from the duty of subjection. Such cases might be regarded as legal precedents without any acknowledgment of papal power. The Pope's part in them had been not 'constitutive' but merely 'declaratory.' The authority had in all cases proceeded from the Folk or its representatives[168].

Monarchy and Republic. When the matter was regarded from this point of view, there could be no deep-set difference between a Monarch and a Republican Magistrate.

This, it is true, was not always consciously perceived. We can hardly, for instance, assert that Leopold of Bebenberg's mode of thought is republican. Yet he expressly teaches that the People of the Empire is *maior ipso principe*, can make laws, especially if there be no Kaiser or if the Kaiser neglect his duty, and can for sufficient cause transfer the Empire from one Folk to another or depose the Emperor. He also teaches that every particular People has just the same rights against its King[169].

Republicanism of Marsilius. Decisively republican, on the other hand, is the system of Marsilius of Padua. With all the consistency of democratic Radicalism it erects an abstract scheme dividing power between the *universitas civium* and the *pars principans*: a scheme which remains the same, whatever be the form of government. With him the 'Legislator' must be the Sovereign; but the People is always and necessarily the 'Legislator,' by the People being meant the Whole Body or a majority of those citizens who are entitled to vote. This inalienable right is to be exercised either in a primary assembly of the People or by its elected representatives. Therefore the Will of the People is the efficient cause of the State. By legislation it gives an articulate form to the State, distributes offices, and binds the various parts into a whole. In the first place it erects the office of Ruler for the discharge of such business as the *universa communitas* cannot itself undertake. But more : the matter, as well as the form, of the Ruler's office proceeds from this Sovereign Legislator. The wielder of Government is to be appointed, corrected, deposed by the Legislator *ad commune conferens*. The Ruler himself is only a part (*pars principans*) of the Whole and always remains inferior to the Whole. By authority granted to him by the Legislator (*per aucto- ritatem a legislatore sibi concessam*) he is the State's secondary and, as it were, instrumental or executive part (*secundaria quasi instrumentalis seu executiva pars*). Therefore in all things he is bound by the laws, and finally, since the incorporate body (*universitas*) is to act by his agency, his government will be at its best when it conforms most closely to the Will of the Whole (*iuxta subditorum suorum voluntatem et con- sensum* [170]).

An essentially different system was developed by Nicolas of Cues in his *Catholic Concordance*; but none the less decisively was it a system of Popular Sovereignty. In his eyes, all earthly power proceeded, like man himself, primarily from God (*principaliter a Deo*); but a God-inspired Will of the Community was the organ of this divine manifestation. It is just in the voluntary consent of the Governed that a Government displays its divine origin : *tunc divina censetur, quando per concordantiam communem a subiectis exoritur.* Therefore all *iurisdictio* and *administratio* are based upon *electio* and upon a freely-willed transfer of power

Cusanus and Popu- lar Sove- reignty.

made by the Community or its majority or representatives. There is no rightful and holy *species dominandi* that is not founded *per viam voluntariae subiectionis et consensus in praesidentium praelationes concordantiales.* Only a Ruler who has been thus appointed is, as bearer of the Common Will, a public and 'common' Person (*ut sic constitutus, quasi in se omnium voluntatem gestans in principando, publica et communis persona ac pater singulorum vocetur*), and only by recognizing himself to be the creature of the Whole does he become the father of its several members (*dum se quasi omnium collective subiectorum sibi creaturam cognoscat, singulorum pater existat*). The function of making laws is by its very nature necessarily reserved for the Community, since all the obligatory force of laws proceeds from the express or silent *consensus* of those who are to be bound. Therefore the Ruler also is bound by the laws. He only receives *iurisdictio* and *administratio* within the scope of his mandate. Even in his jurisdiction and administration he is subject to constant supervision, and, in case he transgresses the limits of his power, he may be judged and deposed by the People. And all this is imprescriptible and inalienable Right bestowed by the law of God and Nature[171].

Popular appeals to the principle of Popular Sovereignty. In similar fashion throughout the fifteenth century in all the theoretical arguments by which men strove to defend the rights of 'the Estates' against the growing might of Monarchy, frequent recourse was had to the People's Sovereignty as to a first principle[172], until that principle, assuming a popular form, penetrated more and more deeply the masses of the folk, and at length took flesh and blood in the revolutions which were accomplished or projected during the Age of the Reformation.

2. Meanwhile thoughts similar to those which had been developed in relation to the State had exercised a decisive influence within the Church. More and more distinctly and sharply men were conceiving the Church as 'a Polity,' and it was natural therefore that in the construction of this Polity they should employ the scheme of categories which had in the first instance been applied to the temporal State. Indeed in the end the Church was regarded as charged with the mission of realizing the ideal of a perfect political Constitution. Thus, besides the transmutation of the specifically ecclesiastical ideals, we may see, in this quarter also, the well-marked evolution of a 'nature-rightly' Doctrine of the State.

A definition which declared the Church to be 'the Congregation of the Faithful' was not to be eradicated, and therefore the doctrine of absolute monarchy, even when at its zenith, was powerless utterly to eliminate the idea of a right vested in the ecclesiastical Community taken as a Whole. However loud might be the tone in which men asserted that the Pope stood above the rest of the Church, had no 'Superior,' and therefore could judge all and be judged of none (*sedes apostolica omnes iudicat et a nemine iudicatur*) : that the Senate of Cardinals, which was always more completely supplanting the Assembly of Bishops, had acquired all its powers merely from the Pope and not from the Church : that even a General Council stood below the Pope, obtained from him authority to assemble and decide, and could neither bind him nor confer authority upon him [173] : none the less, there were two points at which a breach of these principles could not be avoided or could with difficulty be excused as a merely apparent breach. For one thing, the election of a Pope was always recalling the idea that when the

see was vacant the power of the Pope reverted to the
Community, and that therefore the Cardinals, as representatives of the Community, chose a new Monarch [174].
Secondly, the doctrine, hardly doubted in the Middle
Age, that in matters of faith only the Church is
infallible, and that the Pope can err and be deposed
for heresy [175], led to the opinion expressed by many
canonists that in this exceptional case the Pope is subjected to the judgment of the Whole Church (*iudicatur
a tota ecclesia, condemnatur a concilio generali, iudicatur a subditis, ab inferioribus accusari et condemnari
potest*) [176]. It makes no practical difference if, in order
to conceal this breach with the principle of Absolute
Monarchy, men invent the fiction that an heretical
Pope, being spiritually dead, has *ipso facto* ceased to be
Pope, and that the General Council has merely to
declare this accomplished fact in the name of the
Church, of which it has become the sole representative [177].

Supre-
macy of the
Council.

If then in this manner a certain Supremacy of
Council over Pope was still incidentally recognized by
the existing Law of Church, a theoretical explanation
and justification of this Supremacy would soon be forth-
coming. The doctrine that as a general rule the Pope
is above the Universal Church, but in matters of faith
is subject to it and to the Council that represents it,
had hardly ever died out [178]. But if the divine character
of the Pope's right to rule was compatible with his
subjection, even at a single point, to the Church, then
it appeared possible that, without abandonment of the
old and general principle of Papal Supremacy, other
points might be found at which, by way of exception, a
right of the Whole Body might be made good against
its Head. As a matter of fact, there soon were some
who taught that the Conciliar Jurisdiction over the

Pope extended to cases of notorious crime, of schism and of other evils which threatened the welfare of the Whole Church[179]. Moreover, the legal doctrine of acts dictated by necessity was developed in such a manner as to justify in urgent cases an extraordinary procedure on the part of the Whole Church without the Pope and against the Pope[180].

Howbeit, from the beginning of the fourteenth century an ever more triumphant doctrine pressed forward towards a bolder statement of the case. Relying now on those speculative constructions of Society which were supposed to have the warrant of Natural Law, and now upon the Positive Law touching Corporations, it transferred to the Church that theory of Popular Sovereignty which had been elaborated for the State, and in the end it declared in favour of the full Sovereignty of the Universal Church as represented by a Council.

Sovereignty of the ecclesiastical community.

Already John of Paris saw in the Pope only the corporative Head of the Community, related to it merely as every prelate was related to his own ecclesiastical corporation, having only such powers of government as were necessary for the preservation of unity, and, if he transgressed against the common weal, liable to be admonished by the Cardinals and deposed by a Council[181]. But, at this point also, Marsilius of Padua outstripped all his contemporaries. Contesting the divine origin of the Primacy, he saw the Unity of the Visible Church under its Invisible Head represented only by a Council, while to the Roman Bishop, who was to be elected, corrected, deposed by the Council, he allowed no other functions than that of requesting the Temporal Power to summon a Council, that of presiding in it and laying proposals before it, that of recording and publishing its resolutions, and that of

Council and Pope.

threatening transgressors with purely spiritual censures[182]. And then all the propositions which flowed
from the Sovereignty of the Whole were deduced and
stated in elaborate detail by William of Ockham. They
were propositions which theretofore had only been
maintained in isolation from each other, and it was left
for the extremest champions of Councils against Popes
to raise them to the level of a practical programme.
Ockham marshalled all the doubts concerning the
divine origin of the Papal Primacy : doubts which
thenceforth grew always louder[183]. He discussed the
question whether the Church can not freely determine
its own Constitution and perhaps wholly abolish the
monarchical form[184]. He explained the Election of
Popes as the exercise of a right delegated to the
Cardinals by the Community[185]. In no circumstances
would he concede to the Pope more than a limited
power[186], while to a General Council he ascribed the
power of binding him by its resolutions, of sitting in
judgment upon him, of deposing him, and of relin-
quishing him to the temporal arm for punishment[187].
Lastly, he maintained that in case of necessity a
Council might assemble without papal summons and
by virtue of its own inherent power[188].

Theories
of the
Conciliar
Party.

This doctrine of the Sovereignty of the Ecclesiastical Community had already been fully developed
when the writers of the great Conciliar Age, though at
some points they tempered it, erected it as a system
and made it an official programme at Pisa and Constance and Basel. For d'Ailly, Gerson, Zabarella,
Andreas Randuf, Dietrich of Niem and some of their
contemporaries, the whole Constitution of the Church
was based on the thought that the plenitude of ecclesiastical power was in substance indivisible and inalienable, and was vested in the Universal Church repre-

sented by the Council, while the exercise of that power
belonged to the Pope and the Council in common[189].
When the various writers attempted more precisely to
define the relationship of Pope to Council, there were
many variances between them ; but on the whole they
are agreed in ascribing to the Pope the ordinary exercise of a supreme and monarchical power of government, and to the Council a more aboriginal and a fuller
power which is to be employed in regulating, correct-
ing, and, if need be, overruling the papal government[190].   Therefore in the most important acts of
Rulership the co-operation of the Council was requisite.   The Council should rectify abuses of the Pope's
power and might have to judge him, depose him and
even inflict corporal punishment upon him[191].   In order
to exercise these powers, it might assemble itself and
constitute itself without the Pope's permission and
against his will, though in the normal course it should
be summoned by him[192].   During a vacancy of the see,
its suppletive power (*potestas suppletiva*) put it in the
place of the missing Monarch, and then by itself or its
vicars (*per se ipsum vel per organum aliquod vice
omnium*) it could exercise his rights of government[193].
In principle the election of a Pope belonged to the
Council as representing the Whole Church, and when
the Cardinals, as was the regular practice, performed
this function, they were but representatives of the
Council[194].   Attempts, however, were often made to
give to the College of Cardinals an independent position as a third organ of the Church, intermediate between Pope and Council[195].   Gerson and d'Ailly even
believed that in this fashion the ideal of a Mixed
Constitution, compounded of the three 'good polities'
of Aristotle, could be realized in the Church, since the
Pope stands for Monarchy, the College of Cardinals

for Aristocracy, and the Council for Democracy[196]. In truth, however, notwithstanding apparent variations, we see in the works of all these writers a full Sovereignty of the Council as the representative of the Whole Community. In the last resort all other ecclesiastical powers appeared as mere delegations from the Sovereign Assembly : an Assembly whose resolutions were unconditionally binding on the other organs of the Church : an Assembly which, in case of collision, was the sole representative of the Church and indeed stood 'above' the Pope[197]. The Law of God, which set bounds to every power, was, it is true, a limit, though it was the only generally recognized limit of the Council's omnipotence. Gerson, who accepted the divine origin of the Monarchical Constitution of the Church, held therefore that the Papacy, when regarded as an Institution, was unassailable even by the Council[198], while other writers, who suppose a merely historical origin for the Primacy, would allow the Council to modify the monarchical regimen or even to abolish it[199].

Theory of Cusanus.

It is, however, Nicolas of Cues who in the most many-sided fashion carries out the principle of Popular Sovereignty in the Church[200]. For him that principle was an imprescriptible rule of Divine and Natural Law and he maintained a complete parallelism between Church and State. The 'subject' of Church-Right was in his eyes the Whole Body which alone had received a mandate from God (I. c. 12—17). This was true of the Universal Church as well as of the Particular Churches. In the Church therefore, as in the State, all superiority was founded on consent and voluntary submission (II. c. 13—14). True it was, that God co-operated with man in the institution of Ecclesiastical Powers and that all Ecclesiastical Power

was from God (II. c. 19); but it was only the Grace
that was bestowed immediately by God; the Coercive
Force was bestowed by means of a human and voluntary act of conveyance (II. c. 34), and the divine right
of every office, even of the Primacy, had no other
character than that borne by every Temporal Magis-
tracy (I. c. 16; II. c. 13, 34). The medium whereby
definite form was given to that expression of the
General Will, that *communis consensus*, which in all
the various zones of government was necessary for the
conveyance of power, was Election (II. c. 14, 18—19).
By Election were ordained the overseers of the
smaller and larger governmental districts, parsons,
bishops, metropolitans, patriarchs, who thenceforth
represented the Communities of their respective districts, and who when they assembled in Council stood
as a visible presentment of their particular churches
and moreover of the Universal Church (II. c. 1, 16—
19). Therefore the authority of Councils, whatever
their degree, proceeded, not from their Heads, but from
'the common consent of all' (II. c. 8, 13). For this
reason the General Council, since it stood for the
infallible Church (II. c. 3—7), was above the Pope
(II. c. 17—34) and was not dependent on his authority
(II. c. 25), could in case of necessity assemble of its
own motion, and could transact business without him
(II. c. 2, 8). By virtue of the representative character
given by Election, Councils could exercise the power
of legislation, for, since all the binding force of laws is
based upon the *concordantia subiectionalis eorum qui
per eam legem ligantur*, and since therefore Papal
Decretals as well as Provincial Statutes had no source
save this 'common consent,' it followed that canonical
ordinances of all sorts acquired their validity either by
the tacit acceptance that is implied in usage or by the

express consent of the Community (II. c. 8—12). But
further, on the Mandate that is implicit in Election
rested all the jurisdictional and administrative powers
of the several Prelates. By virtue of those powers
the Prelates were the Heads of the Communities
and the presidents of the communal assemblies, but
they were bound by the resolutions of those assemblies
and were responsible to those assemblies for the due
exercise of entrusted offices (II. c. 2, 13—15). And no
other was the case of the Supreme Head of the Church
Universal. He too held his place by Election, an
Election performed by the Cardinals *nomine totius
ecclesiae*. And, albeit the Power of God entered into
the act, authorizing and confirming it, still the Pope
owed his position to the voluntary submission of the
Church Universal. Therefore his only power consisted
of the 'administration and jurisdiction' which had been
conveyed to him (II. c. 13—14, 34). So the Pope was
bound and confined by laws (II. c. 9—10, 20). Like the
King, he was higher than any one of the People, but
of the whole People he was the servant (II. c. 34).
His relation to the General Assembly was that of a
Metropolitan Bishop to the Provincial Council (II. c.
12): by it he could be judged and deposed (II. c. 17—
18). For all this, however, Nicholas of Cues, like
Gerson, regarded this monarchical culminating-point as
an essential and divinely decreed part of the Church's
Constitution (I. c. 14). Also he endeavoured, as did
some others, to interpolate between the democratic
groundwork and the monarchical head an aristocratic
element, which in the case of the Universal Church
consisted of the Cardinals regarded as provincial
delegates, and in the case of the Particular Churches
consisted of the Chapters (II. c. 15). Then he strove
to institute a constitutional link between this Ecclesi-

astical Constitution and the parallel Constitution of the Empire. On the one hand, the temporal rulers in their several provinces and the Emperor in the Whole Church were to manifest their care for the Church by summoning Councils and voting in them (III. c. 8— 11, 13—4), while, on the other hand, the clergy were to take part in the Assemblies of the Empire and of its component territories. To these 'mixed' assemblies—partly ecclesiastical and partly temporal—power to deal with 'mixed' affairs was to be ascribed (III. c. 12, 25, 35).

Upon this same notion of a Sovereignty given by Natural Law to the Community, Gregory of Heimburg, Almain, Aeneas Sylvius in his earlier days, and some later writers constructed their doctrine of Ecclesiastical Law[201]. Those Canonists also who were friendly to the Councils advocated the less extreme propositions of this system and at the same time paid heed to the Law of Corporations[202]. Even the constitutional theory of Antonius Rosellus, albeit strongly monarchical and based on Positive Law, was permeated by the thought of a Popular Sovereignty within the Church[203]. Therefore the earliest scientific reaction in favour of the Papacy, a reaction in which Torquemada was a leader, began with the negation of the principle of Popular Sovereignty, and indeed denounced that principle as radically false and impossible[204]. *Reaction against Popular Sovereignty.*

The constitutional doctrine of the Church thus underwent violent disturbances. Nevertheless one important consequence of the principle of Popular Sovereignty remained undrawn or but partially drawn. The Conciliar Movement did not bestow any active part in the affairs of the Church upon the Laity. At the utmost the theorists would allow a secondary or subordinate place to the Temporal Magistrate. Thus the *Rights of the Laity in the Church.*

exclusive right of the Clergy was not attacked [205]. Indeed Gerson held fast an extremely 'institutional' idea of the Church [i.e. an idea that the Church is rather an Institution than a Fellowship], for he defined the Church Universal in its active potency as the sum total of those essential offices which have been founded by God [206]. And, if upon the other side the Constitution of the Church as a Fellowship was loudly proclaimed and all ecclesiastical power was reposed in the Congregation of the Faithful, all inferences in favour of any active rights of the Laity were excluded by the supposition that every Congregation was perfectly and absolutely represented by the Clerical Council [207].

The Temporal Magistrate as representative of the Laity.

Still even at this point the Reformation was not wholly without medieval precursors. The idea of the general Priesthood of all the Faithful was never quite unrepresented, and also there were some who made the communal principle a foundation for the theoretic construction of the Church's constitution. What is most remarkable in this context is that the theories which went furthest in this direction finally issued in the introduction of the Temporal Magistrature into the Church, for instead of postulating an independent organization of the Ecclesiastical Communes [parishes and the like], men were content to suppose that these were represented by the constituted political powers.

Marsilius and the Laity.

Above all others it is Marsilius in his *Defensor Pacis* who pictures the Church as a Corporation of the Faithful (*universitas fidelium*) wherein the Laity,—for in truth they are Churchmen (*viri ecclesiastici*),—are active members. Between Spiritual and Temporal the difference was not 'personal' but 'real' (II. c. 2). The Clergy were distinguished from the Laity by the Priesthood. This, however, was merely a peculiar faculty of a spiritual kind, and bestowed no external coercive power and no exceptional right of an administrative or jurisdictional sort (II. c. 3—10; III. c. 3, 5, 13—14). Therefore the full powers entrusted by God to the Community of the Faithful were to be exercised by a General Council (II. c. 7, 18, 20, 22), which was to be constituted by all the Faithful, including the Laity, or their Deputies (II. c. 20; III. c. 2). However, as representatives of the Body of the Faithful, the *legislator humanus* and the *principans* were to act: in other words, the Assembly of the People and the Temporal Ruler. Upon them, therefore, lay the duty of summoning the Council, deciding who were its members, controlling and closing its deliberations, and executing its resolutions by force and punishment (II. c. 28, 21; III. c. 33).

Yet more extensive rights were challenged for the Laity by Ockham. He starts from the principle that, albeit the Canon Law would narrow the idea of the Church until it comprised only the Clergy, none the less the Church Universal, being the Congregation of the Faithful, must, according to Holy Writ, embrace the Laity also (*Dial.* I. 5, c. 29—31). Thence he argued in detail that, since Infallibility was guaranteed only to the Church Universal, the true faith might perish in Pope, Cardinals, Roman Church, the whole Clergy, all male and indeed all reasonable members of the Church—for one and all they were but parts of the Church—and yet might survive in the rest of the Church, perhaps in women and babes[208]. Therefore even the Laity might accuse an heretical Pope, and if they had power enough, might punish him (*Dial.* I. 5, c. 30—35). So they could summon a General Council and themselves take part in it; indeed (though the Scholar in Ockham's *Dialogue* thought this a plain absurdity) even women should be admitted, were there

[margin note: Ockham and the Laity.]

need of them (*Dial.* i. 6, c. 85). In Ockham's eye a General Assembly of this sort was by no means impossible. It might, for example, be constructed in such wise that within some limited time every Commune should elect certain delegates, from among whom deputies for the Council should be chosen by the episcopal Synods or temporal Parliaments. In such a Council the *Universitas Fidelium* would in fact be present in the persons of its representatives, and such a Council, like the General Assembly of any other Community or Corporation, would concentrate in itself the power of the Whole Body (*Dial.* i. 6, c. 57, 84, 91—100 ; *Octo qu.* iii. c. 8). The only spiritual rights and powers (*iura spiritualia*) from which Ockham would exclude the Laity are such as have their origin in *Ordo* or *Officium Divinum* ; on the other hand, laymen are capable of all *iura spiritualia* which are concerned with care for the weal of the Church (*propter communem utilitatem ecclesiae*). In particular, according to the *ius naturale*, according to the *ius gentium*, and perhaps according to the *ius divinum*, laymen are entitled to take part in the election of bishops and popes, and are excluded merely by temporary ordinances of human origin. Their ancient right becomes valid once more if there be any defect in the agency which positive law has put in their place. Thus in case of the heresy, the schism or the culpable delay of the Cardinals, the right to elect a Roman bishop lies, as a matter of principle, in the Romans, without distinction between Clergy and People, or else it lies in all Catholics[209]. However, the actual use of this right, as of other rights pertaining to the Whole Community, Ockham made over to the Emperor 'Roman and Catholic,' who, as the Community's Christian Head, might act *vice omnium*, in the name of and under a commission from All, and more especially the Romans[210]. And thus Ockham, like others, introduces the Temporal Magistrate into the Church as the representative of the Laity[211].

VII. *The Idea of Representation.*

To this lively controversy concerning the rights of Rulers and the rights of Communities, medieval doctrine owes the idea of a State with Representative Institutions. It was admitted on all sides that the main object of Public Law must be to decide upon the Apportionment of Power, and, this being so, every power of a political kind appeared always more clearly to bear the character of the constitutional competence of some part of the Body Politic to 'represent' the Whole. It became evident therefore that a theoretical severance must be maintained between the individual personality and the social personality of every human wielder of power, between his own right and his public right, between the private act which affected only the individual and the official act which by virtue of the Constitution bound the Whole Body*. At all these points the Doctrine of the State coincided with the Doctrine of the Corporation, and therefore in this quarter the Publicist had often no more to do than simply to borrow the notions which had been elaborated by the Jurists in their theory of Corporations.

The Representative Constitution.

In the first place, medieval doctrine gave to the Monarch a representative character. However highly his powers might be extolled, the thought that Lord-

Representative character of Monarchy.

---

* In other, and to Englishmen more familiar, words, 'private capacity' and 'politic capacity' were to be distinguished. —*Transl.*

ship is Office had, as we have already seen, always remained a living thought. Pope and Emperor stood for this purpose on a level with any president of a corporation. Therefore, though it was conceded on all hands that the Ruler might have a vested right, and a right that was all his own, in his Lordship, still with equal unanimity men saw as the content of this right merely a call to the temporary assumption of an immortal *dignitas*, and in the concept of that *dignitas* the function of the Ruler was objectified as a constitutionally defined sphere of power *[212].

Politic
capacity.

So it was as the bearer for the time being of a permanent dignity, and not as this or that individual, that the Monarch was to exercise the rights and discharge the duties of Lordship. And within the scope of the powers constitutionally assigned to him, he, as Head, represented the Whole Body. Therefore it was generally agreed in the Church that, as the Prelate is not the Particular Church, so the Pope is not the Universal Church, but merely represents it by virtue of his rank (*intuitu dignitatis*)[213]. The only question for dispute was whether, as a general rule, he by himself represented the Whole Body[214], or whether (as was the case of the president of a Particular Church) his representative power was confined within certain limits, while for a complete representation men must look to a Council[215]. So again, notwithstanding all disputes touching the extent of a Monarch's power, all were agreed that the Emperor was not the Empire, but only, by virtue of his rank, represented the Empire and the Community that was subject to him[216]. The

* Thus, for example, in our English legal doctrine, lordships, dignities, offices, were 'objectified' as 'incorporeal things,' or incorporeal ' objects' of rights, and these things were supposed to endure while their possessors came and went. In such 'things' men might have vested rights, but the things themselves were conceived as constitutionally allotted portions of public power.— *Transl.*

like was the case of every Ruler, whether elective or
hereditary[217]. This being so, endeavours were made
with increasing success to formulate in theory and
effect in practice a distinction between the public and
private capacities of the Monarch[218], between his private
property and the State's property which was under his
care[219], between those private acts of his which only
affected him as an individual and those acts of government which would bind his successors[220]. In this
instance the Church might serve as a model for the
Empire and the State, for within the Church distinctions of this kind had long been observed.

Then, on the other hand, it became apparent that
the powers ascribed to the Community of the People
were not the private rights of a sum of individuals, but
the public right of a constitutionally compounded
Assembly. Even the advocates of an inalienable
Sovereignty of the People did not identify the Whole
with the mere Body of the State, for beside the Body
there was a Head with rights of its own. They
declared at the outset that in all cases it was 'collectively' and not 'distributively' that the Community was
entitled to exercise supreme power[221]. Therefore a line
was to be drawn between the individual and the social
capacities of men[222]. It was not the individual man as
such, but the fully qualified citizen, the 'active burgher,'
as distinguished from mere 'passive burghers,' who
was entitled to participate in the powers that were
ascribed to the Community[223]. Even those citizens
who could vote were thought of, not as an undifferenti-
ated mass, but as an articulated whole, whose composition was affected by differences of rank, of profession
and of office[224]. The exercise of the Popular Sovereignty or of any other right of the Community was
possible only in a properly constituted Assembly, and

*Represen-
tation in
Assem-
blies.*

if and when all formalities had been duly observed[225]. In this context the rules of the Common Law touching the resolutions of Corporations were bodily transferred to Ecclesiastical and Political Assemblies. In particular, during the Conciliar Age when questions of ecclesiastical polity were under discussion—questions about the summons to councils[226], their power of passing resolutions[227], the rights of majorities[228], the mode of reckoning a majority[229]—the rules of Corporation Law were called into play. So also its rules concerning the prevalence of the majority were applied to acts of Political Bodies, and it was in the very words of the Jurists that the majority's power to represent the Whole was stated[230]. Ockham even went so far as to transfer the lore of corporate delict [the torts of corporations] to the relation between Political Communities and that State which comprises all Mankind, in such wise that by a formal sentence of the Corporation of All Mortal Men (*universitas mortalium*) a guilty Nation might be deprived of any preeminence that it had enjoyed and indeed of all part and lot in the rulership of the World-Community[231].

Repre-
senting
and repre-
sented
Assem-
blies.

But, more particularly, to the Law of Corporations we may trace the endeavour to give definite legal shape to that idea of the exercise of the rights of the People by a Representative Assembly which had long been current in the Middle Age, though unknown to Antiquity. Whenever to the right of the Ruler there was opposed a right of the Community—were this right superior to his or were it subordinate—the possibility that the right of the Community would be exercised by means of an Assembly of Representatives was admitted. Indeed in all cases in which either a gathering of the whole people was out of the question, owing to the size of the Community, or the business in hand was not suited to a General Assembly, representative action appeared not only as a possibility but as a necessity. When put into a precise form, the idea was that the Representative Assembly stood in the stead of a Represented Assembly of All, so that the acts of the Representing had exactly the same legal effect as the same acts of the Represented Assembly would have had. Within the ecclesiastical sphere it was on this principle that men based the action of Councils, and especially it was from this principle that were deduced the claims which were asserted on behalf of a General Council. Such a Council, it was said, represented in a perfect and all-sufficing manner the Community of all the members of the Church, in which Community were vested those rights that the Council exercised[232]. A prevailing opinion attributed to this representation a character so perfect that we might call it 'absorptive,' so that, though there might be a distinction in idea, there was no distinction in power between the Council and the Universal Church or Congregation of the Faithful. On the other hand, an opinion which Ockham stated argued conversely that because the Council's position was purely representative, some limit must be set to its power in relation to the *congregatio fidelium*[233]. Then when the representative character of the Council was to be explained, it was usual to refer to the fact that it was composed out of the elected Heads of the various ecclesiastical Communities. Each of these prelates might be supposed to have received at his election a mandate to represent the Community that was subject to him[234]. In Ockham's works we may see even the idea of a General Assembly of Deputies elected, not without the participation of the Laity, to represent all and singular the ecclesiastical communes[235].

M. 5

Repre-
sentation
and Elec-
tion.

In exactly the same fashion the various Assemblies of Estates of larger or smaller territories were regarded as Representations of the People empowered to exercise the People's Rights[236]. In this case also the representative character was supposed to be derived from the mandate given by Election : an Election which every section of the People had made of its own Rulers, but an Election which perhaps had conferred an hereditary right upon some race or some house[237]. On such foundations as these Nicholas of Cues erected a formal system of Representative Parliamentarism. It is true that in this early specimen of that system we see no mechanically planned electoral districts, and the constituencies are organic and corporatively constructed limbs of an articulated People ; still the Assembly stands for the Whole People *in uno compendio repraesentativo*[238]. In a similar sense, at an yet earlier time, Marsilius of Padua had declared in favour of an elective representation of the People, but, in his consistent Radicalism, reserved the exercise of the rights of Sovereignty, properly so called, for a primary or immediate Assembly[239].

Repre-
sentative
character
of Car-
dinals and
Electors.

Then a representative function of a more limited kind was ascribed to the small collegiate bodies which, with certain powers of their own, stood beside the Monarchical Head : for instance, the Electors in the Empire and the Cardinals in the Church. Leopold von Bebenberg was the first to ascribe—but in this he had many followers—the peculiar rights of the Electors, and more especially that of choosing a Kaiser, to a representation by them of the whole Folk of the Empire : a right belonging to the People was exercised by its representatives[240]. So likewise the Cardinals, when they chose a Pope or participated in other acts of Sovereignty, were looked upon as representatives of the ecclesiastical Community[241]. It is in just this context that we see the first development of the principle that every set of men which is a representation of an *universitas* (corporation) must itself be treated as an *universitas*. The surrogate or substitute, so men argued, takes the nature of that for which it stands. Therefore Representatives, who in the first instance are charged with the representation of the several particular communities which compose a People, must, if they are to represent the People as a Whole, act as one single Assembly which resolves and decides in a corporate fashion, and, in the absence of any special provisions for its procedure, ought to observe the rules of the Common Law of Corporations. It was on this ground that Imperialistic Publicists, from the days of Leopold von Bebenberg onward, defended, against the contrary opinion of some Canonists, the thesis that the rules of Corporation Law were applicable to the form and the effect of the choice of an Emperor by the princely Electors[242]. That those rules were applicable to the choice of a Pope and to all other joint acts of the Cardinals was indubitable[243].

VIII. *The Idea of Personality.*

After all that has heretofore been said, we might well expect that the Political Theories of the Middle Age would have laid great stress on the application to Church and State of the idea of Personality, and by so doing would have both enriched that idea and deepened it. The notion of the merely representative function of all the visible wielders of public power would naturally lead onwards to the notion of a represented and invisible 'Subject' of rights and duties. The

Personality of Church and State not theoretically formulated.

Doctrine of Corporations, which was so often cited in this context, was ready to supply the idea of a Juristic Person, and a due consideration of the nature of Church and State might have induced a transmutative process which would have turned the *Persona Ficta* of professional jurisprudence into the concept of a really existing Group-Personality (*Gesammtpersönlichkeit*). Already the Church was conceived, and so was the State, as an organic Whole which, despite its composite character, was a single Being, and the thought might have occurred that the Personality of the Individual consists in a similar permanent Substance within an Organism.

Failure of political theory.

Nothing of this sort happened. The professional lawyers of the Middle Age, it is true, were already operating with the ideal 'Right-Subjectivity' of Church and State, and sometimes their operations were by no means wanting in precision; but the instrument that they were using was merely their 'Fictitious Person,' an instrument forged in the laboratory of Private Law. On the other hand, the Publicists, properly so called, of the Middle Age hardly ever—and this is highly remarkable—make any direct use of the idea of Personality in their theoretical construction of the Body Social, and, when they make an indirect use of it by accepting its results, they become the dependent followers of Legists and Canonists. At this point we may see the beginning of a stream of tendency which has not ceased to flow even in our own day. On the one part, the concept of Legal Personality was confined always more definitely within the boundary of Private Law and became always more arid and sterile. On the other part, the Theory of the State had at its command no instrument which would enable it to put into legal terms the organic nature of the State, and thus was driven to mechanical construction on a basis provided by the Law of Nature.

We have seen above that the Canonists regarded not only each Particular Church but also the Church Universal as a corporate Subject of Rights[244], and that the Civilians simply subsumed Empire and State under the concept of Corporations[245]. Baldus, in particular, formulated with much precision the thought of the State's personality. Thus he explained that the acts of a Government are binding on its successors because the real Subject of the duty is the State's Personality. The Commonwealth, he said, can do no act by itself, but he who rules the Commonwealth acts in virtue of the Commonwealth and of the office which it has conferred upon him. Therefore in the King we must distinguish the private person and the public person. The person of the King is the organ and instrument of an 'intellectual and public person'; and it is this intellectual and public person that must be regarded as the principal, for the law pays more regard to the power of the principal than to the power of the organ. So the true subject of the duty created by an act of the Government is the represented Commonwealth (*ipsa respublica repraesentata*) which never dies, and a subsequent Ruler is liable in its name[246]. However, Baldus is the very man who lets us see clearly that he regards the State's Personality merely in the light of the prevalent 'Fiction Theory' of the Corporation. This appears plainly from his refusal to attribute Will to the State. For this reason he holds that jurisdiction delegated by the Prince ceases at the death of the delegator. If Gulielmus de Cuneo has argued to the contrary, urging that the Empire continues to exist and therefore that the delegator is not dead, he has (so says Baldus) overlooked the fact that here we have to do, not with the Empire, but with the Emperor ; for, be it granted that the Empire remains unchanged, still the Will which is expressed in the act of delegation is the Emperor's, not the Empire's, for the Empire has no Mind and therefore no Will, since Will is mental. (*Imperium non habet animum, ergo non habet velle nec nolle, quia animi sunt.*) Will is matter of fact; and mere matter of fact, as distinguished from matter of law, we cannot thus transfer from Emperor to Empire[247].

Reasons for the failure to grasp the State's Personality.

If therefore the Publicists when they had occasion to employ the concept of an ideal Person had only at their disposal this 'Fictitious' Person that the Jurists had fashioned, we may easily understand that, at the critically decisive points in the discussion of questions touching the whereabouts of the State's Power, the Publicists altogether refrained from speaking of the State's Personality. The rights that lay debatable between Ruler and Community were being ever more definitely brought within the growing idea of Sovereignty, and, this being so, a merely Artificial and Fictitious Person became an ever less competent 'Subject' for such rights. Moreover, in the controversies about the partition and limitations of Public Power men felt little need to penetrate beyond the visible wielders of that Power. And above all, the Doctrine of the State which prevailed in Classical Antiquity identified the State, when considered as a Subject of Rights and Duties, with its visible Sovereign, and this antique Doctrine was becoming the starting-point for theorists.

The State's Personality divided.

And so it fell out that even in medieval theory we may already see that the single Personality of the State is torn asunder into two 'Subjects' corresponding respectively to the Ruler and the Assembly of the People. Between them there is a conflict as to which has the higher and completer right; but they are thought of as two distinct Subjects each with rights of a contractual kind valid against the other and with duties of a contractual kind owed to the other; and in their connexion consists the Body Politic.

In so far as the Ruler was the 'Subject' of the State's power, the notion of a personified *Dignitas* enabled men to separate, both in the ecclesiastical and in the temporal groups, the rights which belonged to the Ruler as Ruler from those which belonged to him as an individual man[248]. But thereby an expression for the Personality of the State as a Whole had not been gained, for in the State there was a place also for the Community as distinguished from the Ruler. Rather we must say that within the State a separate Ruler-Personality [such as the English 'Crown'] was constructed. This Ruler-Personality would outlive the various Rulers who from time to time were invested with it; it endured in the shape of a personified Office. However, in a Monarchy, so long as the throne was occupied, this Personality was absorbed by the visible occupant[249], and in a Republic it took body in the Assembly which exercised the rights of Sovereignty : an Assembly which was pictured in visible form as a living Collective Ruler[250]. The Ruler's Personality.

And then on the other hand, in so far as the Community was a 'Subject' of rights, and stood apart from and either above or below the Ruler, this 'Subject' could not be identified with the Whole organized and unified Body, since the Head was being left out of account. Rather a separate 'Subject' was made of 'the People': a 'Subject' that could be contrasted with 'the Government*.' Then it is true that the The People's Personality.

---

* Thus at a later day King James II. was conceived to have broken a contract made with, not the State, but 'the People.'—*Transl.*

People when thus conceived was personified in the guise of an *universitas* and could be distinguished from the individuals that were comprised within it[251]; but, the impulse towards an organic construction having been repressed, men were steadily driven onwards to a mode of thought which explained the right-possessing *universitas* to be in the last resort merely a sum of individuals, bound into unity by Jurisprudence, and differing only from the plurality of its members for the time being in that those members were 'to be taken collectively' and not 'distributively.' This mode of thought appears in a pregnant fashion among the champions of the rights of the Ecclesiastical Community. They simply identify the Universal Church, (which is by definition the *Universitas Fidelium*,) with a 'collective' sum of all faithful people[252]. Torquemada therefore could attack the Conciliar Theory at this very point. He undertook to prove that the Universal Church as defined by his opponents was not even a possibly competent wielder of the ecclesiastical power that was ascribed to it. For, he argued, a Community taken as Whole cannot have rights of which the major part of its members are incapable, and of the Faithful the major part will consist of women and laymen; besides it would follow that all the members of the Church would have equal rights and the consent of all would be necessary for every act of Sovereignty[253]. Similarly in temporal affairs just the most energetic champions of Popular Sovereignty regard the Sovereign People as the merely collective sum of all individuals[254]. The influence of this 'individual-collective' explication of the idea of the People becomes always more evident in the theories that men hold touching the base and limits of the representation of the Whole by the Majority or by Conciliar Bodies or by the Ruler[255].

Thus the path to the idea of 'State-Sovereignty' The idea of the State's Sovereignty is missed. was barred for medieval theory, and already there were planted in that theory the germs of those later systems of 'Nature-Right'—the system of Ruler-Sovereignty, the system of Popular Sovereignty and the system of Divided Sovereignty—which endeavoured to construe the 'Right-Subjectivity' of the State now in a centralistic, now in an atomistic, but always in a purely mechanical fashion.

Before, however, we turn our attention to these modern elements in the medieval doctrine, we must, in order to complete our picture, cast a glance at the relation and interaction between the idea of the State and the idea of Right (Law).

IX. *The State and Law.*

When the Middle Age began to theorize over the The State freeing itself from the Law. relation of the State to Law, the old Germanic idea of a 'Right-State' [Reign of Law] had already shown its insufficiency. It was the idea of a State which existed only in the Law and for the Law, and whose whole life was bound by a legal order that regulated alike all public and all private relationships. In the Church there had been from all time a Power established which found its origin and its goal outside and beyond a mere scheme of Law and which might be contrasted with that scheme. So also State-Power, so soon as it became conscious of its own existence, began to strive for a similar emancipation from the fetters of the Law. Jurisprudence and Philosophy, so soon as they felt the first rustle of the breath of Classical Antiquity, began to vie with each other in finding a theoretical expression for an idea of the State which should

be independent of the idea of Law. Almost unanimously medieval Publicists are agreed that the State
is based on no foundation of mere Law, but upon moral
or natural necessity: that it has for its aim the pro-
motion of welfare: that the realization of Law is but
one of the appropriate means to this end: and that
the State's relation to Law is not merely subservient
and receptive, but is creative and dominant.

Law above
State and
State
above
Law.But, notwithstanding these acquisitions from Classical Antiquity,—for such in their essence they were—
Medieval Doctrine, while it was truly medieval, never
surrendered the thought that Law is by its origin
of equal rank with the State and does not depend upon
the State for its existence. To base the State upon some
ground of Law, to make it the outcome of a legal act,
the medieval Publicist felt himself absolutely bound.
Also his doctrine was permeated by the conviction
that the State stood charged with a mission to realize
the idea of Law: an idea which was given to man
before the establishment of any earthly Power, and
which no such Power could destroy. It was never
doubtful that the highest Might, were it spiritual or
were it temporal, was confined by truly legal limitations.

Natural
Law and
Positive
Law.How then was it thinkable that, on the one
hand, Law ought to exist by, for and under the
State, and that, on the other hand, the State ought
to exist by, for and under the Law? The thought
that State and Law exist by, for and under each
other was foreign to the Middle Age. It solved
the problem by opposing to Positive Law the idea
of Natural Law. This idea, which came to it from
Classical Antiquity, it proceeded to elaborate.

The idea of
Natural
Law.This is not the place in which to expound the
medieval doctrine of Nature-Right or Natural Law

or to pursue its evolution through the innumerable learned controversies that beset it. The work of development was done partly by Legists and Decretists on the ground provided by the texts of Roman and Canon Law, and partly by Divines and Philosophers on the ground of Patristic and Classical Philosophy. Thomas Aquinas drew the great outlines for the following centuries. To say more would be needless, for, however many disputes there might be touching the origin of Natural Law and the ground of its obligatory force, all were agreed that there was Natural Law, which, on the one hand, radiated from a principle transcending earthly power, and, on the other hand, was true and perfectly binding Law[256]. Men supposed therefore that before the State existed the *Lex Naturalis* already prevailed as an obligatory statute, and that immediately or mediately from this flowed those rules of right to which the State owed even the possibility of its own rightful origin. And men also taught that the highest power on earth was subject to the rules of Natural Law. They stood above the Pope and above the Kaiser, above the Ruler and above the Sovereign People, nay, above the whole Community of Mortals. Neither statute nor act of government, neither resolution of the People nor custom could break the bounds that thus were set. Whatever contradicted the eternal and immutable principles of Natural Law was utterly void and would bind no one[257].

This force was ascribed, not merely to the *Ius Naturale* in the strictest sense of that term, but also to the revealed *Ius Divinum* and to the *Ius Commune Gentium* which were placed alongside of it. The revealed Law of God stood to the Law of Nature (properly so-called) in this relation, namely, that, while

The Law of God, of Nature, and of Nations.

the latter was implanted by God in Natural Reason for the attainment of earthly ends, the former was communicated by God to man in a supernatural way and for a supramundane purpose [258]. Then the *Ius Gentium* (thereby being meant such Law as all Nations agreed in recognizing) was regarded as the sum of those rules which flowed from the pure Law of Nature when account was taken of the relationships which were introduced by that deterioration of human nature which was caused by the Fall of Man. Since the constituted Power in Church and State had not created this Law of Nations but had received it, it was therefore held to partake of the immutability and sanctity of Natural Law [259].

Limits of Natural Law. The deeper were the inroads that were made into the domain of ecclesiastical and temporal legislation by this idea of a Law of Nature which even legislators might not infringe, the more urgent was the need for a definition of the principle which set limits to a law-giver's power. As to the breadth and import of the principle there were abundant controversies. But the very elasticity of the limiting idea could in all circumstances save the principle. Men agreed that the rules of Natural Law could not be altogether abrogated by Positive Law, but still those rules might be, and ought to be, modified and developed, amplified and restricted, regard being had to special cases. In this sense a distinction was often drawn between the immutable first principles and the mutable secondary rules, which might even be regarded as bearing an hypothetical character. This distinction was applied to the true *Ius Naturale* [260], as well as to the *Ius Divinum* [261] and the *Ius Gentium* [262].

The Sovereign above Positive Law. The reverse side of this exaltation of Natural Law we may see in the doctrine of the absolute subjection of Positive Law (*ius civile*) to the Sovereign Power. This doctrine, which worked a revolution in the world of archaic German ideas, taught that the *Ius Civile* was the freely created product of the Power of a Community, an instrument mutable in accordance with estimates of utility, a set of rules that had no force of their own[263]. It followed that in every Community the wielder of Sovereignty stood above the Positive Law that prevailed therein. Nay, always more decisively, men found the distinguishing note of Sovereignty, ecclesiastical or temporal, in the fact that the Sovereign was not bound by any human law.

The advocates of Ruler's-Sovereignty identified Positive Law with the expressly or tacitly declared Will of the Ruler. They placed the Ruler before and above the statutes made by him or his predecessors. They taught that he for his part was not bound by a statute, but might in every single case apply or break it as need might be. Even from the twelfth century onwards, Jurisprudence laid stress on those Roman texts that made for this result. Thence it might take the comparison of the Ruler to a *lex animata* : thence the assertion *Quod Principi placuit legis habet vigorem* : and thence above all a sentence destined to be, from century to century, a focus of controversial literature, namely, *Princeps legibus solutus est.* Furnished with these, the lawyers could thereout fashion other maxims, in particular that which the Popes applied to themselves : *Omnia iura habet Princeps in pectore suo.* Philosophical theory assented. It found the specific difference between the true Monarch and the Republican Magistrate exactly at this point. The latter was bound by the laws made by the People or by him and the People. The former wandered around as a *lex animata,* and in every single case might modify the

The Prince not bound by Law.

previously existing law by virtue of a word that was
drawn from him by the concrete needs of the moment[264].
Nor were there wanting men who from this *potestas
legibus soluta* would draw absolutistic consequences, of
which the Pope in the Church and the Kaiser, or
a little later every Sovereign, in the State would reap
the profit[265].

Positive Law and the Community. Against this doctrine a protest was made by all
those writers who ascribed Sovereignty or even a share
of Sovereignty to the People; and their protest was
sharply formulated. Whereas the maintainers of
'Ruler's-Sovereignty' declared that only in Republics
were the laws founded on the Will of the People and
therefore superior to the Magistrate[266], the champions
of the theory which accepted Popular Sovereignty as
a first principle proclaimed that, no matter what was
the form of government, the binding force of Statute
always had its source in the consent of the Community.
Therefore they would hear nothing of any Ruler who
was above the laws: no, not though he were Pope or
Kaiser[267]. A separation of the legislative from the
executive power begins to be suggested at this point,
and it afterwards becomes of the highest importance in
the development of the idea of the Reign of Law
(*Rechtsstaat*)[268]. However, what was at issue in the
first instance was only the whereabouts of Sovereignty,
and not the relation between Sovereign Power and
Law, for the one party claimed for the Sovereign
Assembly, (in Church or State as the case might be,)
exactly the same superiority to Positive Law which the
other party granted to the Monarch[269].

Natural Rights and Positive Rights. Medieval theory therefore was unanimous that the
power of the State stood below the rules of Natural
and above the rules of Positive Law. That being so,
an analogous distinction had to be drawn in the matter

of the State's relation to two classes of Rights and
Duties.

A Right that was conceived to fall within Positive
Law was regarded as being, like the rule whence it
flowed, the outcome of a concession made by the State,
and was subject to the Sovereign's disposal. Men did
not allow that a vested right, if acquired by a title
derived from Positive Law, could as a matter of
principle be valid as against the Power of the State.

Already, as is well known, the jurist Martinus
[circ. 1150] ascribed to the Emperor a true ownership
of all things, and therefore a free power of disposal
over the rights of private persons. He relied in
particular on some words in the Code (c. 7, 37, l. 3):
quum omnia Principis esse intelligantur. On the
ecclesiastical side a similar doctrine was asserted in
favour of the Pope[270]. For all this, however, a contrary doctrine, which was already maintained by
Bulgarus [circ. 1150], was constantly gaining ground.
It taught that above private ownership there stood
only a Superiority on the part of the State, which was
sometimes expressly called a mere *iurisdictio et protectio*, and which, even when it was supposed to be
a sort of *dominium*, a sort of over-ownership, was still
treated in a purely 'publicistic' manner[271]. However,
it was just out of this Superiority that men developed
the theory—a theory strange to archaic German law—
of a Right of Expropriation, by virtue whereof the
State, whenever Reason of State demanded this, might
modify private rights or abrogate them[272].

Thus the history of the Theory of Expropriation
takes, in the main, the form of a process whereby
definite bounds are set to an expropriatory right. It
was generally agreed that the Supreme Power may
interfere with acquired rights 'for good cause,' but not

Marginal notes: Eminent domain. — The theory of Expropriation.

arbitrarily. For some this was an absolute principle of law[273], and even those who would allow the Sovereign, either in all cases or at least in certain cases, to transgress it, still regarded it as a general rule[274]. As a 'sufficient cause,' besides forfeiture for crime and many other multifarious matters, we see Public Necessity, to which Private Right must yield in case of collision. However, we may hear with increasing stress the assertion that, when there is expropriation for the good of the public, compensation should be made at public expense[275]; but from this rule exceptions will be made, sometimes for the case of general Statutes which affect all individuals alike[276], and sometimes for cases of necessity[277].

Natural Law, Property and Contract. Now it is, however, highly characteristic of Medieval Doctrine that the ground of Positive Law did not seem to it capable of supporting this protection of acquired rights. On the contrary, the sanctity as against the Sovereign of any such right was only to be maintained if and in so far as the right in question could be based outside Positive Law on some ground of Natural Law. In this context two propositions became the foundation of the whole doctrine. First: the institution of property had its roots in the *Ius Gentium*: in Law therefore which flowed out of the pure Law of Nature without the aid of the State, and in Law which was when as yet the State was not. Thence it followed that particular rights which had been acquired by virtue of this Institution in no wise owed their existence exclusively to the State[278]. Secondly: the binding force of Contracts descended from the Law Natural, so that the Sovereign, though he could not bind himself or his successors by Statute, could bind himself and his successors to his subjects by Contract. Thence it followed that every right which the State

had conferred by way of Contract was unassailable by
the State, though here again an exception was made
in favour of interferences proceeding *ex iusta causa*[279].
If, on the other hand, a private right could vouch
for its existence no title of Natural Law, then doctrinal
consistency denied a similar protection to this 'merely
positive right'[280]. This struck in particular at those
rights which were held to fall under the rubric of
'privileges' unilaterally conceded by the State and
sanctioned only by Positive Law. An ever growing
opinion deemed that rights of this class were always
freely revocable at the instance of the public weal[281].

Thus as regards acquired rights, the relative degree
of protection which was due to any such right was
held to be derived from and measured by the foundation in Natural Law of the 'title' by which in the
given case that right had been acquired. On the other
hand, absolute protection against Positive Law was
due to those rights which were directly conferred by
pure Natural Law without the intermediation of any
entitling act [e.g. the right to life], and which therefore
were not conditioned by any title and could not be
displaced by a title that was adverse.

Innate Rights and Acquired Rights.

In this sense Medieval Doctrine was already filled
with the thought of the inborn and indestructible rights
of the Individual. The formulation and classification
of such rights belonged to a later stage in the growth
of the theory of Natural Law. Still, as a matter of
principle, a recognition of their existence may be found
already in the medieval Philosophy of Right when it
attributes an absolute and objective validity to the
highest maxims of Natural and Divine Law. Moreover, a fugitive glance at Medieval Doctrine suffices
to perceive how throughout it all, in sharp contrast
to the theories of Antiquity, runs the thought of the

The Rights of Man.

absolute and imperishable value of the Individual : a thought revealed by Christianity and grasped in all its profundity by the Germanic Spirit. That every individual by virtue of his eternal destination is at the core somewhat holy and indestructible even in relation to the Highest Power : that the smallest part has a value of its own, and not merely because it is part of a whole : that every man is to be regarded by the Community, never as a mere instrument, but also as an end :—all this is not merely suggested, but is more or less clearly expressed[282].

Rights of the Community. On the other hand occurred the thought of the original and essential rights of Superiority which belonged to the Whole Body. Here, once more, the Church had set up a model : a model of a Power in the Community which, by virtue of Divine Law, was necessarily implicated in the Community's existence and therefore was absolutely one and indivisible and inalienable. The same necessity, the same oneness, indivisibility and inalienability were soon claimed for the plenitude of the Imperial Power by Legists and Publicists. Thus could they demonstrate against the Church the nullity of the Donation of Constantine[283], and thus could they demonstrate against other temporal rulers the impossibility of any complete liberation by privilege or prescription from the power of the Empire[284]. What in this context was said of the Empire became in the end bare theory ; but, soon afterwards it gained practical value by being transferred from the Empire to the State. It was from this point outwards that, with the aid of legal and philosophic argument, was laid the doctrinal foundation upon which in course of time the towering Modern State, (absorbing meanwhile into itself the feudal and patrimonial rights of the Middle Age,) could take, and actually took, its stand. There arose the doctrine of a State Power, precedent and superior to all Positive Law, founded by the very Law of Nature, possessing an immutable sphere of action : of a State Power which, being an aboriginal and essential attribute of the Community, was the correlate of the inborn rights of individual men. Thenceforward, with ever-increasing distinctness, were formulated those indestructible rights of Superiority which are implicit in the idea of the State : rights which needed no title in Positive Law and could not be diminished by any title which that Law could bestow[285]. And then the notion of Sovereignty received its culminating attribute, when (however highly the Supreme Power might be extolled) men asserted that even itself could not destroy itself. If, on the one hand, the prevailing doctrine hence deduced the inalienable rights of the Crown[286], there were, even in the Middle Age, those who would establish by similar reasoning the inalienable rights of the People. Indeed, the attribute of indestructibility was applied to that original Sovereignty, which a common opinion attributed to the Community, and we may already see assertions of the logically reasoned conclusion that, by virtue of Divine and Natural Law, the Sovereignty of the People is absolutely indestructible[287]. Hand in hand with this went a theoretical process which distinguished those rights of Superiority which belonged to the very essence of the State from fiscal rights casually acquired by the State and held by it in the same manner as that in which a private man might hold them[288]. And thus it fell out that, as the doctrine of Nature Right became victorious, men began to grasp, as a matter of principle, that separation of *Ius Publicum* from *Ius Privatum* which they had learned from the Romans. That contrast had at one time seemed to them hardly more than a matter of words ;

soon, however, it was becoming ever more decisively a main outline in the ground-plan of all constructive Jurisprudence[289].

Transgression of limits by the State. In the course of these discussions of the relationship of the State to Law, a deep difference of opinion began to reveal itself, and to cleave the Medieval doctrine in twain, so soon as questions were raised as to the effects of a transgression by the State Power of the limits that Law set to its action.

Void acts of State. The properly Medieval and never completely obsolete theory declared that every act of the Sovereign which broke the bounds drawn by Natural Law was formally null and void. As null and void therefore every judge and every other magistrate who had to apply the law was to treat, not only every unlawful executive act, but every unlawful statute, even though it were published by Pope or Emperor[290]. Furthermore, the unlawful order or unlawful act was null and void for the individual subjects of the State. It was just for this cause that their duty of obedience was conceived as a conditional duty, and that the right of actively resisting tyrannical measures was conceded to them[291].

Formal omnipotence of the State. This truly Medieval mode of thought was in harmony with the actual practice of the age of feudalism and the age in which the Community appeared as a legal system of 'Estates.' But, as the idea of Sovereignty took a sharper outline, theorists began to hold that in the legal sphere the Sovereign was formally omnipotent. Then the prevalent opinion found itself once more compelled to declare that in a Monarchy both the legislative and the executive acts of the Monarch are equipped with this formal omnipotence. On the other hand, the doctrine of Popular Sovereignty made exactly at this point a fruitful application of its principle of a Separation of Powers, since it would allow this formal omnipotence only to acts of legislation. When this point of view had been attained, all limitations of the State Power began to look like no more than the claims which Righteousness makes upon a Sovereign Will. If that Will knowingly and unambiguously rejected such claims, it none the less made a law which was formally binding: a law which was externally binding on individual men, and on the Courts also[292].

None the less, there still was life in the notion that a duty of the State which was deducible from Natural Law was a legal duty. Although there was no sharp severance of Natural Law from Morality, the limits drawn round the legitimate sphere of Supreme Power were not regarded as merely ethical precepts. They were regarded and elaborated as rules which controlled external action, and so were contrasted with purely ethical claims made upon internal freedom[293]. No one doubted that the maxims of Divine and Natural Law bore the character of true rules of true Law, even when they were not to be enforced by compulsory processes. No one doubted that a true and genuine Law existed which preceded the State and stood outside and above the State. No one doubted that formal Right [or Law] might be material Unright [or Unlaw], and that formal Unright might be material Right[294]. No one doubted that the formally unconditional duty of obedience that is incumbent on subjects was materially limited by the Law of God and Nature. No one doubted that the words of Holy Writ 'We must obey God rather than man' contained a rule of Law for all places and all ages, or that the meanest of subjects would be doing Right [Law] if in conformity with the dictates of his conscience he refused obedience to the

The State and Natural Law.

Sovereign Power and steadfastly bore the consequence, or, again, that such a subject if he took the opposite course would be doing not Right [Law] but Unright [Unlaw][295]. And we should go far wrong if we supposed that the distinction between formal Right [or Law] and material Right [or Law], a distinction immanent in the idea of a Law of Nature, was but mere inactive theory. To say nothing of indirect consequences, it produced a direct result of far-reaching practical importance. All tribunals, all officials charged with the application of law, were conceived to be in duty bound to bring the acts of the Sovereign into the closest possible conformity with the dictates of material Right [or substantial Justice]. For this purpose they were to employ that exceedingly wide power of 'interpretation' with which they were supposed to be entrusted[296].

The State and Morality. During the Middle Age we can hardly detect even the beginnings of that opinion which would free the Sovereign (whenever he is acting in the interest of the public weal) from the bonds of the Moral Law in general, and therefore from the bonds of the Law of Nature[297]. Therefore when Machiavelli based his lesson for Princes upon this freedom from restraint, this seemed to the men of his time an unheard of innovation and also a monstrous crime. Thus was laid the foundation for a purely 'political' theory of the State, and thenceforward this theory appeared as a rival of the 'nature-rightly' doctrine. But just because there was a competitor and assailant in the field, this old doctrine evolved itself into an ampler form in the course of the next century. More and more the germs which were present in the medieval lore unfolded themselves, and new thoughts about the nature of Human Society were brought to light as the old elements

were systematized and combined. Irresistibly and
incessantly waxed the System of Natural Law, internally growing towards completion, externally extending
the boundaries of its domination over the minds of
men, plunging deeper into the positive doctrines of Law
and Polity, subjecting them to its transmutative power.

X.   *The Beginnings of the Modern State.*

At all these points the Doctrine of the Medieval
Publicists has shown us a double aspect.   Everywhere
beside the formulation of thoughts that were properly
medieval we have detected the genesis of 'antique-
modern' ideas, the growth of which coincides with the
destruction of the social system of the Middle Age and
with the construction of 'nature-rightly' theories of
the State.   It remains for us to set forth by way of
summary this tendency of medieval doctrine to give
birth to the modern idea of the State and to transform
the previously accepted theory of Communities.   We
must attend separately to the more important of those
points at which this tendency exhibits itself[298].

The fundamental fact which chiefly concerns us
when we contemplate this process of evolution is that
in medieval theory itself we may see a drift which
makes for a theoretical concentration of right and
power in the highest and widest group on the one
hand and the individual man on the other, at the cost
of all intermediate groups.   The Sovereignty of the
State and the Sovereignty of the Individual were
steadily on their way towards becoming the two central
axioms from which all theories of social structure
would proceed, and whose relationship to each other
would be the focus of all theoretical controversy.   And
soon we may see that combination which is charac-

[margin note beside second paragraph:] Transmutation of Medieval Doctrine by Antique influence.

[margin note beside third paragraph:] State and Individual obliterate Intermediate Groups.

teristic of the 'nature-rightly' doctrines of a later time : namely, a combination of the Absolutism which is due to the renaissance of the antique idea of the State, with the modern Individualism which unfolds itself from out the Christiano-Germanic thought of Liberty.

Origin of the State in Contract.
As regards the question touching the Origin of the State—its origin in time and its origin in law—the Theory of the Social Contract slowly grew. It was generally agreed that in the beginning there was a State of Nature. At that time 'States' were not, and pure Natural Law prevailed, by virtue whereof all persons were free and equal and all goods were in common. Thus it was universally admitted that the Politic or Civil State was the product of acts done at a later time, and the only moot question was whether this was a mere consequence of the Fall of Man, or whether the State would have come into being, though in some freer and purer form, if mankind had increased in numbers while yet they were innocent[299]. By way of investigating the origin of Political Society, men at first contented themselves with a general discussion of the manner in which *dominium* had made its appearance in the world and the legitimacy of its origin ; and in their concept of *dominium*, Rulership and Ownership were blent. Then, when the question about Ownership had been severed from that about Rulership, we may see coming to the front always more plainly the supposition of the State's origin in a Contract of Subjection made between People and Ruler[300]. Even the partizans of the Church adopt this opinion when they have surrendered the notion that the State originated in mere wrong. But then arose this further question :—How did it happen that this Community itself, whose Will, expressed in an act of transfer, was the origin of the State, came to be a Single Body

competent to perform a legal act and possessing a
transferable power over its members? At this point
the idea of a Divine Creation of the State began to
fail, for however certain men might be that the Will
of God was the ultimate cause of Politic Society, still
this cause fell back into the position of a *causa remota*
working through human agency[301]. As a more proxi-
mate cause the 'politic nature' which God has implanted in mankind could be introduced; and Aristotle
might be vouched. We can not say that there were
absolutely no representatives of a theory of organic
development, which would teach that the State had
grown out of that aboriginal Community, the Family,
in a purely natural, direct and necessary fashion[302]. Still
the weightier opinion was that Nature (like God) had
worked only as *causa remota* or *causa impulsiva*: that
is, as the source of a need for and of an impulse
towards the social life, or, in short, as a more or less
compulsory motive for the foundation of the State.
More and more decisively was expressed the opinion
that the very union of men in a political bond was an
act of rational, human Will[303]. Occasionally there may
appear the notion that the State was an Institution
which was founded, as other human institutions [e.g.
monasteries or colleges] were founded, by certain
definite Founders, either in peaceful wise or by some
act of violence[304]; but, in the main, there was a general
inclination towards the hypothesis of some original,
creative, act of Will of the whole uniting Community.
This joint act was compared to the self-constitution of
a corporation[305]. But men did not construct for this
purpose any legal concept that was specially adapted
to the case. The learning of Corporations developed
by the lawyers had no such concept to offer, for they
also, despite the distinction between *universitas* and

societas, [between Corporation and Partnership,] confused the single act whereby a Community unifies
itself, with a mere obligatory contract made among
individuals, and they regarded the peculiar unity of the
Corporation as something that came to it from without
by virtue of a concession made by the State. Thus in
the end the Medieval Doctrine already brings the
hypothetical act of political union under the category
of a Contract of Partnership or 'Social' Contract[306].
On the one hand, therefore, proclamation was made
of the original Sovereignty of the Individual as the
source of all political obligation[307]. In this manner a
base was won for the construction of Natural Rights
of Man, which, since they were not comprised in the
Contract, were unaffected by it and could not be
impaired by the State. On the other hand, since the
Sovereignty of the State, when once it was erected,
rested on the indestructible foundation of a Contract
sanctioned by the Law of Nature, conclusions which
reached far in the direction of the State's Absolutism
could be drawn by those who formulated the terms of
the Contract[308].

The Final Cause of the State.
   If Philosophy was to find the terms of that fictitious
Contract which provided a basis of Natural Law for
the State and the State's power, it could not but be
that the decisive word about this matter would be
sought in the purpose which the State and its power
are designed to fulfil. If, on the one part, the idea
was retained that every individual had a final cause of
his own, which was independent of and stood outside
and above all political and communal life[309]—and here
was a divergence from Classical Antiquity—so, on the
other part, the final cause of the State was always
being enlarged—and here was a departure from the
earlier Middle Age, though at times we may still hear

echoes of the old Germanic idea that the State's one
function is the maintenance of peace and law[310]. In imitation of classical thought, men defined the State's purpose
to be a happy and virtuous life : the realization of the
public weal and civic morality. True, that, according to
the prevailing doctrine, the function of the State had a
limit, and a necessary complement, in the function of
the Church : a function making for a higher aim than
that of the State, namely, for inward virtue and supramundane bliss[311]. But an always stronger assault was
being made upon the Church's monopoly of culture.
An independent spiritual and moral mission was
claimed for the State[312], until at length there were
some who would ascribe to the State the care for all
the interests of the Community, whether those interests
were material or whether they were spiritual[313].

If, however, the contents of the Institutes of Natural Law were to be discovered by a consideration
of their final cause, this same final cause would also
be the measure of those indestructible rights that per-
tained to the 'Subjects' of Natural Law. From the
final cause of the Individual flow the innate and inalienable rights of liberty, and so from the final cause
of the Politic Community flow—and from of old the
Church might here serve as a model—the State's
innate and inalienable rights of superiority. From the
rights thus bestowed Positive Law could take, and to
them it could add, nothing. If, as a matter of fact, it
contravenes them, it must admit itself over-ruled. The
maxim *Salus publica suprema lex* entered on its reign,
and a good legal title had been found on which Revolution, whether it came from above or from below,
could support itself when it endeavoured to bring the
traditional law into conformity with the postulates of
the Law of Nature.

Natural Rights and the Final Cause of the State.

Revolu-
tionary
elements
in Natural
Law.

In truth Medieval Doctrine prepared the way for the great revolutions in Church and State, and this it did by attributing a real working validity as rules of Natural Law to a system constructed of abstract premisses and planned in accordance with the dictates of expediency. The whole internal structure of the State was subjected ever more and more to criticism proceeding from the Rationalist's stand-point. The value of the structure was tested by reference to its power of accomplishing a purpose and was measured by reference to an ideal and 'nature-rightly' State. The steering of public affairs was likened to the steering of a ship; it is a free activity consciously directed towards the attainment of a goal[314]. Thus there arose the idea of an Art of Government, and people undertook to teach it in detail[315]. There was disputation about the best form of government and the most suitable laws, and out of this grew a demand for such a transformation of Public Law as would bring it into accord with theoretical principles. Through the last centuries of the Middle Age, alike in Church and Empire, unbroken and always louder, rings the cry for 'Reformation'!

Develop-
ment of
Sove-
reignty.

Turning now to the fundamental concepts of Public Law, the resuscitation and further development of the classical idea of Sovereignty will appear to us as the main exploit achieved in this department by the prevalent endeavour to construct constitutions which shall conform to Natural Law. Men found the essence of all political organization in a separation of Rulers and Ruled. Also they took over from the antique world the doctrine of the Forms of Government and of the distinctions that exist between them. And so they came to the opinion that in every State some one visible Ruler, a man or a ruling assembly, is the 'Subject' of a Sovereign Power over the Ruled[316]. And then, when, in contrast to the theory of 'Ruler's Sovereignty,' men developed the theory of a Popular Sovereignty, existing everywhere and always, the partizans of this doctrine did not once more call in question the newly acquired idea of Sovereignty, but transferred it to an Assembly which represents the People[317]. The Medieval notion of Sovereignty, it is true, always differed in principle from that exalted notion which prevailed in after times. For one thing, there was unanimous agreement that the Sovereign Power, though raised above all Positive, is limited by Natural Law[318]. Secondly, it was as unanimously agreed that the idea of the Sovereign by no means excludes an independent legal claim of non-sovereign subjects to participate in the power of the State. On the contrary, advocates of 'Ruler's Sovereignty' expressly maintained a political right of the People, and advocates of the People's Sovereignty expressly maintained a political right of the Ruler, so that even the extremest theories gave to the State somewhat of a 'constitutional' character. Therefore it was thought possible to combine the Sovereignty of the Monarch with what was in principle a Limited Monarchy[319]. Therefore also the idea of a Mixed Constitution could be developed without facing awkward questions[320]. Therefore again the beginnings of a doctrine which teaches the Separation of Powers could be reared on a basis of Popular Sovereignty[321]. And therefore also the Representative System could be theoretically elaborated[322]. None the less, the idea of Sovereignty, when once it had been formulated, irresistibly pressed forwards towards the conclusion that in the last resort some one Ruler or some one Assembly must be the 'Subject' of the Supreme Power, and that in case of conflict the State is incorporate only in this one man or this one Assembly.

State and Individual in immediate contact.

The State Power, thus focussed at a single point, made, over all members of the State, ever fresh claims to all such rights of Superiority as were comprised within the idea and measure of the State's final cause and were compatible with those rights of Liberty of which the Individual could not be deprived[323]. And just because the rights of Superiority flowed from the very idea of State Power, that Power, with increasing insistence, claimed to exercise them over all individuals equally and with equal directness and immediacy[324]. If then, on the one hand, the Individual just in so far as he belongs to the Community is fully and wholly absorbed into the State[325], so, on the other hand, there is a strong tendency to emancipate the Individual from all bonds that are not of the State's making.

The State an exclusive group.

There was, moreover, a steady advance of the notion that the State is an exclusive Community. In phrases which tell of the Antique World men spoke of the State simply as 'Human Society.' The State is the all-comprehensive, and therefore the one and only, expression of that common life which stands above the life of the individual.

State and Church.

This thought, it is true, came at once into conflict with the ascription of a higher, or even an equal, right to the Church. And it was only with a great saving-clause for the rights of the Church that the prevalent doctrine of the Middle Age received the antique idea of the State. Still in the fourteenth and fifteenth centuries theory was preparing the way for the subsequent absorption of Church in State. One medieval publicist there was who dared to project a system, logically elaborated even into details, wherein the Church was a State Institution, Church property was State property, spiritual offices were offices of State, the government of the Church was part of the

government of the State, and the sovereign Ecclesiastical Community was identical with the Political
Assembly of the Citizens. He was Marsilius of
Padua[326]. No one followed him the whole way. Howbeit, isolated consequences of the same principle were
drawn even in the Middle Age by other opponents
of the Hierarchy. Already an unlimited power of
suppressing abuses of ecclesiastical office was claimed
for the State[327]. Already, with more or less distinctness, Church property was treated as public property and placed, should the *salus publica* require it,
at the disposal of the State[328]. Already powers of
the State which reach far down even into the internal
affairs of the Church were being deduced from the
demand that in temporal matters the Church should
be subject to the temporal Magistrate[329]. Already the
classical sentence which told how the *ius sacrum* was
a part of the *ius publicum* was once more beginning
to reveal its original meaning[330].

If, however, we leave out of sight the State's rela- State and
tion to the Church, we see that, when Medieval Empire.
Doctrine first takes shape, the idea of the State, which
had been derived from the Antique World, was en-
feebled and well-nigh suffocated by the consequences
that were flowing from the medieval idea of the Empire :
an idea which itself was being formulated by theory.
The thought of a concentration at a single point of the
whole life of the Community not only stood in sharp
contradiction to actual facts and popular opinions, but
also was opposed in theory to what might seem an
insurmountable bulwark, namely to the medieval
thought of an harmoniously articulated Universal Community whose structure from top to bottom was of the
federalistic kind[331]. Nevertheless that antique concept
of the State, when once it had found admission, worked

and worked unceasingly and with deadly certainty until it had completely shattered this proud edifice of medieval thought. We may see theory trying to hold fast the mere shadow of this stately idea, even when what should have corresponded to it in the world of fact, the Medieval Empire, had long lain in ruins. And so also we may see in theory the new edifice of the Modern State being roofed and tiled when in the world of fact just the first courses of this new edifice are beginning to arise amidst the ruins of the old.

Definition of the State.

When Aristotle's *Politics* had begun their new life, the current definition taught that the State is the highest and completest of Communities and a Community that is self-sufficing[332]. It is evident that, so soon as men are taking this definition in earnest, only some one among the various subordinated and super-ordinated Communities can be regarded as being the State. For a while this logical consequence might be evaded by a grossly illogical device. The πόλις or *civitas* that the ancients had defined was discovered by medieval Philosophy in a medieval town, and, by virtue of the ideal of the organic structure of the whole Human Race, the community of this πόλις or *civitas* was subordinated to a *regnum* and to the *imperium* : that is, to higher and wider communities in which it found its completion and its limitations. Thus, no sooner has the medieval thinker given his definition, than he is withdrawing it without the slightest embarrassment : his superlative becomes a comparative, and the absolute attribute becomes relative[333]. Then, on the other hand, the lawyers, with the *Corpus Iuris* before them, explained that the Empire is the one true State[334]; but they defined *civitas* and *populus* and even *regnum* in such a manner that these terms could be

applied to provinces and to rural or urban communes[335];
and then, as a matter of fact, they went on applying the
concept of 'The State' to communities that were much
smaller than the Empire[336]. Still the antique idea,
when once it had been grasped, was sure to triumph
over this confused thinking. Indeed we may see that
the Philosophic Theory of the State often sets to work
with the assumption that there cannot be two States
one above the other, and that above the State there is
no room for a World-State, while below the State
there is only room for mere communes[337]. Then in
Jurisprudence, from the days of Bartolus onwards,
an ever sharper distinction was being drawn between
communities which had and those which had not an
external *Superior*, and communities of the latter kind
were being placed on a level with the *Imperium*[338].
The differences between *civitas*, *regnum* and *imperium*
became mere differences in size instead of being joints
in the organic articulation of a single body, and at the
same time the concept of the State became the exclusive property of a community which recognizes no
external superior (*universitas superiorem non recognoscens*)[339].

Thus already in the Middle Age the idea of the
State arrived at theoretical completion, and the attribute of External Sovereignty became the distinguishing mark of the State. The *Imperium Mundi*, which
rose above the Sovereign States, had evaporated into
an unsubstantial shadow, and at any rate was stripped
of the character of a State, even when its bare existence was not denied. For States within the State
there was thenceforth no room, and all the smaller
groups had to be brought under the rubric 'Communes
and Corporations'[340].

The State
and other
Communi-
ties.

From the concentration of 'State Life' at a single

Precarious position of Communities within the State. point there by no means follows as logically necessary a similar concentration of all 'Community Life.' The medieval idea of the organic articulation of Mankind might live on, though but in miniature, within each separate State. It might become the idea of the organic articulation of the Nation. And up to a certain degree this actually happened. The Romano-Canonical Theory of Corporations, although it decomposed and radically transmuted the German notion of the autonomous life of communities and fellowships, always insured to the non-sovereign community a certain independent life of its own, a sphere of rights within the domain of Public Law, a sphere that belonged to it merely because it was a community, and lastly, an organic interposition between the Individual and the Community of All. Even among political theorists there were not wanting some who in the last centuries of the Middle Age—centuries brimful of vigorous corporate life—sought to oppose to that centralization which had triumphed in the Church and was threatening the State, a scientific statement of the idea of corporative articulation and a logically deduced justification of the claims that could be made on behalf of the smaller groups as beings with rights of their own and an intrinsic value[341].

Centralization of Communal life. For all this, however, even in the Middle Age the drift of Theory set incessantly towards an exaltation of the Sovereignty of the State which ended in the exclusive representation by the State of all the common interests and common life of the Community. In this direction Philosophy with giant strides was outstripping Jurisprudence.

Philosophic theory and Rights of Lordship. For those rights of Lordship of Germanic origin which subsisted within the State and beneath the Sovereign's Power, Jurisprudence might long provide a secure place. It had accepted the *ius feudorum*, and was prepared to treat offices as objects of proprietary rights. But Political and Philosophical Theories could find no room whatever in their abstract systems for feudal and patrimonial powers[342]. On the contrary, this was just the point whence spread the thought that all subordinate public power is a mere delegation of the Sovereign Power[343]. Also this was just the point whence spread a process which transmuted the medieval concept of Office, in such wise that every office appeared merely as a commission to use the Power of the State : to use, that is, in a certain manner, a power which is in substance one and untransferable. When that process is completed, every officer appears as the freely chosen instrument of the Sovereign Will[344].

A similar attitude was taken by the abstract theories of Politics and Philosophy in relation to those independent Rights of Fellowships which had their source in Germanic Law. For a long time Jurisprudence was prepared to give them a home ; but Philosophical Theory looked askance at them. The Doctrine of the State that was reared upon a classical ground-work had nothing to say of groups that mediated between the State and the Individual. This being so, the domain of Natural Law was closed to the Corporation, and its very existence was based upon the ground of a Positive Law which the State had made and might at any time alter. And then as the sphere of the State's Might on the one hand, and the sphere of the Individual's Liberty on the other, became the exclusive and all-sufficing starting-points for a Philosophy of Law, the end was that the Corporation could find a place in Public Law only as a part of the State and a place in Private Law only as an artificial Individual, while all in actual life that might seem to conflict with this

Philosophic theory and the Rights of Fellowships.

7—2

doctrine was regarded as the outcome of privileges which the State had bestowed and in the interest of the public might at any time revoke. While the Middle Age endured, it was but rarely that the consequences of these opinions were expressly drawn[345]. Howbeit, Philosophic Doctrine was on the one hand filling itself full of the antique idea of the State, and on the other hand it was saving therefrom and developing the Christiano-Germanic idea of Freedom and depositing this in the theory of Natural Law. And as this work proceeded towards the attainment of ever more distinct results, the keener were the weapons which Medieval Doctrine was forging for that combat which fills the subsequent centuries. A combat it was in which the Sovereign State and the Sovereign Individual contended over the delimitation of the provinces assigned to them by Natural Law, and in the course of that struggle all intermediate groups were first degraded into the position of the more or less arbitrarily fashioned creatures of mere Positive Law, and in the end were obliterated.

NOTES.

1. Too little attention has hitherto been paid to the influence on political theory of the work done by the Legists and Canonists. Really it is from their great commentaries that the purely political writers borrow their whole equipment of legal ideas. Thus it is characteristic that nothing is said of Bartolus and much is made of Ubertus de Lampugnano and his lecture on the Empire delivered at Prague in 1380 (*Zeitschr. f. gesch. Rechtswis.* II. pp. 246—256). But this is a reproduction almost verbatim of Bartolus's Commentary on l. 24 Dig. de capt. 49, 15. Only a few ornaments have been added, such as the jest about the Greek Emperor being still an Emperor at least in that sort in which the king on the chess-board is a king. ^{Importance of the Jurists.}

2. This sequence of ideas may best be seen in Dante's work, where it serves as a foundation for his Theory of the State. Comp. e.g. Monarchia, I. c. 7 (also c. 6) on the correspondence between the *universitas humana* with, on the one hand, the World-Whole, and, on the other hand, those smaller communities whose *totum* this *universitas* is. But Dante takes the core of this thought from Aquinas: see especially Summa contra gentiles III. q. 76—83, and De regimine principum I. c. 12. And long before this we meet the same ideas similarly formulated; in particular the parallelism of macrocosm and microcosm: thus in Joh. Saresb. Polycr. (see below Note 10) and Hugo Floriac. De regia et sacerdot. pot. I. c. 1. Then compare Alvar. Pelag. De planctu eccl. I. a 37 R, and Somn. Virid. I. c. 37—48. The last splendid example of the development of this fundamental thought is the 'Catholic Concordance' of Nicolas Cusanus; especially I. c. 1—4. ^{Macrocosm and Microcosm.}

3. The application to the Order of Human Society of propositions derived from Augustine and teaching the principle of 'Unity before Plurality' is effected by Aquinas in particular. He employs the maxim *Omnis multitudo derivatur ab uno*, and sees the ^{Unity as source and goal.}

prototypes of the State in the World with its One God, in the Microcosm of Man with its single soul, in the unifying principle which prevails among the powers of the soul, and which prevails also in the natural body and in the animal kingdom.   See De reg. princ. I. c. 2, 3, 12 ; also Summa contra gentil. III. q. 81.   But the kernel of this mode of thought is older ; e.g. Hugo Floriac. I. c. 1 brings in a comparison with the unity of the World-Whole and with that of the human body.   Similar thoughts are developed by Aegid. Rom. De regim. princ. III. 2, c. 3 : since all *multitudo ab uno procedit*, it must *in unum aliquod reduci* : since among the heavenly bodies we see the rule of the *primum mobile*, in the body the rule of the heart, in a compound body the rule of one element, among bees the rule of a queen, so the State needs a single government.   With higher genius, Dante, Mon. I. c. 5—16, bases the demand for a *unum regens* in every Whole on the types of an *ordinatio ad unum*, found in the World-Whole (c. 7), among the heavenly bodies (c. 9), and every-where on earth.   Similar thoughts in Alv. Pel. I. a. 40 ; Joh. Paris. c. 1 ; Anton. Ros. II. c. 5—7 ; Laelius (in Goldast II. p. 1595 ff.) ; Petrus de Andlo I. c. 8.   Then a mystical development is given to the idea by Nicolas Cusanus, who finds an image of the Trinity throughout the Unity of the articulated world : thus God, Angels, Men in the Church Triumphant ; Sacrament, Priesthood, Folk in the Church Militant ; Spirit, Soul, Body in Man.   See Conc. Cath. ; and also De auctor. praes. in Düx, I. p. 475 ff.

Partial Wholes.

4.   See Thom. Aq. Comm. ad Ethic. lect. 1 (Op. ed. Parm. XXI. p. 2) : hoc totum, quod est civilis multitudo vel domestica familia, habet solam unitatem ordinis, secundum quam non est aliquid simpliciter unum ; et ideo pars eius totius potest habere operationem quae non est operatio totius ;...habet nihilominus et ipsum totum aliquam operationem, quae non est propria alicuius partium.   De reg. princ. I. c. 1 : since the Many bound together 'secundum propria quidem differunt, secundum autem commune uniuntur,' there must be 'moventia ad proprium bonum unius cuiusque,' as well as a 'movens ad bonum commune multorum.'

The Praises of Unity.

5.   In high terms Dante, c. 15, lauds the Principle of Unity as the source of all good, for the *maxime ens* must be the *maxime unum*, and the *maxime unum* must be the *maxime bonum*.   Similarly Thom. Aq. De reg. princ. I. c. 3 ; comp. Summa contra gentil. IV. c. 1 ff. Nay, 'binarius numerus infamis.'   Papal theory accuses its opponents of heresy, since they 'ponunt dua principia.'   See e.g. Boniface VIII. in the bull Unam sanctam of 1302 (c. 1 Extrav. comm. I. 8), and the letter in Raynald. Ann. 1302 nr. 12 ; also what

is said by the Clerk in Quaestio in utramque part. p. 105 ; Joh. Andr. upon c. 13, X. 4, 17 ; Panorm. upon c. 13, X. 2, 1.

6.   Dante, I. c. 3 and 4, endeavours to define the common purpose of Mankind.   He finds it in the continuous activity of the whole potency of Reason, primarily the speculative, secondarily the practical.   This is the 'operatio propria universitatis humanae'; the individual man, the household, the *civitas* and the *regnum particulare* are insufficient for it.   For the achievement of it only a World-Realm will serve, and the *propinquissimum medium* is the establishment of an Universal Peace.   Comp. III. c. 16.

The Purpose of Corporate Mankind.

7.   Already in 829 the episcopal utterances about Church and State at the Councils of Worms and Paris, afterwards appended to the Capitulary of Worms, begin with the principle (grounded on words of S. Paul) 'universalis sancta ecclesia Dei *unum corpus* manifeste esse credatur eiusque caput Christus.'   On this follows the doctrine, warranted by Gelasius and Fulgentius, that 'principaliter itaque totius sanctae Dei ecclesiae corpus in duas eximias personas, in sacerdotalem videlicet et regalem...divisum esse novimus'; and lastly the professional duties of the priesthood on the one hand and the kingship on the other are particularized.   See Concil. Paris. in Mansi XIV. p. 605 ff.; Const. Worm. in Mon. Germ. Leg. I. p. 333, c. 2—3, p. 333 ff., p. 346 ff.; also Hefele Conciliengesch. IV. p. 57 ff. and 72 ff.   To the like effect Jonas of Orléans (ob. 843), De institutione regia, in d'Achéry, Spicileg., ed. nov. Paris 1723, I. p. 324. Similar thoughts from Agobard of Lyons (ob. 842) and Hinkmar of Reims (ob. 882).   After this the picture of Mankind as one body with a God-willed spiritual and temporal constitution is common. Thus in Gregor. VII., e.g. lib. I. ep. 19, ann. 1073 ; Ivo of Chartres, e.g. ep. 106, p. 125, ep. 214, p. 217 ff.; S. Bernard, ep. 244 ad Conr. Reg. ann. 1146, p. 440 ff. (also in Goldast II. 67—68); Gerhoh of Reichersberg, De corrupto statu eccl., praef. p. 11 ; Thomas of Canterbury, ep. 179, p. 652 ; Hugo Floriac. I. c. 1 and II. pp. 46, 50 ; Innocent III., e.g. Registr. sup. neg. Rom. Imp. ep. 2, 18 and 79, pp. 997, 1012, 1162.   Throughout Aquinas: see e.g. Summa Theol. II. 1, q. 81, a. 1 (multi homines ex Adam derivati sunt tanquam multa membra unius corporis) and III. q. 8, a. 1 and 2 (genus humanum consideratur quasi unum corpus, quod vocatur mysticum, cuius caput est ipse Christus et quantum ad animas et quantum ad corpora) ; Lect. 2 ad Rom. 12 ; Lect. 3 ad 1 Corinth. 12.   See also Vincent. Bellov. Spec. doctr. lib. VII. c. 31 (duo latera corporis unius). On innumerable occasions Theologians and Canonists employ the term *ecclesia* to describe a Realm of All Mankind, including its

The Universal Church and the Commonwealth of Mankind.

temporal constitution: e.g. August. Triumph. I. q. 1, a. 6; Joh. Andr. upon c. 13, X. 4, 17; Panorm. upon c. 13, X. 2, 1. On the other hand, Engelbert of Volkersdorf, De ortu et fine c. 15, 17 and 18, is the first expressly to argue that Mankind is one people with only one true law and one true *consensus*, and must therefore be one true *respublica*. Then to the like effect Dante, Mon. I. c. 3, 5—9. Lupold. Bebenb., c. 15. Petrarca, Ep. VII. and VIII. Alvar. Pelag. I. a. 13 F, a. 37 Q and R, a. 40 and 45 (unum corpus mysticum, una communitas et unus populus, una civilitas et politia Christiana). Quaestio in utramque partem, p. 102 ff. Ockham, Octo qu. III. c. 1 (totum genus humanum est unus populus; universitas mortalium est una communitas volentium habere communionem ad invicem) and c. 9; also Dial. III. tr. 2, l. 1, c. 1 (univ. mortalium, unus populus, unus grex, unum corpus, una civitas, unum collegium, unum regnum; connexio inter omnes mortales); ibid. l. 3, c. 17 and 22. Somn. Virid. II. c. 305—312; Nic. Cus. Conc. Cath. III. c. 1 and 41.

Priesthood and Realm.

8. As is shewn by all the passages cited in our last note, the whole Middle Age is filled by the thought which finds a typical expression in the Summa mag. Stephani Tornacensis (1165—1177) praef.: in eadem civitate sub uno rege duo populi sunt, et secundum duos populos duae vitae, duo principatus, duplex iurisdictionis ordo procedit: the *civitas* is the *ecclesia*, the king is Christ, the two folks are the clergy and the laity, the two lives are the spiritual and the temporal, the two *principatus* are *sacerdotium et regnum*, the two spheres of law the *divinum et humanum*. References to the spiritual and bodily sides of humanity become common, and the purposes of the two Orders are found respectively in this world and the next.— Occasionally Science, the *studium*, is introduced as a third and independent province of life. See Ptolom. Luc. De reg. princ. II. c. 16 in fine : in qualibet monarchia ab initio saeculi *tria* se invicem comitata sunt : divinus cultus, sapientia scholastica et saecularis potestas. Jordan. Osnabr. c. 5, p. 71 : the Romans received the *sacerdotium*, the Germans the *imperium*, the French the *studium*; these are the three courses in the edifice of the Catholic Church; the *sacerdotium* at Rome is the foundation, the *studium* at Paris the roof, the *imperium* at Aachen, Arles, Milan and Rome the four walls.

Temporal Power of the Pope and the Principle of Unity.

9. When Boniface VIII. [in the famous bull Unam Sanctam] put the sum and substance of the ecclesiastical claims into a compendious form (c. 1, Extrav. com. I. 8), he placed in the forefront an emphatic statement of the principle of Unity. But the same principle had long been the base of the assertions of the popes and their partizans. The argument that could be drawn from the superior

worth of Spiritual Power could become a proof of the subjection of Temporal Power only by virtue of the self-evident proposition that an *ordinatio ad unum*, in the sense that we have explained above, is requisite for all mankind. The consequences deduced from a comparison of the two Powers to body and soul, or sun and moon, would have lacked cogency, had any doubt been felt touching the validity of a comparison of the whole body of mankind to a single organism or to a celestial vault enlightened by a single luminary. Also the argument which speaks of the two swords is only cogent if we may take for granted that God has destined both swords for the protection of a one and only Church. And so it is with other arguments. Then from the fourteenth century onwards appeals to the *argumentum unitatis*, coupled with references to the decretal of Boniface, are freely made by the ecclesiastical party. We even see the downright statement that, since it would be heretical to derive the universe from two principles, so also it must be heretical to suppose two co-equal Vicars on earth (ponere duos vicarios aequales in terris). See e.g. John Andr. upon c. 13, X. 4, 17; Panorm. upon c. 13, X. 2, 1; August. Triumph. I. q. 1, a. 6 and q. 22, a. 3 (the *tota machina mundialis* is single, therefore there can be but one *principatus*). Petrus de Andlo II. c. 9. See also the arguments drawn from the *unitas principii* by the Clerk in Somn. Virid. I. c. 37, 43, 45, 47, 101; also the arguments for and against unity in Quaest. in utramque partem, p. 102 ff.; in Ockham, Octo qu. I. c. 1, 5, 18; III. c. 1 and 9, also c. 8; Dial. III. tr. 1, l. 2, c. 1 and 30; and Anton. Rosell. I. c. 3, 4, 19, 39—55.

10. This absorption of the State by the Church is already clearly proclaimed, so far as concerns its first principle, by Gregory VII. Nothing less than this lies in the extension that he gives to the 'potestas ligandi in coelo et in terra' committed to S. Peter, and to the 'Pasce oves meas.' He asks (Registrum, lib. 4, ep. 2, ann. 1076, p. 242—243): 'Quod si sancta sedes apostolica divinitus sibi collata *principali* potestate *spiritualia* decernens diiudicat, cur non et *saecularia*?' And again (lib. 8, ep. 21, ann. 1080, p. 279): 'Cui ergo aperiendi claudendique coeli data potestas est, de terra iudicare non licet?' And again (lib. 4, ep. 24, ann. 1077, p. 455): 'Si enim coelestia et spiritualia sedes b. Petri solvit et iudicat, quanto magis terrena et saecularia.' Compare also lib. 4, ep. 23, p. 279, and lib. 1, ep. 63, p. 82, and the statement of papal rights in the Dictatus papae II. 55ᵃ, p. 174—6.—But the system is for the first time scientifically developed by John of Salisbury. For him the *respublica* is a body fashioned by God in the likeness of the macrocosm of

Absorption of State in Church.

Nature and the microcosm of man ; in it the Priesthood, being the Soul, rules the rest and has even to govern, erect, depose the Head ; Polycrat. IV. c. 1—4 and 6, V. c. 2—6, VI. c. 21.   Similarly Thomas of Canterbury, ep. 179 ad Henr. II. Reg. Angl., p. 652 : 'Ecclesia enim Dei in duobus constat ordinibus, clero et populo ;...in populo sunt reges, principes, duces, comites et aliae potestates, qui saecularia habent tractare negotia, ut totum reducant ad pacem et unitatem Ecclesiae.'   See also Ivo of Chartres, ep. 106, p. 125 ; S. Bernard, ep. 256, and De consid. lib. 4, c. 3 ; S. Anselm. Cantuar. Comm. in Matth. c. 26.   Then Innocent III. gave this doctrine the juristic shape in which it passed into the Canon Law.   See especially c. 34, X. 1, 6 ; c. 6, X. 1, 33 ; c. 13, X. 2, 1 ; c. 13, X. 4, 17 ; also lib. 2, ep. 202, ann. 1199, in Migne, vol. 214, p. 759 : Petro non solum universalem ecclesiam, sed totum reliquit saeculum gubernandum. Innocent IV. expressed the same thought in a yet sharper form. See the letter to Frederick II. in v. Wessenberg, Die grossen Kirchen-versammlungen, vol. I. (2 ed. Konstanz, 1845), p. 305—6.   Also Comm. on c. 13, X. 4, 17   In principle Thom. Aquinas stands on the same ground.   See De reg. princ. I. c. 14—15 ; Summa Theol. II. 2, q. 60, a. 6, ad. 3 ; Opusc. contra errores Graecorum, libell. II. c. 32—38 (the Pope head of the *respublica Christi*).   Yet more strongly, Aegidius Romanus, De pot. eccl. I. c. 2—9, II. c. 4—5, 10—11, III. c. 12.   When Boniface VIII. has given to this doctrine a final form [Unam sanctam, c. 1, Extrav. com. I. 8] it is widely spread abroad by the canonists.   See in particular Aug. Triumph. I. q. 1, a. 6 (the *ecclesia* is identical with the *communitas totius orbis*, which comprehends both the *corporale et spirituale*) and a. 8.   Alvar. Pelag. I. a. 13 and 37 : the Church has the spiritual and temporal power.   Also a. 40 : she is the true *politia*, of which the State is only part ; both powers are 'partes integrales unius potestatis'; they have the same *finis supranaturalis*, since the temporal is but a mean of the spiritual.   Also a. 59 D: 'partes distinctae unius potestatis.'

Insufficiency of an Invisible Unity.

11.   See especially Thom. Aquin. Summa contra gentil. IV. c. 76, p. 625—6: a refutation of the argument that Christ's headship would suffice to secure the requisite unity: His corporal presence should be represented by a Monarch.   Also Alvar. Pel. I. a. 40 D (against Dante).

Temporal Sovereignty of the Pope.

12.   Among the Popes themselves this is expressly proclaimed by Gregory VII. (see passages cited in Note 10; also lib. I. ep. 55[a], ann. 1075, p. 174 : quod solus possit uti imperialibus insigniis); also by Innocent III. (see Note 10; in particular, in c. 13, X. 4, 17 he deduces the proposition 'quod non solum in Ecclesiae patrimonio,

super quo plenam in temporalibus gerimus potestatem, verum etiam
in aliis regionibus, certis causis inspectis, temporalem iurisdictionem
casualiter exercemus' from the divine mandate that he has as 'eius
vicarius, qui est sacerdos in aeternum secundum ordinem Melchisedech, constitutus a Deo iudex vivorum et mortuorum'; compare
Reg. sup. neg. Imp. ep. 18, p. 1012: 'vicarius illius, cuius est terra
et plenitudo eius, orbis terrarum et universi qui habitant in eo');
Innocent IV. (see Note 10); Boniface VIII. (c. 1, Extrav. comm.
I. 8: 'subesse Romano pontifici omni humanae creaturae declara-
mus, dicimus, definimus et pronuntiamus omnino esse de necessitate
salutis'; he called himself Caesar and Emperor, comp. v. Wessenberg,
Kirchenversammlungen, I. p. 307).—Among the Canonists, already
in cent. xii. many say 'Papa ipse verus Imperator'; comp. Summa
Colon. (1160—1170) and Paris. (circ. 1170) upon c. 3, C. 2, q. 6, v.
eorum, and c. 7, C. 2, q. 3 dict. Grat. in Schulte, Sitzungsber. [Vienna
Acad.] vol. 64, pp. 111, 131. Also Gloss. ordin. upon c. 1, Dist. 22,
v. *coelestis*. So too Thom. Aquinas says 'nisi forte potestati spirituali etiam saecularis potestas coniungatur, sicut in Papa, qui utrius-
que potestatis apicem tenet, sc. spiritualis et saecularis, hoc illo
disponente qui est sacerdos et rex in aeternum, sec. ordinem
Melchisedech etc.'; in libr. II. Sent. dist. 44, ad. 4 (Op. VI.). Ptolom.
Luc., De regim. princ. III. c. 10: Peter and his successors have been
appointed by Christ to be both Priests and Kings, so that the Pope
is the *caput in corpore mystico* and from him all the sense and movement of the body flow: in temporals also, for these depend upon
spirituals, like body upon soul; ib. c. 13—19. Similarly Aegid.
Rom. I. c. 2—3; Aug. Triumph. I. q. 1, a. 7—9; II. q. 36; Petrus
de Andlo II. c. 9. Yet more definitely Alvar. Pelag. I. a. 13,
especially c and G; a. 37, R nr. 19 (est simpliciter praelatus omnium
et monarcha), and Bb (papa universalis monarcha totius populi
Christiani et de iure totius mundi); a. 52; a. 59 K (Christ and Pope
are in no wise two heads, but one head); but in particular the
reasoning of a. 40: (1) politiae Christianae est unus principatus
absolute: (2) huius politiae Christ. unius unus est princeps regens et
dirigens eam: (3) primus et supremus iste princeps politiae Christ.
est Papa. Opinions which in part go yet further concerning the
verum dominium temporalium are stated and refuted by Joh. Paris.,
proem. and c. 15—43; Ockham, Octo qu. I. c. 2, 7—19; II. c. 7;
Dial. III. tr. 1, l. 1, c. 2 ff.; l. 2, c. 1 ff.; tr. 2, l. 1, c. 18 ff.; Ant. Ros. I.
c. 1—19, and c. 39—55. Comp. also the Clerk in Somn. Virid.
c. 6, 8, 10, 12, 77, 85, 89, 111, 117, 151, 163.

13. From Gregory VII. onwards the Popes and their supporters

Direct
Power of
the Pope
in Tem-
poralities.

are unanimous in holding that, so far as the substance is concerned, the Temporal as well as the Spiritual Power belongs to the Chair of Peter, and that the separation which is commanded by divine law affects only the Administration, not the Substance. The various shades of opinion differ only as to the extent of the right of user committed to the temporal ruler and of the right reserved to the Pope, and, in particular, as to the definition of the cases in which the Pope, notwithstanding the right committed to the secular magistrate, may directly interfere in temporal affairs.—Therefore it is a mistake to represent the great Popes as proclaiming, and the common opinion of the later Middle Age as accepting, only that sort of 'indirect power in temporalities' (in Bellarmine's sense of these terms) which was claimed for the Apostolic See by later theorists. This mistake has been made by Hergenröther, op. cit. 421 ff., Molitor, op. cit. p. 166 ff. and others. The words of Innocent IV. on which Molitor has laid special weight, say merely that as a general rule the spiritual sword is not to meddle with the wielding of the temporal, and it is only to this normal separation in the use of the swords that Innocent's words 'directe, secus indirecte' (c. 13, X. 2, 1) refer. The statements to the effect that the Pope, by virtue of his spiritual power, 'per consequens' rules over temporal affairs, because and in so far as 'temporalia ordinantur ad spiritualia tanquam ad finem,' make no surrender of the fundamental thought of an Universal State in which the plenitude of all power, worldly as well as spiritual, is in principle committed to the Pope. Indeed these same popes and canonists, as Molitor (p. 91 ff.) admits, expressly assert the axiom that the Pope has both swords and commits one of them to other hands merely for use. With this axiom the doctrine that would allow the Pope only a *potestas indirecta* is irreconcilable. For this reason even Torquemada, despite his tendency towards moderation in the statement of papal rights (Summa II. c. 113 ff.), cannot be reckoned among the advocates of this doctrine of 'indirect power,' since in plain words he claims for the Pope *utrumque gladium,* and *in radice* the temporal power (c. 114). As a hint of the doctrine of cent. xvi. we might rather choose a passage in which Gerson ascribes to the Church in worldly affairs 'dominium quoddam directivum, regulativum et ordinativum' (De pot. ecc. c. 12; Op. II. 248).

Inferiority
of Tem-
poral
Power.

14. See Joh. Saresb. IV. c. 3: the Church has both swords: 'sed gladio sanguinis...utitur per manum principis, cui coercendorum corporum contulit potestatem, spiritualium sibi in pontificibus auctoritate reservata: est ergo princeps sacerdotii quidem minister et qui

sacrorum officiorum illam partem exercet, quae sacerdotii manibus videtur indigna.' Aegid. Rom. I. c. 9; August. Triumph. I. q. I, a. 4, q. 43, a. 2; Alvar. Pelag. I. a. 13 and 37.

15. In some form or another, as might be expected, all advo- The cates of the ecclesiastical power maintain, not only the separation of Powers that be are the two powers, but the divine institution of the worldly Magistrature: ordained for this was a revealed truth [Rom. xiii. 1; Matth. xxii. 21]. So even of God. Gregor. VII. lib. 2, ep. 31, lib. 3, ep. 7, lib. 7, ep. 21, 23, 25. Innoc. III. l. 7, ep. 212 (vol. 215, p. 527); Reg. sup. neg. Imp. ep. 2 and 79. Joh. Saresb. Polycr. IV. c. 1, p. 208—209 and VI. c. 25, p. 391—395. Thom. Aquin. in libr. II. Sent. dist. 44, ad. 4 (utraque deducitur a potestate divina). Ptol. Luc. III. c. 1—8. Alv. Pel. I. a. 8, 41 C—K, 56 B. Host. Summa IV. 17. Panorm. on c. 13, X. 2, 1.

16. Resuming the teaching of Augustine, Gregory VII. is the Sinful Origin of first to declare that the temporal power is the work of sin and the the State. devil. See lib. 8, ep. 21, ann. 1080, p. 456—7: 'Quis nesciat reges et duces ab iis habuisse principium, qui Deum ignorantes, superbia, rapinis, perfidia, homicidiis, postremo universis sceleribus, mundi principe diabolo videlicet agitante, super pares, scilicet homines, dominari caeca cupiditate et intolerabili praesumtione affectaverunt?' And again: 'itane dignitas a saecularibus—etiam Deum ignoranti- bus—inventa, non subicietur ei dignitati, quam omnipotentis Dei providentia ad honorem suum invenit mundoque misericorditer tribuit?' See also lib. 4, ep. 2, ann. 1076, p. 243: 'illam quidem (scilicet, regiam dignitatem) superbia humana repperit, hanc (episco- palem) divina pietas instituit; illa vanam gloriam incessanter captat, haec ad coelestem vitam semper aspirat.' Cardinal Deusdedit (ob. 1099), Contra invasores etc. lib. III. sect. 5 et 6 § 12 (in Mai VII. p. 107) argues in like fashion: 'Nec mirum, sacerdotalem auctori- tatem, quam Deus ipse per se ipsum constituit, in huiusmodi causis regiam praecellere potestatem, quam sibi humana praefecit adin- ventio eo quidem permittente, non tamen volente': then the example of the Jews is cited. John of Salisbury, Polycrat. VIII. c. 17—18, 20, says of all *regna* 'iniquitas per se aut praesumpsit aut extorsit a Deo'; the latter was the case of the Jews according to 1 Reg. viii., since 'populus a Deo quem contempserat sibi regem extorsit.'— Hugh of Fleury (Prol. I. c. 1, 4, 12, II. p. 66—68), who himself deduces an immediately divine origin for the royal power from 'Non est potestas nisi a Deo,' describes as a wide-spread error the doctrine which would give to that power a human, and therefore sinful, origin. Innocent III., Reg. sup. neg. Imp. ep. 18, argues for the indestructibility of the Priesthood and the frailty of the

Realm, since the one was instituted by divine ordinance and the other (1 Reg. viii.) 'extortum ad petitionem humanam.' Compare August. Triumph. II. q. 33, a. 1. Also Alvar. Pelag. I. a. 59 G (regnum terrenum, sicut ipsa terrena creatura sibi constituit tanquam ultimum finem,...est malum et diabolicum et opponitur regno coelesti) and 64 D—E (sordida regni temporalis initia).—Gerson, Op. IV. 648: the efficient cause of *dominatio* and of *coercitivum dominium* was sin.—Petr. Andl. I. c. 1: 'fuit itaque solum natura corrupta regimen necessarium regale'; but for the Deluge, instead of ownership and lordship, there would have continued to be, as there will be in another world, liberty, equality and community of goods under the direct government of God. See also Frederick II. in Petr. de Vin. ep. v. c. 1. [In an earlier part of his book, D. G. R. III. 125, 126, Dr Gierke has stated the doctrine of the sinful origin of the State that is found in Augustine's De civitate Dei.]

Ordination of State by Church. 17. Already Honorius Augustodunus, Summa gloria, c. 4, in Migne, vol. 172, pp. 1263—5, declares that, since soul is worthier than body, and priesthood than realm, the realm *iure ordinatur* by the priesthood; as the soul vivifies the body, so the priesthood *constituens ordinat* the realm : 'igitur quia sacerdotium iure regnum constituet, iure regnum sacerdotio subiacebit.'—So again, Hugo a S. Victore, De sacram. lib. II. pars 2, c. 4 : the spiritual power is worthier than the temporal, 'nam spiritualis potestas terrenam potestatem et instituere habet, ut sit, et iudicare habet, si bona non fuerit ; ipsa vero a Deo primum instituta est, et cum deviat, a solo Deo iudicari potest, sicut scriptum est : Spiritualis diiudicat omnia et ipse a nemine iudicatur' : the spiritual is prior in time as well as in worth : thus in the Old Dispensation the priesthood was first instituted by God, and afterwards the royal power was ordained by the priesthood at God's command ; so now in the Church the sacerdotal dignity consecrates the royal power, both sanctifying it by blessing and forming it by institution.—So in the same words Alexander Halensis, Summa Theolog., P. IV. q. x., memb. 5, art. 2. Then Aegid. Rom. De pot. eccl. I. c. 4, and Boniface VIII. in Unam Sanctam : 'nam veritate testante spiritualis potestas terrenam potestatem instituere habet et iudicare, si bona non fuerit.' Compare also Joh. Saresb., above Note 14, and Thomas of Canterbury, who, in the passage cited in Note 10, proceeds to say : 'et quia certum est reges potestatem suam accipere ab Ecclesia, non ipsam ab illis, sed a Christo.' Vincent. Bellovac. lib. VII. c. 32.—A thorough statement by Alvar. Pelag. I. a. 36, 37 (regalis potestas est per sacerdotalem ordinata), 56 B, 59 F—G (the spiritual is efficient and final cause of the temporal

power, and only in this way has the, in itself sinful, terrene realm a
share in the sanctity of the celestial).   August. Triumph. I. q. 1, a. 1
and 3, q. 2, a. 7, II. q. 33, a. 1 and 2 (the *imperium tyrannicum* is
older than the priesthood, but the *imp. politicum, rectum et iustum* is
established by the Popes for the defence and service of the Church).
—Hostiensis, upon c. 8, X. 3, 34, nr. 26, 27.—Panormitanus, upon
c. 13, X. 2, 1.—Konrad v. Megenberg, in Höfler, Aus Avignon,
p. 24 ff.—A relationship of this sort between the two powers is
already implied in the allegorical use of Sun and Moon (e.g. in
Gerhoh v. Reichersberg, praef. c. 3), which becomes official from
the time of Innocent III. onwards: c. 6, X. 1, 33, also lib. 1, ep.
104, vol. 214, p. 377, and Reg. s. neg. Imp. ep. 2, 32 and 179;
for the moon borrows her light from the sun (ep. 104 cit.).   The
yet commoner comparison with Soul and Body effects the same purpose, for the soul was regarded as the formative principle of the body.
See Honorius Augustod. as above, and Ptol. Luc. De reg. princ. III.
c. 10 (sicut ergo corpus per animam habet esse, virtutem et operationem...ita et temp. iurisdict. principum per spiritualem Petri et
eius successorum).

18.   The thought that in the last resort the State is an Ecclesiastical Institution is already being expressed when, on the one hand,
the two powers have assigned to them respectively the ghostly domain
and the corporeal, and, on the other hand, corporeal purposes are
declared to be mere means for ghostly purposes.   See Gregor. VII.,
lib. 8, ep. 21; Innoc. III., Respons. in consist. in Reg. sup. neg.
Imp. ep. 18, p. 1012 ff.; c. 6, X. 1, 33.   Thom. Aquin., De reg.
princ. I. c. 14—5: the priests have the care of the ultimate end;
temporal kings have merely the care of antecedent ends: 'ei ad
quem finis ultimi cura pertinet, subdi debent illi ad quos pertinet
antecedentium finium, et eius imperio dirigi.'   See also Thom. Aq.
in libr. II. Sent. dist. 44 in fine, and Summa Theol. II. 2, q. 60, a. 6
ad. 3.   Vincent. Bellov. lib. VII. 3 and 32.   Aegid. Rom., De pot. eccl.
II. c. 5: 'potestas regia est per pot. eccl. et a pot. eccl. constituta
et ordinata in opus et obsequium ecclesiasticae potestatis.'   Aug.
Triumph. I. q. 1, a. 8: 'temporalia et corporalia...ad spiritualia
ordinantur tanquam instrumenta et organa.'   Alv. Pel. I. a. 37
P and R, a. 40 and 56.   Durandus a S. Porciano, De origine iurisdictionis, qu. 3: 'temporalia quae ordinantur ad spiritualia tanquam
ad finem.'   Panorm. c. 13, X. 2, 1.

19.   To this effect already Deusdedit, Contra invasores, lib. III.
sect. 5 et 6 § 13, p. 108.   Petri Exceptiones, I. c. 2, in Savigny,
Gesch. des r. R., II. 322.   Dictum Gratiani upon c. 6, Dist. 10.

The State an Ecclesiastical Institution.

The sphere of Temporal is defined by

Spiritual Law.

Petr. Blesensis jun. Specul. c. 16. Vincent. Bellovac. lib. VII. c. 33. Aug. Triumph. I. q. 1, a. 3, and II. q. 44, a. 1—8. Alv. Pelag. I. a. 44. Ockham, Octo qu. III. c. 9.

Subjection of Temporal Power.

20. See Gregor. VII., lib. 1, ep. 63; lib. 4, ep. 2, ep. 23, ep. 24; lib. 8, ep. 21 (especially p. 464). Cardinal Deusdedit, Contra invasores, lib. III. per totum. Honorius Augustod., Summa gloria, p. 1265: 'iure regnum sacerdotio subiacebit' (above Note 17). Joh. Saresb. v. c. 2, p. 252. Thom. Cantuar., epist. 177—184, p. 648 ff. Ivo of Chartres, ep. 106, Henrico Anglorum Regi, p. 125 : 'regnum terrenum coelesti regno, quod Ecclesiae commissum est, subditum esse semper cogitatis ; sicut enim sensus animalis subditus debet esse rationi, ita potestas terrena subdita esse debet ecclesiastico regimini ; et quantum valet corpus nisi regatur ab anima, tantum valet terrena potestas nisi informetur et regatur ecclesiastica disciplina ; et sicut pacatum est regnum corporis cum iam non resistit caro spiritui, sic in pace possidetur regnum mundi, cum iam resistere non molitur regno Dei': You (King Henry) are not *dominus*, but *servus servorum Dei* ; be their *protector*, *non possessor*. Comp. ep. 60, p. 70 ff. If Ivo here and elsewhere (ep. 214, p. 217 ff., and ep. 238, p. 245) expressly states that the *ecclesia* can only flourish if Priesthood and Realm be united, while every discord between the two powers must rend the church, and if he exhorts the Pope (ep. 238) to do his part in the production of unity,—with a saving for the majesty of the apostolic see,—still the legal relation of Realm to Priesthood is, in Ivo's eyes, a complete subjection.—To the same effect Alex. Halensis, III. q. 40, m. 2. Rolandus (Alex. III.), Summa, p. 5, D. 10. Innocent III., in c. 6, X. 1, 33. Thom. Aquin. De reg. princ. I. c. 14 (Romano pontifici omnes reges populi Christ. oportet esse subditos, sicut ipsi domino Jesu Christo) ; Opusc. contra impugn. relig. 11 c. 4, concl. 1 ; Summa Theol. II. 1, q. 60, a. 6, ad. 3 (potestas saecularis subditur spirituali, sicut corpus animae) ; in lib. II. Sent. d. 44 ; Quodl. 12, q. 13, a. 19, ad. 2. Aegid. Rom. De pot. eccl. I. c. 7 (two swords, like soul and body, quorum unus alteri debet esse subiectus) ; II. c. 4, 10 and 12. Boniface VIII., in Unam Sanctam : Oportet autem gladium sub gladio esse et temporalem auctoritatem spirituali subiici potestati. August. Triumph. I. q. 1, a. 1 and 3, II. q. 36, 38, 44, a. 1 (Papa est medius inter Deum et populum Christianum ;...medius inter Deum et imperatorem ;...a quo imperatori respublica commissa). Alv. Pel. I. a. 13, 37 Q—R, 56, 59. And. Isern. I. Feud. 29, pr. nr. 2. Barthol. Soc. III. cons. 99, nr. 18. Cardin. Alex. c. 3, D. 10. The Commentary on c. 6, X. 1, 33. Comp. also Höfler, Kaiserthum, 57 ff., 80 ff., 137 ff.—Comparisons

with gold and lead, heaven and earth, sun and moon, soul and body, frequently recur, and the last of these, if taken in earnest, must make for an unconditional subjection of the State, as in the above-cited words of Ivo.

21. See John of Salisbury in Note 14 and Thomas of Canterbury in Note 10. Summa Parisiensis (above Note 12): imperator vicarius eius. Ptol. Luc. III. c. 17: imperium ad exequendum regimen fidelium secundum mandatum pontificis ordinatur, ut merito dici possint ipsorum executores et cooperatores Dei ad gubernandum populum Christianum. Aegid. Rom. De pot. eccl. c. 5. Hostiensis upon c. 8, X. 3, 34, nr. 26—7. August. Triumph. I. q. 1, a. 8 (princes are quasi ministri et stipendiarii ipsius papae et ipsius ecclesiae, they receive an office and are remunerated de thesauro ipsius ecclesiae); q. 44 and 45; II. q. 35, a. 1, and 38, a. 2—4 (the Emperor is minister papae); I. q. 22, a. 3 (the Emperor is likened to a proconsul). Alv. Pel. I. a. 40: as the Church, which is Cosmopolis, can give (by baptism) and take away the right of citizenship, so she distributes offices among her citizens; sacerdotal consecration and unction first give temporal lordship over God's holy people, and these priestly acts must be regarded as approval and confirmation; a. 56 B and P; also a. 13; a. 40 K (sicut anima utitur corpore ut instrumento,...sic papa...utitur officio imperatoris ut instrumento); a. 52—54 (all worldly and ghostly offices are 'gradus in ecclesia'). The Clerk in Somn. Virid. II. c. 163. Comp. in Joh. Par. prooem. the confutation of the statement that praelati et principes are only tutores, procuratores and dispensatores of the Pope's verum dominium temporalium.

[margin: Temporal Rulers as Servants of Church and Pope.]

22. Apparently Goffredus abbas Vindocinensis (Migne, vol. 157, p. 220) is the first allegorically to explain the two swords mentioned in Evang. Lucae, c. 22, v. 38, as being material and spiritual swords, which are to be used in defence of the Church; but he only uses this allegory to support a demand for an amicable union between the two powers. Gerhoh Reichersp. (Migne, vol. 194, p. 111) goes no further. Bernard of Clairvaux (ep. 256, ann. 1146, in Migne, vol. 182, p. 463) seems the first to explain the allegory in the manner that was afterwards adopted by the Church's champions: Petri uterque est, alter suo nutu, alter sua manu: see also De consider. IV. c. 3, in Migne, vol. 186, p. 776. Then already with John of Salisbury, Polycrat. IV. c. 3, the Prince receives one sword from the hand of the Church; the Church *has* that sword (habet et ipsum), but uses it 'per principis manum.' So S. Anselm, Comm. in Matth. c. 26. Among the Popes, Innoc. III., Gregor. IX., Innoc. IV., and

[margin: The High Church Doctrine of the Two Swords.]

Bonif. VIII. (Unam sanctam, also speech in the Roman synod, in Hefele, Konciliengesch., VI. § 689) raised this theory to the rank of an official doctrine. It was conceded by some of the Emperors, such as Otto IV., Frederick II., Albert (1302 and 1303); see Höfler, pp. 86, 134. Thenceforward it was a self-evident axiom for the Canonists, and Prosdocimus de Comitibus, nr. 55, can reckon the two theories of the Two Swords as 'a difference between the *leges* and the *canones*.' Comp. Glossa Ord. on c. 1, Dist. 22. v. *coelestis*: argumentum quod papa habet utrumque gladium, scil. spir. et temp. (The text that is being glossed, from Petrus Damianus, Opusc. IV. admits of various interpretations:—beato aeternae vitae clavigero terreni simul et coelestis imperii iura commisit.) Quotation from Alanus in Lup. Beb. c. 9, p. 368. Gloss. Ord. on c. 13, X. 1, 2: verum executionem gladii temporalis imperatoribus et regibus commisit ecclesia; quaedam enim possumus aliis committere quae nobis non possumus retinere.' Commentaries on c. 34, X. 1, 6, c. 1, X. 1, 7, c. 13, X. 2, 1, c. 10, X. 2, 2 by Innocentius, Zabarella, Ant. Butrigarius, Felinus and Decius. Thus e.g. Panormitanus holds that the imperium is 'non immediate a Deo, sed per debitam et subalternatam emanationem a vicario Christi Jesu, apud quem sunt iura coelestis et terreni imperii': in this sense are to be understood the words 'non est potestas nisi a Deo'; but we may also apply them to mean that according to the will of God one Sword belongs to temporal rulers 'respectu exercitii.' See further Aegid. Rom. De pot. eccl. I. c. 7—9. Schwabensp. c. 1. Aug. Triumph. I. q. 1, a. 1, and II. q. 36, a. 1—4. Alv. Pelag. I. a. 13, 37 S (dominus legitimus…utilis) and Z, 40 K, 59 D (the Pope is always primum movens, even when the Prince is proximum movens), II. a. 57; Konr. Megenb. in Höfler, aus Avignon, p. 24 ff. Petrus a Monte, in Tr. U. J. XIII. 1, f. 152 ff. Petrus de Andlo, II. c. 9. Turrecremata, Summa de eccl. II. c. 114. Naturally a few legists take the same view, e.g. Bartolus, l. 1, § 1, Dig. 48, 17, and Paul. Cast. l. 8, Dig. 1, 3, nr. 6; and some feudists, e.g. Andr. de Isern. II. Feud. 55, nr. 87. All the arguments *pro* and *con* are collected by Ockham, who distinguishes with exactitude various nice shades of the doctrine 'Imperium a Papa': see Octo qu. I. c. 2, 18—19 and on the other side c. 6—17; also see II. c. 1—4, 12, 15, and on the other side c. 6—14; VIII. c. 1; Dial. III. tr. 2, l. 1, c. 18—25.

Emperors and Temporal Rulers as Pope's Vassals.

23. Comp. e.g. Innoc. IV. upon c. 10, X. 2, 2, nr. 1; Thom. Aquin. Quodl. 12, q. 13, a. 19, ad 2: Reges sunt vassalli ecclesiae. Clement V. in Clem. un. de iureiurando, 2, 9, and the commentaries thereon. Aug. Triumph. I. q. 1, a. 1; II. q. 38, a. 4; Alv. Pel. I.

a. 13 B, a. 40, a. 57 ; Konr. Megenb., in Höfler, aus Avignon, p. 24 ff.; Petr. Andl. II. c. 2 ; Panorm. c. 13, X. 2, 1.

24. According to S. Bernard, De consider. IV. c. 3, the temporal sword is to be wielded 'ad nutum sacerdotis et ad iussum imperatoris.' Gregory IX. (Raynald, ann. 1233, nr. 1) repeats this but omits the last half of the phrase. Aegid. Rom., De pot. eccl. I. c. 8—9, says that the Pope has both swords, 'sed decet Ecclesiam habere materialem gladium non ad usum sed ad nutum.' See also Notes 20 and 21.

[margin: The Temporal Sword at the Disposal of the Church.]

25. Innocent III. is the first sharply to distinguish between (1) the normal use that is made of the spiritual sword when the acts of temporal rulers are subjected to ecclesiastical jurisdiction, and (2) the exceptional cases in which the Pope directly uses the temporal sword. See in particular c. 13, X. 2, 1 (lib. 7, ep. 42, ann. 1204) on the one side, and on the other c. 13, X. 4, 17. So also Innocent IV.: compare the letter of 1245 in Hefele, v. 1001: nec curabimus *de cetero* gladio uti materiali, sed tantum spirituali contra Fridericum. Encyclica of 1246 : spiritualiter de temporalibus iudicare. Innoc. Comm. upon c. 13, X. 2, 1.—Hostiensis, Summa, 4, 17 : sicut contra et super et praeter naturalem et humanam rationem Filius Dei incarnatus et natus est, sic iurisdictio spiritualis, quam Ecclesiae reliquit, contra et super et praeter naturam iurisdictionis trahit ad se principalem iurisdictionem temporalem, si id, quod de iurisdictione spirituali est, in ea incidit. Petrus Paludanus, De causa immediata eccl. pot. a. 4: Papa est superior in spiritualibus et per consequens in temporalibus, quantum necesse est pro bono spirituali.—Johan. Andr. c. 13, X. 4, 17 : temporalia per quandam consequentiam. Turrecremata, II. c. 113 ff.—On the other hand, in the argumentation of Gregory VII. lib. 4, ep. 2, and lib. 8, ep. 21, the right that he claims of deposing the Kaiser is thoroughly fused with a right to excommunicate the Kaiser. Similarly, those later writers, who will hardly allow any independence to the temporal sword, do not clearly distinguish between the ordinary use of spiritual power in the correction of Rulers and an extraordinary use of temporal power by the Pope. See e.g. Joh. Saresb. Polycr. IV. c. 1—4 ; Aegid. Rom. De pot. eccl. I. c. 2—4, II. c. 4 and esp. III. c. 4—8 ; August. Triumph. I. q. 1, a. 1 (institui, regulari et ordinari si bona sit, condemnari et iudicari si bona non sit) ; Alv. Pel. I. a. 37, 56, 58 ; Cler. in Somn. Virid. II. c. 18, 22, 24, 26, 28, 32, 69, 139.

[margin: Direct use by the Church of the Temporal Sword.]

26. So Innocent III. in c. 13, X. 4, 17 : there should be no invasion into *ius alienum* ; what is Caesar's should be given to Caesar. And to the same effect what is said of the separation of

[margin: The Church should respect the]

Rights of Rulers. the swords and their duty of mutual aid: Reg. sup. neg. Imp. ep. 2, vol. 216, p. 997, and ep. 179, p. 1162, also lib. 7, ep. 54 and 79, vol. 215, p. 339 and 361, lib. 10, ep. 141, p. 1235, lib. 11, ep. 28, p. 1358. Innocent IV. Comment on 13, X. 4, 17: nam temporalia et spiritualia diversa sunt, et diversos iudices habent, nec unus iudex habet se intromittere de pertinentibus ad alium, licet se ad invicem iuvare debeant.—Hostiensis, Summa, 4, 17: iurisdictiones distinctae; ...nec debet se intromittere de subditis Imperatoris, nisi forte in casibus.—Gloss. Ord. upon c. 13, X. 4, 17; and upon c. 13, X. 2, 1: non ergo de temporali iurisdictione debet intromittere se Papa nisi in subsidium. Ant. Butr. on c. 13, X. 4, 17; Joh. Andr. on c. 13, X. 2, 1; Panorm. on c. 13, X. 2, 1; Turrecremata, 11. c. 113.

Extra-ordinary Use of Temporal Power by the Church. 27. S. Bernard, De consider. 1. c. 6: ubi necessitas exigit... incidenter...causa quidem urgente.—Innocent III. in c. 13, X. 4, 17: the power may be used *casualiter* if *causae multum arduae* require it. (As to *casualiter* and the variant *carnaliter*, see Molitor, p. 61 ff.)— Gloss. Ord. l. c.: in subsidium. Host. upon c. 13, X. 2, 1; Thom. Aquin. Sum. Theol. 11. 2, q. 60, a. 6, ad. 3; Joh. Andr. c. 13, X. 2, 1; Ant. Butr. c. 13, X. 4, 17: non regulariter; Panorm. l. c.: in a case of necessity, if there are *ardua negotia*.

Translation of the Empire by the Pope. 28. Gregory VII. lib. 8, ep. 21, ann. 1080, p. 464: quapropter quos sancta Ecclesia sua sponte ad regimen vel imperium deliberato consilio advocat, (iis) non pro transitoria gloria sed pro multorum salute, humiliter obediant.—S. Bernard, ep. 236; Landulf. Col. De transl. Imp., c. 8; Ptol. Luc. III. c. 10; Aug. Triumph. II. q. 37, a. 5: regnorum omnium translatio auctoritate papae facta fuit vel alicuius qui ipsum figurabat: e.g. Samuel, Daniel and so forth. Also q. 46, a. 3: est Dei vice omnium regnorum provisor.—Konrad v. Megenburg, in Höfler, aus Avignon, p. 24 f.: the transfer should be made in accordance with divine law, not arbitrarily.—Panorm. c. 13, X. 2, 1: hinc est quod imperium transferre potest de certo genere personarum ad aliud genus.—Turrecremata, II. c. 115; Ockham, Octo qu. IV. c. 4, and VIII. c. 3; Dial. III. tr. 2, l. 1, c. 20.

Translatio Imperii. 29. Innocent III. in c. 34, X. 1, 6, and all the Commentaries upon this canon. Ptol. Luc. III. c. 18; Land. Col. c. 3—8; Aug. Triumph. II. q. 37, a. 1—4. Alv. Pel. I. a. 13 F and 41; Andr. Isern. prooem. Feud. nr. 37; Petr. Andl. I. c. 13—15, II. c. 3; cf. Ockham, Octo qu. IV. c. 5.

Papal Appointment of Kaisers and Kings. 30. See above Notes 17 and 21, and below Note 34. Already Gregory VII. claims this right, as appears from c. 3, C. 15, q. 6, a passage from a letter of his (ann. 1080) to Bishop Hermann of Metz: Alius item Romanus Pontifex, Zacharias scilicet, regem

Francorum non tam pro suis iniquitatibus, quam pro eo, quod tantae potestati erat inutilis, a regno deposuit, et Pipinum, Karoli imperatoris patrem, in eius loco substituit, omnesque Francigenas a iuramento fidelitatis, quod illi fecerant, absolvit. In the two letters of 1077, lib. 4, ep. 23 and 24, p. 275 ff., he claims to decide a disputed succession to the throne, and charges all men to obey him whom he confirms *in regia dignitate.*

31. As to the supposed institution of the Prince-Electors by Gregory V. and his right to institute them, see Land. Col. c. 9; Ptol. Luc. III. c. 10 and 19; Aug. Triumph. II. q. 35 ; Alv. Pelag. I. a. 13 F, 21, 27 Z and Dd, 40 E—F, 45 ; Zabarell. c. 34 § *verum,* X. 1, 6, nr. 8. Ptolemy of Lucca, Augustinus Triumphus, and Alvarius argue that the Church may at any time for good and reasonable cause change the mode of election, give the right of election to another nation, or itself exercise the right, institute an hereditary empire etc. Augustinus and Alvarius say straight out that the Pope elects the Emperor by the agency of the Prince-Electors (per eos), for a principal may choose instruments and ministers as he pleases. *The Pope and the German Electors.*

32. Honorius Augustod. p. 1264; Imperator Romanus *debet ab Apostolico eligi* consensu principum et acclamatione plebis, in caput populi constitui, a Papa consecrari et coronari. Innoc. III. in c. 34, X. 1, 6. Innoc. IV. Compost., Joh. And., Zabar., Panorm., Ant. Butr., Felin., Decius on this canon. Aug. Triumph. II. q. 38—41. Alv. Pel. I. a. 13, 40, 43, 57 ; Petr. de Andlo, II. c. 2, 4—7; Marcus, I. q. 938; Turrecrem. II. c. 115. *The Pope's Part in the Election of an Emperor.*

33. Innoc. IV. upon c. 10, X. 2, 2, nr. 1—2, and c. 7, X. 1, 10, nr. 3: the Pope appoints a curator for a king incompetent to rule. Durant. Spec. I. 1 de legato § 6, nr. 15 and 17. Andr. Isern. II. Feud. 55, nr. 87. Alv. Pel. I. a. 13 F, 37 S, 56 N. Petr. Andl. II. c. 10 (but it is otherwise under the Golden Bull). Hier. Zanetinus, diff. nr. 101. Turrecrem. II. c. 115. This principle was practically applied by Clement V. See also Ficker, Forschungen, II. 458 ff. *The Pope's Guardianship of the vacant Realm.*

34. Gregory VII. endeavoured, not only practically to use these powers, but also theoretically to deduce them from the superiority of the spiritual power, since the bearer of the keys can be judged by none and himself must judge the temporal rulers : Nescitis quia angelos iudicabimus ? quanto magis saecularia ! He appealed to the deeds of his predecessors, more particularly Gregory I. and Zacharias. See lib. 1, ep. 55[a], p. 175, lib. 4, ep. 2 and 24, lib. 8, ep. 21 ; c. 3, C. 15, q. 6 (above Note 30), c. 4 eod. He is followed in this by Gregory IX., Innocent IV., John XXII., Nicholas V. Comp. *The Pope's power to depose Rulers and free Subjects from the Oath of Fealty.*

Dictum Gratiani P. II. C. 15, q. 6. Joh. Saresb. Polycrat. IV. c. 3, p. 213: dignitatem principis conferre et auferre, and V. c. 6. Landulf. Col. c. 4. Thom. Aq. Summa Theol. II. 2, q. 10, a. 10, and q. 12, a. 2. Innoc. IV. on c. 27, X. 2, 27, nr. 6. Aegid. Rom. De pot. eccl. I. c. 2—5. Host. c. 8, X. 3, 34, nr. 26—27. Dur. Spec. l. c. nr. 17. Aug. Triumph. I. q. 1, a. 1 and 3; q. 6; q. 26, a. 4; q. 46, a. 1; II. q. 40, a. 1—4; q. 45, a. 3; q. 46, a. 1—2. Alv. Pel. I. a. 13 B, 21, 37 R, 40 F (eccl. Rom. cuius est regna transferre et reges de sua sede deponere); 56 E (duty of protecting nations against the tyranny of kings); II. a. 29 and 30. Zabar. c. 34 § *verum*, X. 1, 6, nr. 7. Panorm. eod. c. nr. 7—9, and c. 13, X. 4, 17 (deponit causis exigentibus). Phil. Dec. c. 1, X. 2, 19, nr. 8. Some legists took this side: Bartol., l. 11, C. 1, 14, nr. 4; Baldus, ead. l. nr. 6.

The Pope's power over Rulers other than the Emperor. 35. See e.g. Aug. Triumph. II. q. 45 and 46; the Clerk in Somn. Virid. II. c. 76 ff., 92 ff., 163.—It is true that some special claims could be made against the Kaiser (see e.g. Alv. Pelag. I. a. 42 G and a. 44 E), because he was an elected prince, and because there was 'specialis coniunctio inter imperatorem et papam'; and the imperialist partizans point out that their adversaries would set the Emperor below other Monarchs (see e.g. Ockham, Dial. III. tr. 2, l. 1, c. 20). Still in the main Frederick II. was quite right when in his famous letter he laid stress on the solidarity of the interests of all temporal rulers who were equally threatened by the Pope. See Petr. de Vin. ep. 1. c. 2, 3, 34.

Reminiscences of the Subjection of Church to Realm. 36. For Abp. Reinald of Köln in 1162 (Watterich, Pont. Rom. vitae II. 530 and 533) there was still life in the thought that the Church of Rome is the Empire's church, and the Pope is a bishop of the Empire. Then in cent. xiv. it begins to be common for the opponents of ecclesiastical claims to appeal to history and to speak of the position held by the church under the old Roman Emperors, the Frankish Emperors, the Ottos and Henry III.

37. Ockham, Octo q. III. c. 3 and 8, Dial. III. tr. 2, l. 1, c. 1, and l. 3, c. 17 and 22. Comp. also Anton. Rosell. I. c. 61—63.

Church and State are co-ordinate. 38. This had previously been the teaching of the Church herself. Henry IV. (ann. 1076 in M. G. L. II. p. 48) is the first to oppose it to the growing ecclesiastical claims. Pet. Crassus, p. 28 ff., fully develops it: God instituted two laws, two peoples, two powers among Mankind. So Wenrich, p. 214 ff.; Wido, De scismate, lib. II.; Walram Naumb., De unitate eccl., lib. I.; Sigebert episc. adv. Paschalem, ann. 1103; Tractatus de investitura, ann. 1109. Appeals to it are made by Frederick I. (e.g. ann. 1152 in Jaffé Mon. Corb. p. 500 and ann. 1157, M. G. Leg. II. p. 105; comp. ep. Wibaldi, ann. 1152, in Jaffé, l. c. p. 502), Frederick II. (e.g. Pet. de Vin. ep. I. c. 1, 9, 31, V. c. 1) and later Emperors. It is adopted by most of the Legists; they follow in this the glosses, especially that on Auth. coll. 1. 6, prooem. v. *conferens generi.* Many of the older Canonists held the same opinion, connecting it with the words of Gelasius and Nicholas I. which appeared in the Decretum as c. 8, D. 10, c. 6, D. 96, c. 10, D. ead. Among them are Stephanus (above Note 8) and Huguccio (as to whom see Lup. Beb. c. 9, and against him Aug. Triumph. II. q. 36, a. 4). So also some of the older Theologians, such as Peter Damiani (Opusc. IV. in Migne, vol. 145, p. 71—72 and 86—87, lib. 4, ep. 9 ad Firm. ep. and lib. 7, ep. 3 ad Henr. Reg. p. 121) and Gerhoh of Reichersberg (Syntagma, 180—3). Then it is defended by Hugo Floriac. (I. c. 12, p. 43 ff., and II. p. 46 ff., and 65); Otto Frising.; Eberh. Bamberg. (ob. 1172, see Höfler, Kaiser-thum, p. 61); Eike v. Repgow in the Sachsenspiegel, I. a. 1; Johann v. Buch, Gloss. on Sachsensp. I. a. 1, and III. a. 57, § 1; Vridank, p. 152, v. 12—19, and other German poets.—Then Dante (Mon. III. c. 16) endeavoured to give it a deeper philosophical foundation. To biblical, historical and legal, he added physical and metaphysical arguments, for he endeavoured to show that to the double nature and double end of man there must correspond a *duplex directivum* ordained by God. Comp. also Joh. Paris. c. 4—10: potestates distinctae et una in aliam non reducitur. Lup. Bebenb. c. 10: pot. distinctae et divisae. Quaestio in utramque part. p. 96—102. Ockham, Octo qu. I. c. 1, 3—5 and 20 (where a distinction is drawn between two opinions, viz. that the two powers cannot be united, and that, though they could be united, an ordinance of God forbids their union); Dial. III. tr. 2, l. 2, c. 1—4. Disput. int. mil. et cler. pp. 667—682. Miles in Somn. Virid. I. c. 1—16 and 39 ff., II. c. 116: Deus duas iurisdictiones distinxit, duos populos, duas vitas, duo genera militum. Petr. de Aliac. in Gerson, Op. 1. 678. Gerson, IV. 650. Randuf, De mod. un. c. 15. Theod. a Niem, De schism. III. c. 7; Priv. et iura imp. p. 785. Nic. Cus. III. c. 1—2, 5, 31, 41. Aen. Sylv. c. 7. Greg. Heimb. Admon. I. p. 557—563. Ant. Ros. I. c. 20—38 and 41: Deus duos constituit vicarios. Almain, Expos. on Qu. I. c. 6—7, declares the second of the two opinions discussed by Ockham to be the true one.

39. Pet. Crassus, p. 28 ff. Sachsensp. I. a. 3, § 3. Joh. Paris. c. 18, p. 195. Ockham, Octo qu. I. c. 15 and III. c. 2. Somn. Virid. I. c. 70 ff. and 103 ff. Franc. Curt. sen. Cons. 43, nr. 4. — Temporal Law is not dependent on the Canons.

40. See esp. Pet. Crassus, p. 26: divinitus datum. Wenrich in Martene, I. p. 220. Emp. Frederick I. ann. 1157 and 1159, in

Imperium non dependet ab ecclesia.

M. G. L. pp. 105, 118 : a solo Deo imperium. Cinus upon l. 1, C. 1, 1, nr. 2—3, and Auth. cassa on l. 12, C. 1, 3, nr. 2 : Imp. et Papa aeque principaliter sunt constituti a Deo. Damasus, Broc. M. III. br. 19. Dante, Mon. lib. III. throughout. Quaestio in utr. part. a. 1, 2, 3, 5. Joh. Paris. c. 5 : et ambae oriuntur ab una suprema potestate, scil. divina, immediate ; c. 10, 15—22. Marsil. Pat. Def. pac. II. c. 27. Declarations at Lahnstein and Rense, in Ficker, zur Gesch. des Kurv. v. R. p. 699 ff. Miles in Somn. Vir. 1. c. 57—69, 74—78, 88—102, 146—163. Disput. int. mil. et cler. p. 677. Baldus, l. 1, C. 1, 1, nr. 1—12 ; sup. pace Const. v. 'hoc quod non,' nr. 8—13. Joh. ab Imola, l. 1. Dig. de V. O. nr. 22—27. Joh. And. Nov. s. c. 13, X. 4, 17. Theod. a Niem., De schism. III. c. 7 ; Priv. aut iur. imp. p. 785. Nic. Cus., Conc. cath. III. c. 3 and 5. Ant. Ros. I. c. 11, 20—38, 47—49 and 56. Declarations of Frederick I. (Höfler, p. 64 ff.) and Frederick II. (in Pet. de Vin. ep. I. c. 1, p. 93 ; c. 9, p. 122 ; c. 11, p. 126 ; c. 25 ; III. c. 4, p. 68 ; v. c. 1). Passages from the poets in Höfler, p. 105—7. For intermediate opinions, which he rejects, see Joh. Paris. c. 11 ; also Lup. Bebenb. c. 9. Ockham elaborately discusses the many possible shades of the doctrine *Imperium a Deo* : Octo qu. II. c. 1, 3, 5 ; IV. c. 8—9 ; VIII. c. 5 ; Dial. III. tr. 2, l. 1, c. 25—28.

Imperialists on the Papal Claims.

41. A feudal relationship between Emperor and Pope is unanimously denied : the Kaiser only swears to defend : Lup. Bebenb. c. 9, p. 368—70, and c. 13, p. 391—4 ; Ockham, Octo qu. II. c. 11 ; VIII. c. 1 and 5 ; Dial. III. tr. 2, l. 1, c. 21 ; the definition of rights in Ficker, Kurverein, p. 710 ; Ant. Ros. I. c. 9, 47, 71. On the other hand, but few men flatly deny the power of the Pope to act as supreme judge over the Emperor or allow only purely spiritual censures *ratione peccati* : among the few are Frederick II. (Petri de Vin. ep. I. c. 3) and Marsilius. Others admit that there is such a power to be used in extraordinary cases, or explain the acts of jurisdiction which the Popes have really performed as the outcome of voluntary submission. Of this more below. There is much hesitation over the Translatio Imperii [from Greeks to Germans] and its legal justification : also over the part played by the Pope in the Election of an Emperor. Marsilius (II. 26) denies to the Pope any right of examining the election. Usually some right of deciding, for certain ecclesiastical purposes, who is *de facto* Emperor is allowed to the Pope. See e.g. Lup. Bebenb. c. 10, p. 370—4 ; Ockham, Octo qu. II. c. 10 ; Dial. III. tr. 2, l. 1, c. 21 ; Ant. Ros. I. c. 48. Lupold v. Bebenburg (c. 12) goes further, and concedes a power to solve doubts in cases of double election, since the law of God gives the

Pope power to decide *dubia iuris*, and the law of necessity gives him power to decide *dubia facti.* He even maintains (c. 11, 13 and 16) that the coronation is no bare ceremony, for, though the Election gives the Elect imperial power over the lands held by Charles the Great before the Translatio Imperii, it is the coronation which makes him Emperor of the rest of the world. This opinion (see against it Ockham, Oct. q. IV. c. 1—3 and 7) failed to obtain supporters. At any rate after the Kurverein [meeting and declaration of the Electors] at Rense, the imperialist party held that the unction and coronation were mere solemnities, which played no greater part in the case of the elected emperor than that which they played in the case of an hereditary king; they in no way attested a papal overlordship. Comp. Joh. Paris. c. 19; Articuli of 1338 in Böhmer, Fontes IV. p. 594, a. 2; Documents in Ficker, Kurverein von Rense, pp. 699 ff. esp. p. 710, a. 4; Marsil. Pat. II. c. 26 and De transl. imp. c. 12; Ockham, Octo qu. II. c. 10; V. c. 1—10; VI. c. 1—2; VII. c. 1—2; VIII. c. 1 ff.; and Dial. III. tr. 2, l. 1, c. 21; Somn. Virid. I. c. 166—9; Joh. de Anan. c. 6, X. 1, 6, nr. 7. (At a later time the Church Party had recourse to the supposition of a *privilegium* bestowing on the Emperor Elect the *ius administrandi ante coronationem.*) Ecclesiastical claims to a guardianship of the Empire were disputed by Marsilius and Ockham; but the latter admitted that they might perhaps be founded upon an *auctoritas* proceeding from the Empire itself: Octo qu. II. c. 14; and Dial. III. tr. 2, l. 1, c. 22.

42. The principle that Christ's kingdom is not of this world was interpreted in numberless ways by the anti-clerical opposition. The commonest exposition comes to this, that *ex iure divino* the Church has no worldly *iurisdictio*, and as regards property can only demand so much as is necessary for her support and divine service; but that she is capable of acquiring by title of Positive Law (ex concessione et permissione principum) a wider field of lordship and ownership, and also may in case of necessity exercise worldly rights. Comp. Joh. de Paris. prooem. and c. 13—14. Ockham, Octo q. I. c. 6, ad. 2, 7—9, 10, II. c. 6, III. c. 1—2, VIII. c. 5; Dial. I. 6, c. 3, III. tr. 1, l. 1, c. 9, 13, 15, l. 2, c. 2 and 29, tr. 2, l. 1, c. 19 and 24. Michael Cesena, ep. d. a. 1333 (Goldast, II. 1238 ff.). Quaest. in utramque, a. 3. Disput. p. 677 ff. Somn. Virid. I. c. 1—16, II. c. 1 ff. and 303; Petr. de Aliac., I. 667 and 674 ff.; Greg. Heimb. a. 1433 (Gold. I. 560 ff. and II. 1604 ff.); Ant. Ros. c. 20—38 and 50. These principles in themselves remained unaffected by the ever renewed complaints of the growing worldliness of the Church (e.g.

[margin note: The Church is a purely Spiritual Realm.]

Dante, II. c. 12—13), and by the dispute among the Franciscans touching Evangelical Poverty. Still hardly ever were there wanting extremer opinions which flatly denied the Church's competence to wield worldly power or to hold any—or any unnecessary—property. This is the case of Marsilius, who therefore (but in this he stands nearly alone) denies to the Church any 'coactive jurisdiction,' and therefore any coercion of consciences, even in purely spiritual matters. See also Wyclif, Supplem. Trialogi, p. 407 ff., and art. **17**; Hus, Determ. de abl. temporal. a clericis.

Imperialists concede Superior Dignity of the Church.
43. Comp. Sachsensp. I. a. I. Dante, III. c. 16 in fine: despite the separation, the Kaiser should do reverence to the Pope as a first-born son to a father: mortalis illa felicitas quodammodo ad immortalem felicitatem ordinatur. Joh. de Paris. c. 15 and 18. Ockham, Octo qu. I. c. 3 and 14. Somn. Virid. I. c. 83—84. Baldus, l. 11, C. 1, 14, nr. 4, and prooem. Dig. nr. 17—19: the Pope superior to the Emperor, *non simpliciter*, but *in quibusdam*. Similarly Joh. de An. c. 6, X. 1, 33, nr. 6. Comp. Heinrich v. Langenstein, in Hartwig, I. p. 52, n. 1. Ant. Ros. I. c. 63. In this sense it was possible to accept the comparison with Soul and Body: better still, that with Sun and Moon, both of which were created by God, each having its own powers and duties, though the orb of day was the higher.

The Celestial Head gives sufficient Unity to the two Powers.
44. Thus already Hugo Floriac. I. c. 2, and II. pp. 46, 65. Dante, III. c. 12: true it is that Emperor and Pope must *ad unum reduci*; but while, if we consider them as *homines*, the measure will be that of the 'optimus homo, qui est mensura omnium et idea,' if we consider them as office-holders, *ipse Deus* is the *communis unitas* which is super-posed above their *relationes* and *differentialia*. Joh. Paris. c. 18—19: una est ecclesia, unus populus, unum corpus mysticum; but the unity rests in Christ, and under Him the Priesthood and Realm are two distinct offices: as distinct as the offices of teacher and physician when held by one man. Quaest. in utramque p. 103, ad. 4—5. Ockham, Octo qu. I. c. 1 and 18; Dial. III. tr. 1, l. 2, c. 1 and 30. Miles in Somn. Virid. I. c. 38, 46, 48, 102, II. c. 102, 305—312. Anton. Ros. I. c. 42.

Church and State in co-operation.
45. It need hardly be said that even the Popes and their supporters often teach that amicable relations between Priesthood and Realm are a necessary condition for the weal of Christendom. Thus Gregory VII. with great emphasis: lib. 1, ep. 19, ann. 1073, p. 302. Ivo of Chartres (above, Note 20). S. Bernard, ep. 244, p. 440 ff.; De consid. II. c. 8. Innocent III. (above, Note 26). Innocent IV. (above, Note 26). But what is peculiar to the opponents of Church-Sovereignty is the doctrine that in this world

the Unity of the two powers goes no further than the establishment of these good relations. Thus already Hugo Floriac. prol. I. c. 3, 12, II. p. 46, 50 : God instituted, hallowed and connected the two powers, by which in this present life the Holy Church is ruled and governed, and He desired their inward harmony : they are the two eyes of the *corpus ecclesiae*, the two lights *in tota mundi fabrica*, two pillars, two wings. See also Const. Frider. II. ann. 1220, § 7 in M. G. L. II. p. 236. Sachsensp. I, a. I, with the gloss to this art. and to III. art. 57. Also Declaration of the Princes of the Empire, ann. 1274, in Raynald, ann. nr. 11 : et ii duo gladii in domo domini constituti, intimae dilectionis foedere copulati, exsurgant in reformationem universi populi Christiani. Likewise Rudolf I.; see also citations in Höfler, p. 121 ff. Eng. Volk. De ortu, c. 22. Joh. Paris. c. 14. Definition of Rights in Ficker, op. cit. p. 710, art. 4, ann. 1338. Quaest. in utramque partem, p. 105, ad. 11. Ockham, Octo q. I. c. 3 and 14. Miles in Somn. Virid. I. c. 49—54. Ant. Ros. III. c. 15— 18. Johannes in Introduction to the Brünner Schöffenbuch. But the idea of 'harmonious concordance' between two powers which are two vital functions of the one mystical body attains its most splendid form in the hands of Nicholas of Cues: especially, III. c. 1, 12 and 14.

46. Hugh of Fleury teaches on the one hand that the bishops are subject to the royal power, 'non natura, sed ordine, ut universitas regni ad unum redigatur principium,' even as Christ is subject to the Father (I. c. 3, and II. p. 58 and 65), and, on the other hand, that kings are subject to the spiritual power (I. c. 7, p. 30 ff., c. 9—10, II. pp. 53—5, 59—60). He blames Gregory VII. (II. p. 58), and even concedes the royal appointment of bishops, subject however to the approval of the ecclesiastical power and to spiritual investiture (I. c. 5, and II. p. 57). Joh. Par. c. 14. Qu. in utr. a. 4. Ock. Oct. qu. III. c. 3, 8 and Dial. III. tr. 2, l. 1, c. 24. Som. Vir. II. c. 112, 114, 124. Theod. a Niem, Priv. p. 785. Nic. Cus. III. c. 1, 4. Ant. Ros. I. 47, 48, 56, 63, 64, III. c. 16, 21 and the summary in 56: the *monarchia divina* and *monarchia temporalis* are co-ordinated by God; each is subject to the other in that other's province; and 'mixed' affairs should be treated by 'mixed' councils. As to particulars:—the subjection of Emperor and Princes to the Church *ratione fidei et peccati* is conceded (see Host. de accus. nr. 7 and see the admission in the Sachsenspiegel, III. a. 54, § 3 and 57, § 1, that the Kaiser is within the 'rightful' ban of the Church); also princes are in duty bound to lend to the Church the aid of the lay arm (Dictum Gratiani before Dist. 97 and after c. 28, C. 23, q. 8; Const. of 1220, § 7, M. G. L. II. 236 ; Sachsensp. I. a. 1; Gerson,

Superiority of Church in Spirituals and of State in Temporals.

IV. 606 and 619); but, on the other hand, a temporal jurisdiction over the priesthood in temporal causes is asserted (Ockham, Octo qu. III. c. 2; and Dial. I. 6, c. 1—65, 91—100, III. tr. 2, l. 3, c. 16—23; Ant. Ros. I. c. 29, 30, 53, 63; Gloss on Sachsensp. I. a. 1).

Occasional interference of Pope in Temporal Affairs. 47. Joh. Paris. c. 14 and 18 (per accidens). Lup. Bebenb. c. 12, p. 379, 385, 386 (necessitas facti aut iuris). Ockham, Octo qu. I. c. 11, II. c. 4, 7—9, 12, 14, III. c. 2, IV. c. 3, VIII. c. 5, and Dial. III. tr. 1, l. 1, c. 16 and l. 3, c. 4 (casualiter in defectum iudicis). Somn. Virid. I. c. 150—151, 164—165, II. c. 4—12, 136. Ant. Ros. III. c. 22. Gloss on Sachsensp. I. a. 1, III. a. 52 and 57. Klagspiegel, 119.

Occasional interference of Kaiser in Spiritual Affairs. 48. Petrus Crassus, pp. 27 and 31 (right to summon a Council); p. 48 (right to sit in judgment on a Pope). Hugo Floriac. II. pp. 57—9 (appointment of Popes and decision of ecclesiastical disputes). Nilus arch. Thessal. De primatu, l. II. p. 38. Joh. Paris. c. 14. Mich. de Caes. ep. Gold. II. pp. 1244—1261. Petrarca, ep. XV. ib. 1365. Ockham, Octo q. I. c. 12, 17, II. c. 7, III. c. 8, IV. c. 6; Dial. III. tr. 2, l. 2, c. 2—15, l. 3, c. 2 and 4. Randuf, De mod. un. c. 15 and 20. Nic. Cus. III. c. 15 and 40 (the Emperor may himself undertake ecclesiastical reforms). Zabar. c. 6, X. 1, 6, nr. 15, and De schism. p. 689 ff. Greg. Heimb. in Gold. I. 561—563. Ant. Ros. I. c. 48, II. c. 24, 25, III. c. 3. Decius, Cons. 151, nr. 13.— Even the papalists concede certain rights which they explain as flowing from the Emperor's *advocatia* over the Church (Gloss on c. 34, X. 1, 6, v. *carebit*): thus the right to call a Council is conceded by Aug. Triumph. I. q. 3, a. 2, and q. 5, a. 6, by Petrus a Monte, II. nr. 5, and others, but contested by Alv. Pel. I. a. 22. The papalists help themselves over historical instances of the exercise of imperial rights (especially in the matter of papal elections) by referring such instances to concessions which the Church has revoked: e.g. Landulf. Col. De transl. Imp. c. 6; Aug. Triumph. I. q. 2, a. 7; Alv. Pel. I. a. 1, and 37 Bb and CC.

Unity within the Church. 49. See esp. Thom. Aquin. Summa cont. gent. IV. 76 (sicut est una ecclesia, ita oportet esse unum populum Christianum, with one *caput* and one *regimen*); Lect. 2 ad Ephes. IV. (the *ecclesia* as *civitas* etc.); Comm. ad Ps. 45. Alv. Pel. I. a. 7, 13, 24—8, 36—8 and esp. 63.

The Church and the Infidels. 50. For this reason the power of the Church and of its earthly Head comprises, though to a disputable extent, all the infidels in the world, nay, it covers all past and future Mankind and so reaches into heaven and hell. See Thom. Aquin. Sum. Theol. II. 2, q. 10—12, and III. q. 8, a. 1—3; Host. upon c. 8, X. 3, 34; Aegid. Rom. De pot. eccl. II. c. 7; Aug. Triumph. I. q. 18, 23—4 and 29—35; Alv. Pel. I. a. 13 A, 37 F—N, 40, 57; Somn. Virid. II. 35; Ant. Ros. IV c. I.

51. In the eyes of the papalists this is self-evident. Gloss on c. 3, X. 1, 41, v. *minoris*: ecclesia fungitur iure imperii. Hostiensis, Summa de r. i. i. nr. 4: ecclesia respublica est, quia ius publicum consistit in sacris et in sacerdotibus. Thom. Aquin. as above in Note 49. Alvarius Pelagius, I. a. 61—3, goes furthest: the Church is a *regnum*, and indeed the one universal, holy and complete Realm; and to it the whole of the 'Aristotelic-Thomistic' theory of the State is applied.—But even the Opposition disputes only the worldly nature of the Church, and does not deny to it the character of a *politia* with magistrature and coercive power; see above Note 42. Gerson and other writers of the same group declare that the Church is a *communitas, respublica, politia iuris*, to which everyone must belong; see e.g. Gerson, Op. III. p. 27; Randuf, De modis uniendi, c. 2 (ib. II. p. 163): ecclesia Christi est inter omnes respublicas aut societates recte ordinatas a Christo superior.—The treatment of heresy as *crimen laesae maiestatis* (Innoc. III. and Gerson, III. pp. 33, 63) and all coercion of conscience have their roots here. *The Church is a State, Polity or Common wealth.*

52. Ockham, Octo qu. I. c. 1 and 30, and III. c. 2 and 8; Dial. III. tr. 2, l. 1, c. 3 and 8, l. 3, c. 17. See also Gerson, Trilogus, Op. II. p. 88, for some similar opinions that were expressed in his day.— Marsilius denies to the Church coercive power even in spirituals, and this implies the negation of the necessity of External Unity. Gregory of Heimburg, I. p. 557 ff. goes near to this. *The necessity of External Unity doubted.*

52 a. See Lechner, Joh. v. Wiclif, I. p. 541, and II. p. 233.

53. See above all Dante, Mon. I. Also Engelb. Volk., De ortu, c. 14, 15, 17—18; De reg. princ. VII. c. 32. Ockham, Dial. III. tr. 2, l. 1, c. 1. Petrarca, ep. VII. (et in terra et in coelo optima semper fuit unitas principatus) and ep. VIII. p. 1355. Ant. Ros. I. c. 5—7. Aen. Sylv. c. 4, 10, 12. *The Church as conceived by Wyclif and Hus. Universality of the Empire.*

54. Following in the steps of Augustine, De civit. Dei, v. c. 15, theorists elaborately prove that the Romans subdued the world *de iure*, though at times they were guilty of violence. The chief argument consists in the many miraculous 'judgments' in which God manifested his choice of the Romans, on account of their political virtues, to be the wielders of that *officium imperii* for which they were the *aptum organum*. Thereby He legitimated their wars and victories. Also it is opined that in all their conquests they unselfishly kept 'the common good' before their eyes, and that this end justified the means. Comp. esp. Dante, II. c. 1—11; Engelb. *Legitimacy of the Roman Empire.*

Volk. De ortu, 15, 18; Petrarca, ep. VII. p. 1355; Baldus, l. 1, C. 1, 1; Aen. Sylv. c. 3—5; Petr. de Andlo, I. c. 4—10; Ant. Ros. v. c. 1—2, 15—24; and so also ecclesiastical writers (e.g. Ptol. Luc. III. c. 4—6; Alv. Pel. I. a. 42) even though they do not allow that this *imperium* was *verum*. Then the lawyers add references to the Corpus Iuris (esp. l. 9, D. 14, 2), to the legitimacy of the titles (*testamenta* and *bella iusta*) by which dominion was acquired, and to the retroactive validation by voluntary subjection. Comp. Engelb. Volk. c. 11; Ockham, Dial. III. tr. 2, l. 1, c. 27 and l. 2, c. 5: consensus maioris partis mundi: a corrupt intent does not prevent acquisition of rights. Ant. Ros. v. c. 1—30: an elaborate demonstration of the legitimacy of the Empire according to ius divinum, naturale, gentium et civile.

Transfer of the Empire. 55. Comp. Jord. Osnab. c. 1, p. 43 ff. and c. 8. Dante, Mon. II. c. 12—3. Eng. Volk. c. 11 and 20. Ockham, Octo qu. II. c. 5, IV. c. 3, VIII. c. 3 and Dial. III. tr. 2, l. 2, c. 5. Aen. Sylv. c. 6—8: general utility required, Nature invented, God granted, His Son hallowed, the consent of men confirmed, the Roman empire. Ant. Ros. v. c. 18 and 29.—The strictly ecclesiastical doctrine differed a little from this:—Christ Himself took over the Empire, allowing Augustus to govern as His Vicar; He then substituted for Himself Peter and Peter's successors, and the subsequent emperors were their vicars; and finally He caused Constantine to recognize this relationship by the so-called Donation; Ptol. Luc. III. c. 13—18; Petr. de Andlo, I. c. 11 and 13; comp. Ockham, Octo qu. II. c. 15.—Men are unanimous that the existing *Reich* is identical with that of the Caesars; Petr. Crassus, p. 26; Dante, l. c.; Ockham, Octo q. II. c. 5, IV. c. 3, 5, 7, VIII. c. 3, Dial. III. tr. 2, l. 1, c. 25 and 27. Only Lupold v. Bebenburg brings into play the rights that Karl the Great had before he was crowned Emperor; and against this Ockham, Octo qu. IV. 3, protests.—Also men are unanimous that the present Greek Emperor is no longer a true Emperor, since he is no longer united to the true Church: Joh. Gal. in appar. Tancr. upon Comp. III. in Schulte, Abhand. [Vienna Acad.] vol. 66, p. 131; Gloss upon c. 34, X. 1, 6, v. *transtulit in Germanos*; Bartolus, l. 24, Dig. de capt. 49, 15; Ubertus de Lampugnano, op. cit.; Joh. de Platea, l. un. Cod. 11, 20; Tengler, Laiensp. 56.

Universal Extent of the Empire. 56. S. Bernh. ep. ad Lothar. in Gold. p. 66; ad Conr. ib. p. 67. Otto Frising. Gesta, I. c. 23, Chron. VII. c. 34. Land. Col. De transl. c. 10: super omnes reges et nationes est dominus mundi. Gl. on II. Feud. 53 pr. Pet. de Vin. ep. I. c. 1, 2; VI. c. 30. Alv. Pel. I. a. 37 and 57; II. a. 29. Lup. Bebenb. c. 11, 13, 16. Ockham,

Octo q. IV. c. 5 and VIII. c. 3. Gloss on Sachsensp. III. a. 57. Baldus, l. 1, Cod. 1, 1, nr. 1 ff. and II. Feud. 53 pr. Theod. a Niem. p. 785. Randuf, De mod. un. c. 5 and 14 (p. 167 and 180). Alex. Tart. l. 26, Dig. 36, 1, nr. 2. Aen. Sylv. c. 10. Pet. de Andlo II. c. 2. Tengler, Laiensp. 56. The Empire comprises *de iure* even the infidels; Joh. Gal. and Gloss on c. 34, X. 1, 6; Eng. Volk. c. 18 (for even they are bound to us *iure naturali vel gentium*); Ockham, Dial. III. tr. 2, l. 2, c. 5; Ant. Ros. I. c. 56.—The content of the imperial rights is variously defined. Lupold of Bebenburg, c. 15, distinguished imperial and mediatized lands: in the latter the Emperor has immediate jurisdiction only over the rulers and a mediate jurisdiction over the subjects in case of default of justice, or the like. Ockham, Octo qu. IV. c. 3, 8, 9, VIII. c. 4: the Emperor is a Superior with right to decide matters that the king cannot decide, and with power to perform certain 'reserved' acts; also (v. c. 6) with power to make new kings in provinces that have none. Aeneas Sylvius still asserts a true feudal lordship over all princes and peoples; they all have their temporalities from the Kaiser and owe him obedience (c. 10); he has a right of 'correction,' may issue commands *pro salute communi*, impose taxes, demand auxiliary troops, right of transit, provisions (c. 14); he may decide disputes among sovereigns. Petr. de Andlo (II. c. 8): legislation, protective lordship, taxation, suzerain power. Nich. of Cues (III. c. 6—7) pares down the *imperium mundi* until it is a general care for the common weal of Christianity especially in matters of faith.

57. Jordan. Osnabr. c. 1, p. 43 ff. and c. 10, p. 90. Engelb. Volk. c. 20—4. Aug. Triumph. II. p. 42. Baldus sup. pace Const. v. *imp. clem.* nr. 8. Joh. de Platea, l. 2, C. 11, 9, nr. 2. Aen. Sylv. c. 8. Ant. Ros. I. c. 67. Petr. de Andlo, II. c. 20.

The Empire is indestructible de facto.

58. The most important employment of this principle is the invalidation of the Donation of Constantine. Dante III. c. 10 (scissa esset tunica inconsutilis: superius dominium, cuius unitas divisionem non patitur); Quaestio in utramque p. 106, ad. 14; Ant. Ros. I. c. 64—6, 70. See below, Note 283. But the principle is also turned against kings and republics. Lup. Bebenb. c. 11 and 15: true, that by privilege or prescription hereditary kingships may be founded and kings may acquire imperial rights in their realms and so far as concerns (*quoad*) their subjects; but this is only prescription *quoad quid*, and the Kaiser's suzerainty is always reserved. Ockham, Octo q. III. c. 7, IV. c. 3—5, VIII. 3—4; Dial. III. tr. 2, l. 1, c. 18, l. 2, c. 5—9, 23. Alv. Pel. II. a. 29. Baldus, l. 1, Cod. I. 1, nr. 13—22 and II. Feud. 53 pr. Alex. Tart. l. 26, Dig. 36, 1, nr. 4. Aen.

The Empire is indestructible de iure.

Sylvius, c. 11—13 : it would be against the *ius naturae*, the common weal, the command of Christ. Petr. de Andl. II. c. 8 : both swords are equally indivisible. Bertach. v. *imperium.*

59. Land. Col. De transl. c. 10. Quaestio in utramque p. 98, 102, art. 5, 106, ad. 14. Andr. de Is. prooem. Feud. nr. 29—35. Nicol. Neap. l. 6, § 1, Dig. 27, 1, nr. 2. Hier. Zanetinus, Diff. nr. 102.

60. Comp. Eng. Volk. c. 18. Baldus, II. Feud. 53 pr.: the Empire would still remain *universale*, for *universale* and *integrum* are not all one. Comp. prooem. Dig. nr. 22—35. Nic. Cus. Conc. III. c. 1, 6, 7 : it is 'imperium mundi a maiori parte mundi,' and because the imperial rights still remain, at least so far as concerns the protection of the Christian faith.

61. John of Paris, c. 3 : whereas in the Church unity is required by divine law, the faithful laity, moved by a natural instinct, which is of God, should live in different States ; this difference is justified by the differences between soul and body, word and hand, unity of church-property and division of lay folk's property, unity of faith and diversity of laws ; also appeal is made to Augustine ; comp. c. 16, 22, p. 210—2. To the same effect, but with a 'perhaps,' Gerson, II. 238. Disputatio, p. 686—7. Somn. Virid. I. c. 36: only within each particular realm need there be unity.—So Marsilius, though he leaves the question open, remarks that the unity of the world does not prove the necessity of an *unicus principatus*, since a *pluralitas* can constitute a unity (Def. Pac. I. c. 17; in Transl. Imp. c. 12 he omits Landulf's mention of the *imperium mundi*).—On the other side, see Eng. Volk. c. 16 and 18 ; Ant. Ros. II. c. 4 and 7. And, in particular, Ockham, Dial. III. tr. 2, l. 1, c. 1—10. Of the five possible views that Ockham mentions he seems to prefer the fifth, viz. that, according to circumstances, sometimes unity, sometimes severance will be desirable. Comp. l. 2, c. 6—9.

62. See Aegid. Rom. De reg. princ. II. 1, c. 2. Engelb. Volk. De ortu, c. 15, 17, 18: as the example of Universal Nature shows a building-up towards Unity, so the *ordo totius communitatis publicae* shows an ever-recurring 'subalternation' until a single point is reached: above every common weal stands a commoner: every lower end is means to a higher end : the sum total of this-worldly ends is means to an other-wordly end : the 'felicity' of every narrower depends on that of some wider community, and thus in the last resort on the felicity of the Empire. Dante, I. c. 3 and 5. See also Aug. Triumph. I. q. 1, a. 6. As to the structure of the Chuch, see Gierke, D. G. R. vol. III. § 8.

63. [The difficulty of finding an exact equivalent for the

German *Zweck* has hampered the translator. Our author means that in the medieval scheme each Partial Whole, e.g. a village commune, has a *Sonderzweck*, an aim, object, purpose or end peculiar to it, and distinct from the *Zweck* of any larger whole, e.g. the kingdom.] Dante (I. c. 3 and 5), in particular, makes this plain. For him, every composite Being (plura ordinata ad unum) has its *Sonderzweck* which makes it a unit. This is the case with the *homo singularis*, the *communitas domestica*, the *vicus*, the *civitas*, the *regnum*. No one, however, more beautifully expresses the idea of an organic articulation in unity and a relative independence of members in a 'harmonious concord' of the whole body than does Nicholas of Cues, e.g. II. c. 27—28. Comp. also Ant. Ros. I. c. 6.

64. See Aegid. Col. II. 1, c. 2 and Dante l. c. (they throw *provincia* and *regnum* into one); Ockham, Dial. III. tr. 1, l. 2, c. 3—5. [Elsewhere, D. G. R. III. 356, Dr Gierke has stated the doctrine of the legists. They incline towards a triple gradation of local *universitates*, (1) *vicus, villa, castrum, oppidum*, (2) *civitas*, a city-territory, such as may be found in Italy, (3) *provincia* or *regnum*.]— Thom. Aquin. De reg. princ. I. c. 1, distinguishes *familia, civitas, provincia* (*regnum*). Engelb. Volk. in one of his writings (De reg. prin. II. c. 2—3) stops at the *civitas*, which also embraces the *regnum*; in another (De ortu, c. 7 and 12) he says that Aristotle distinguished five communities (*domus, vicus, civitas, provincia, regnum*, to which *imperium* must be added,) while Augustine made only three (*domus, urbs, orbis*).—Aug. Triumph. l. c., makes five *communitates* in the mystical body of the Church: the *vicus* with a parson, the *civitas* with a bishop, *provincia* with archbishop, *regnum* with patriarch, *communitas totius orbis* with pope.—Ant. Ros. I. c. 6, distinguishes as standing above the individual and the household, five 'corpora mystica universitatum': (1) *communitas unius vici, castri, oppidi*, under *parochus* and *magister*; (2) *civitatis* under bishop and *defensor*; (3) *provinciae* under archbishop and *praeses*; (4) *regni* under *primas* and *rex*; (5) *universi orbis* under Pope and Kaiser.

[margin: The graduated Articulation of Communities.]

65. This rich development of thought has been overlooked by van Krieken, Die sog. organische Staatstheorie, pp. 26—39; also Held, Staat u. Gesellschaft, p. 575 is incorrect.

66. In what follows we shall only pay heed to those sides of the Organic Comparison [i.e. the comparison of the body politic to the body natural] which become of importance in legal theory. We may, however, notice in passing its connexion with some of the pictorial concepts of ecclesiastical law (e.g. the spiritual marriage of the prelate with his church, the family relationship of a daughter-

[margin: 'The Organic Comparison.']

church to a mother-church) and with some poetical allegories: as e.g. the statue of Nebuchadnezzar's dream (cf. Gerson, IV. 662) or the installation of the Empire (Lup. Beb. ritmat. querul. in Boehmer, Fontes, I. 479). The application to the Church of 'the Six Ages' (Gold. I. p. 25 ff. c. 3—7) and the remarks as to the Ages and Faults of the Empire in Eng. Volk. De ortu et fine, c. 21 and 23, show the same tendency.

The Mystical Body and the Pope as its Head.

67. See e.g. B. Gregor. in c. 1, Dist. 89. Concil. Paris. ann. 829 (above, Note 7). Jonas of Orléans (above, Note 7). Gregory VII. (above, Note 45). Ivo of Chartres (above, Note 20). S. Bern. Ep. of 1146 (above, Note 7). Gerhoh of Reichersp. (above, Note 7). Thom. Aquin. (above, Note 7). Ptol. Luc. De reg. princ. III. c. 10 (above, Note 12). Gl. on c. 14, X. 5, 31, v. *unum corpus.* Innoc. c. 4, X. 2, 12, nr. 3. Alv. Pel. I. a. 13. Joh. Andr. c. 4, X. 1, 6, nr. 13. Domin. Gem. c. 17 in Sexto 1, 6, nr. 4—16.

Bicephal- ism would be mon- strous.

68. Alv. Pel. I. a. 13 F and a. 37 R—Q. Somn. Virid. II. c. 6 ff. Ockham, Dial. III. tr. 1, l. 2, c. 1. Aug. Triumph. I. q. 5, a. 1 and q. 19, a. 2: the Pope is 'caput universalis ecclesiae...et capitis est influere vitam omnibus membris.' Elsewhere (I. q. 1, a. 1 and 6) he makes the Pope the vitalizing heart, and then (I. q. 19, a. 2) says that he is not contradicting himself, since in metaphorical discourse comparisons may be varied so as to bring out various likenesses. Johannes Andreae, Nov. s. c. 13, X. 4, 17. Card. Alex. D. 15, and c. 3, D. 21. Ludov. Rom. Cons. 345, nr. 3 ff. Petrus a Monte, De prim. pap. I. nr. 16 (Tr. U. J. XIII. 1, p. 144).

Need for a Temporal Head.

69. Engelb. Volk. De ortu, c. 15, 17, 18. Petrarca, Ep. VII.. the *orbis universus*, being a *magnum corpus*, can only have *unum caput temporale*, for, if an *animal biceps* would be a monster, how much more a many-headed beast. Similarly in Ep. VIII. Nic. Cus. III. c. 1 and 41. Ant. Ros. I. c. 67. Petr. de Andlo, II. c. 2.

70. The Knight in Somn. Virid. II. c. 305—12.

Possibility of Many- headed- ness.

71. Lup. Bebenb. c. 15, pp. 399, 401: not *duo capita in solidum*, but a *caput mediatum* below a *caput immediatum*, like kings below the Emperor, and bishops below an archbishop. Quaestio in utramque partem, p. 103. Ockham, Dial. III. tr. 1, l. 2, c. 1 and 30: quamvis corpus naturale esset monstruosum si haberet duo capita...tamen corpus mysticum potest habere plura capita spiritualia, quorum unum sit sub alio: so priests and king, whose head is God.

The Priesthood as Soul of the Body Politic.

72. [Elsewhere, D. G. R. III. 112, our author has traced this comparison far back to the Apostolic Constitutions, Chrysostom, Gregory of Nazianzus and Isidore of Pelusium.] Ivo of Chartres, Ep. 106 (above, Note 20). Joh. Saresb. v. c. 2, 3—5. Alex. Hal.

III. q. 40, m. 2. Hugo de S. Vict. De sacram. l. II. p. 2, c. 4.
Honor. Augustod. Summa gloria de praecel. sacerd. in Migne, vol. 172.
Innocent III. in c. 6, X. 1, 33; Reg. sup. neg. imp. Ep. 18. Thom.
Aquin. Summa, II. 2, q. 60, art. 6, ad 3 (potestas saecularis subditur
spirituali, sicut corpus animae). Ptol. Luc. III. c. 10. Alv. Pel.
I. a. 37 R. Cler. in Somn. Virid. I. c. 37, 43, 45, 47, 101.

73. The knight in Somn. Virid. (I. c. 38, 44, 46, 48, 102, The
II. 102) asserts that Christ alone is the Soul, while the spiritual and Representation of
temporal powers are the two principal members, head and heart, Soul by
equally directed by the Soul, but endowed with separate powers and the Priesthood ques-
activities.—On the other hand, Marsilius sees the priesthood as no tioned. ·
more than one among many members.

74. Nic. Cus. I. c. 1—6, III. c. 1, 10, 41. [The main part of The
this note has been taken into our text. Cusanus proceeds to show Catholic
Concord-
the parallelism between spiritual and temporal assemblies: e.g. ance of
between the Cardinals and the Prince-Electors.] Nicholas
v. Cues.

75. Joh. Saresb. v. c. 2 : est respublica corpus quoddam, quod The Body
divini muneris beneficio animatur et summae aequitatis agitur nutu Mystical,
Moral,
et regitur quodam moderamine rationis. Vincent Bellovac. Spec. Politic.
doctr. VII. c. 8 : to the like effect : de corpore reipublicae mystico.
Hugo Floriac. I. c. 2 : corpus regni : also c. 1, 3, 4. Thom. Aquin.
De reg. princ. I. c. 1, 12—14; Summa Theol. II. 1, q. 81, a. 1 : in
civilibus omnes homines qui sunt unius communitatis reputantur
quasi unum corpus et tota communitas quasi unus homo. Ptol. Luc.
II. c. 7 : quodlibet regnum sive civitas sive castrum sive quodcunque
aliud collegium assimilatur humano corpori; IV. c. 23. Eng. Volk.
De reg. princ. III. c. 16 : civitas vel regnum est quasi quoddam
unum corpus animatum; c. 19: corpus naturale; corpus morale et
politicum. Mars. Pat. I. c. 15. Ockham, Octo q. VIII. c. 5, p. 385;
Dial. III. tr. 1, l. 2, c. 1; tr. 2, l. 1, c. 1. Gerson, IV. 598, 600, 601.
Zabar. c. 4, X. 3, 10, nr. 2—3 : ad similitudinem corporis humani.
Aen. Sylv. c. 18 : mysticum reipublicae corpus. Ant. Ros. I. c. 6 :
five-fold corpus mysticum (above, Note 64). Martinus Laudens. De
repress. (Tr. U. J. XII. 279) nr. 5 and 6 : universitas est corpus
mysticum quod continet partes suas, i.e. singulos de universitate.
Bertach. v. *capitulum*, f. 150, nr. 4.

76. Joh. Saresb. v. c. 1 ff. The servants of Religion are the Anthropo-
Soul of the Body and therefore have *principatum totius corporis*, the morphic
conceits.
prince is the head, the senate the heart, the court the sides, officers
and judges are the eyes, ears and tongue, the executive officials are
the unarmed and the army is the armed hand, the financial department is belly and intestines, landfolk, handicraftsmen and the like

are the feet, so that the State exceeds the centipede *numerositate pedum* ; the protection of the folk is the shoeing ; the distress of these feet is the State's gout (vi. c. 20).

The beginnings of Anthropomorphism.

77. Joh. Saresb. v. c. 1. Compare Wyttenbach, Plutarchi Moralia, Oxonii 1795, I. p. lxviii ff. ; Schaarschmidt, Joh. Saresberiensis, Leipzig 1862, p. 123.—The incitement to comparison of particular pieces of the State with particular members of the human body is due in part to the words of St Paul (see esp. in c. 1, Dist. 89, the application of the idea of *membra in corpore* to the divers *officia* of the Church, where the Apostle is vouched) ; and is also due to a continuous tradition of the pictorial phrases of classical writers. This may be seen already in Lex Wisigoth. II. 1, § 4 ; also in the ancient Introduction to the Institutes in Fitting, Juristische Schriften des früheren Mittelalters (Halle 1876), p. 148, § 20: Princeps quasi primum caput...illustres quasi oculi...spectabiles manus...clarissimi thorax...pedanei pedes : and so in the Church.

Anthropomorphism continued.

78. Thus Vincent. Bellovac. Spec. doct. VII. c. 8—14 ; close agreement with John of Salisbury. Ptol. Luc. II. c. 7, IV. c. 11 and 25 ; vouching the Policraticus. Engelb. Volk. De reg. princ. III. c. 16 : the rulers are the soul, the citizens the various limbs : 'cui deputatur a natura unumquodque simile membrum in corpore.' Aen. Sylv. c. 18.—Marsilius is freer from these vagaries, notwithstanding the use that he makes of his knowledge of medicine.

The Anthropomorphism and State-Medicine of Cusanus.

79. Nic. Cus. I. c. 10, 14—17, and III. c. 41. In the 'Spiritual Life,' which in its totality represents the soul, Christ Himself is the single heart, whence in the guise of arteries the *canones* branch in every direction, so that even the Pope does not stand above them but must fill himself with them. In the 'Corporal Life' the offices from the Kaiser's downwards are the several limbs, the *leges* are the nerves, and the *leges imperiales* are the brain, so that by them the head, that is, the Emperor, must be bound. The *patria* is the skeleton and the flesh is represented by changing and perishing *homines.* The health of the State consists in the harmony of the four temperaments. Diseases of the body politic should be treated by the Emperor in accordance with the counsel of books and of experienced state-physicians. He should himself test the medicine by taste, smell and sight that it may suit time and place, and then bring it to the teeth (privy council), stomach (grand council) and liver (judicial tribunal) for digestion and distribution. If preservative measures fail, then in the last resort he must proceed to amputation, but this will be *cum dolore compassionis.*

80. Joh. Saresb. VI. c. 20—5.

81. Thom. Aquin. Summa Theol. III. q. 8: a demonstration Some Theories of Thom. Aquinas. that 'tota ecclesia dicitur unum corpus mysticum per similitudinem ad naturale corpus humanum': Christ the head, all rational creatures the members of this body. Aquinas remarks, however, that this is similitude, not identity. As points of difference he notices that past and future men are members of the mystical body, and that parts of it are in their turn independent bodies, so that there may be divers heads and heads of heads (*caput capitis*) corresponding to its manifold articulation. Then the various Conditions of Grace are pictured as internal degrees of membership (art. 3). Then he explains Original Sin by saying that all born of Adam may be considered *ut unus homo*, and also *tanquam multa membra unius corporis*, but that the act of one member of the natural body, e.g. the hand, 'non est voluntarius voluntate ipsius manus, sed voluntate animae quae primo movet membrum': Summa Theol. I. q. 81, a. I. With the same idea of the Body Mystical he connects the doctrine of the seven sacraments; whereof two operate for the spiritual and bodily maintenance and increase of the Whole, and five for the placing of Individuals in the way of grace: Summa Theol. III. q. 65 ff.; Summa cont. gentil. IV. q. 58 ff.; Lect. 2 ad Rom. 12. Also the differences of ecclesiastical office and calling he deduces from the necessary existence of divers members in the one body with the one soul; Lect. 2 ad Rom. 12; Lect. 3 ad I. Corinth. 12. Comp. Alv. Pel. I. a. 63. Also Catechism. Rom. P. II. c. 7, q. 6.

82. Ptol. Luc. IV. c. 23: therefore Augustine compares the State Harmony of Organic Forces. to a melodious song, while Aristotle likens it to a *naturale et organicum corpus*.

83. Aegid. Rom. De reg. princ. I. 2, c. 12; comp. I. I, c. 13; Co-ordination of Limbs. III. I, c. 5 and 8; III. 2, c. 34; III. 3, c. I and c. 23 (wars the medicine of human society).

84. Eng. Volk. De reg. princ. c. 16. In c. 18—31 the Goods of State and Goods of Individual. parallelism is displayed in the matter of the five internal *bona* (sanitas, pulchritudo, magnitudo, robur, potentia agonistica regni) and the six external *bona* (nobilitas, amicitia, divitiae, honorabilitas, potentia, bona fortuna regni).

85. Mars. Pat. I. c. 2, and for the details c. 15. Comp. c. 8, 17, and II. c. 24.

86. Ockham, Octo qu. I. c. 11, and VIII. c. 5, p. 385. Thus, Mutually Suppletive Power among Organs. e g. the lame try to walk with their hands and those who are handless must take to biting: sic in corpore mystico et in collegio seu universitate, uno deficiente, alius, si habet potestatem, supplet defectum eius. Comp. Dial. III. tr. 2, l. 3, c. 2 and 4, where the common and

specific functions of clergy and laity as divers members of the Church are distinguished, and at the same time it is remarked that in the mystical body there is a much greater call than there is in the natural body for one member to discharge in cases of necessity the functions assigned to another by positive law.

The Idea of Membership. — 87. Joh. Saresb.; see above, Note 75. Thom. Aq. De reg. princ. I. c. 12; Summa Theol. II. 2, q. 58, a. 5, III. q. 8, a. 1, and above, Note 81. Aegid. Rom.; above Note 83. Eng. Volk. III. c. 16. Alv. Pel. I. a. 63: ecclesia est...unum totum ex multis partibus constitutum et sicut unum corpus ex multis membris compactum: in details he follows the learning of S. Thomas. Baldus, prooem. Feud. nr. 32: imperium est in similitudine corporis humani, a quo, si abscinderetur auricula, non esset corpus perfectum sed monstruosum. Nic. Cus.; above, Note 79. Aen. Sylv. c. 18. Ant. Ros. I. c. 67 and 69.

Likeness and Unlikeness among Members. — 88. Comp. the definition of *ordo* (obtained from Aug. De civ. Dei, l. 19, c. 13) in Hug. Floriac. I. c. 1 and 12, p. 45 and Ptol. Luc. IV. 9: parium et disparium rerum sua cuique loca tribuens dispositio. Then Thom. Aq. (Summa Theol. I. q. 96, a. 3) starting from this, concludes that, even had there been no Fall of Man, inequality among men would have developed itself 'ex natura absque defectu naturae'; for 'quae a Deo sunt, ordinata sunt' and 'ordo autem maxime videtur in disparitate consistere.' See also Summa adversus gentiles, III. c. 81.—Then all Estates, groups, professional gilds and the like appear as *partes civitatis* to writers who rely on Aristotle: especially to Marsilius (II. c. 5), who distinguishes three *partes vel officia civitatis* (in a strict sense), namely, the military, priestly and judicial orders, and three *partes vel officia civitatis* (in a wider sense) namely, agriculture, handicraft and trade. A similar idea is applied to the Church; e.g. by Aquinas: see above Note 81. Alv. Pel. I. a. 63 G: the triple distinction in the Church (despite its unity) according to *status, officia et gradus* is likened to the triple distinction among carnal members according to their natures, their tasks and their beauties. See also Randuf, De mod. un. c. 2 (membra inaequaliter composita), 7 and 17.

Mediate Articulation. — 89. Alv. Pel. I. a. 36 C: there are indivisible members, whose parts would not be members; e.g. in the Church the faithful man; and there are divisible members, whose parts in their turn are members, as e.g. the 'particular churches' and ecclesiastical colleges. Antonius de Butrio, c. 4, X. 1, 6, nr. 14—5: membra de membro. Marsil. Patav. II. 24: in the *regimen civile*, as well as in the *regimen ecclesiasticum*, the analogy of the *animal* requires a manifold and graduated articulation ; otherwise there would be monstrosity ; finger must be directly joined, not to head but to hand ; then hand to arm, arm to shoulder, shoulder to neck, neck to head. Nic. Cus. II. c. 27. [Elsewhere, D. G. R. III. 251, our author gives other illustrations from Innocent IV., Johannes Andreae and others.]

90. Already S. Bernard (De consid. III. p. 82) exhorts the Pope to pay regard to the *potestates mediocres et inferiores* ; otherwise he will be putting the thumb above the hand and alongside the arm and so will create a monster: 'tale est si in Christi corpore membra aliter locas quam disposuit ipse.' Marsilius (II. c. 24) employs the same picture when complaining that the Popes have impaired the form of Christ's mystical body by disturbing its organic articulation, while that body's substance is impaired by the corruption of the clergy. The champions of the conciliar party have recourse to the same analogy for proof that the mystical body will perish if all power be concentrated in its highest member. See Randuf, c. 17 (183); Greg. Heimb. De pot. eccl. II. p. 1615 ff. *Papal Absolutism and the Mediate Articulation of the Church.*

91. Ptol. Luc. II. 26, where, besides the organization of the natural body, that of the heavenly spheres is adduced. Marsil. Pat. I. c. 2 and 5 : see above, p. 26. Also Thom. Aquin. Summa cont. gentil. III. c. 76—83. Alv. Pelag. I. a. 63 c (*ordinatio*). Eng. Volk. III. c. 21 : in ordinatione debita et proportione ad invicem...partium. Nicol. Cus. III. c. 1 : omnia quae a Deo sunt, ordinata necessario sunt. Petr. de Andlo, I. c. 3. *Organization and Interdependence.*

92. Joh. Saresb. l. c. Thom. Aq. Summa Theol. I. q. 81, a. 1; Lect. 2 ad Rom. 12 : in corpore humano quaedam sunt actiones quae solum principalibus membris conveniunt, et quaedam etiam soli capiti; sed in ecclesia vicem capitis tenet papa et vicem principalium membrorum praelati maiores ut episcopi ; ergo etc.—Ptol. Luc. II. c. 23 : debet...quilibet in suo gradu debitam habere dispositionem et operationem. Marsil. Pat. I. c. 2 (above, p. 26) and c. 8 : upon the formation and separation of the parts of the State, there must follow the allotment and regulation of their *officia*, 'ad instar naturae animalis.' Alv. Pel. I. a. 63 G : diversi actus. Ockham ; above, Note 86. *The Idea of Function.*

93. The difference between an organ and a mere limb is suggested by Eng. Volk. III. c. 16 : *pars civitatis* and *pars regni*. Comp. also Marsil. Patav. I. c. 5 ; above, Note 88. *The Idea of Organ.*

94. Thom. Aq. Summa Theol. I. q. 96, a. 4 : quandoque multa ordinantur ad unum, semper invenitur unum ut principale et dirigens ; Summa cont. gentil. IV. q. 76. Ptol. Luc. IV. c. 23 : there must be a *summum movens* controlling all movements of the limbs; *The Governing Part.*

with this is compatible 'in qualibet parte corporis operatio propria primis motibus correspondens et in alterutrum subministrans.' Similarly Dante.   Comp. Aegid. Col. III. 2, c. 34 : the king as soul of the body.   Marsil. Pat. I. c. 17 : in the State, as in the *animal bene compositum*, there must be a *primum principium et movens*; otherwise the organism must needs 'aut in contraria ferri aut omnimodo quiescere':—this is the *pars principans*.   Joh. Par. c. 1 : quemadmodum corpus hominis et cuiuslibet animalis deflueret, nisi esset aliqua vis regitiva communis in corpore ad omnium membrorum commune bonum intendens, so every multitude of men needs a unifying and governing force.   In closely similar words, Petr. de Andlo, I. c. 3, who then adds that among the *summi moventes* there must be *unus supremus* (the Kaiser), in relation to whom the members that are moved by the other *moventes* are *membra de membro*.

95.   See above, Notes 67 ff.

Connexion with a Rightful Head.

96.   This argument is often adduced on the papal side to show that the Church cannot exist without the Pope, and that no one who is not connected with the Pope can belong to the Church.   Comp. e.g. Alv. Pel. I. a. 7, 13, 24, 28, 36, 38 ; Card. Alex. D. 15 summa.

Need for a single Head denied.

97.   It is urged that there may be unity although there are many rulers; that the *principatus* as an institution is distinguishable from its occupant for the time being ; that the mystical body may be headless for a time : in particular the Church, which always retains its celestial Head.   Thus, Ockham, Dial. I. 5, c. 13 and 24, maintains the possibility of the continued existence of the Church after severance from the *ecclesia Romana* ; for, he expressly says, though the similitude between the mystical body of Christ and the natural body of man holds good at many points, still there are points at which it fails. To the same effect Petr. Alliac. in Gerson, Opera, I. 692 and II. 112; Gerson, De aufer. pap. II. 209 ff.; Randuf, De mod. un. c. 2, ib. 163; Nic. Cus. I. c. 14 and 17.

The State a work of Human Reason.

98.   Comp. Thom. Aq. Comment. ad Polit. p. 366 (ratio...constituens civitatem).   He teaches that the constitution of the Church is the work of God (Summa adv. gentil. IV. c. 76), but regards the creation of the State as a task for the kingly office, which here imitates the creation of the World by God and of the Body by the Soul (De reg. princ. I. c. 13).   Ptol. Luc. IV. c. 23.   Aegid. Rom. De reg. princ. III. 1, c. 1, and III. 2, c. 32.   Eng. Volk. De Ortu, c. 1 (ratio imitata naturam).   Aen. Sylv. c. 1, 2, 4.—More of this below in Note 303.

Marsilius on the

99.   Mars. Pat. I. c. 15.   In the natural organism Nature, the *causa movens*, first makes the heart which is the first and indispensable

portion, and bestows on it heat as its proper force, whereby the heart then, as the proper organ for this purpose, constitutes, separates, differentiates and connects all the other parts, and afterwards maintains, protects and repairs them. On the other hand, the creative principle of the State is the rational 'anima universitatis vel eius valentioris partis.' This, following the model set by Nature, generates a *pars prima, perfectior et nobilior*, answering to the heart, and being the Princeship (*principatus*). On this the said *anima* bestows an active power, analogous to vital heat, namely, the *auctoritas iudicandi, praecipiendi et exequendi*. Thus the Princeship is empowered and authorized to institute the other parts of the State. But, just as the heart can only work in the form and power that Nature has given to it, so the Princeship has received in the Law (*lex*) a regulator of its proceedings. In accordance with the measure set by the Law, the Princeship must establish the different parts of the State, equip them with their *officia*, reward and punish them, conserve them, promote their co-operation, and prevent disturbance among them. Even when the State's life is started, the Ruling power, like the heart, can never stand still for an instant without peril. *[margin: Origin of the State.]*

100. Thom. Aq. Summa Theol. II. 1, q. 91, a. 1: tota communitas universi gubernatur ratione divina; and therefore the *ipsa ratio gubernationis rerum*, which exists in God *sicut in principe universitatis*, has the nature of a *lex*, and indeed of a *lex aeterna*. Comp. ib. 1. q. 103 (although according to a. 6 'Deus gubernat quaedam mediantibus aliis') and II. 1, q. 93, a. 3; Summa cont. gentil. III. q. 76—7. Dante, I. c. 7, and III. c. 16. And see above, Notes 7, 8, 11, 44, 67, 71. *[margin: The Divine Monarchy.]*

101. See above, Note 15. John of Salisbury (Policr. IV. c. 1, pp. 208—9, and VI. c. 25, pp. 391—5) is especially earnest in the maintenance of the divine origin of temporal power. Ptol. Luc. (III. c. 1—8) gives elaborate proof of the proposition 'Omne dominium est a Deo': it is so *ratione entis* (for the *ens primum* is the *principium*); and it is so *ratione finis* (for all the purposes of government must culminate in God, who is *ultimus finis*). Even *dominium tyrannicum* is of God, who suffers it to exist as a method of chastisement, but Himself will not leave tyrants unpunished. Then Alv. Pel. (I. a. 8 and 41 C—K) repeats this, but expressly says that it does not disprove the sinful origin of the State. He (I. a. 56 B) distinguishes: *materialiter et inchoative* the temporal power proceeds from natural instinct and therefore from God: *perfecte et formaliter* it derives its *esse* from the spiritual power 'quae a Deo speciali modo derivatur.' *[margin: Divine Origin of the State.]*

102. See above, Notes 38, 40, 44, and, as to the Roman Empire, Notes 53—55.

103. Alv. Pel. I. a. 12, 13 U and X, 18. Aug. Triumph. I. q. 1, a. 1; a. 5: the papal power comes from God *specialius* than any other power, God being immediately active in election, government and protection; still He does not immediately generate each particular pope (as He generated Adam, Eve and Christ), but this happens *mediante homine*, as in the generation of other men; but the electoral college only has the *designatio personae*, for *auctoritas et officium*, being *quid formale in papatu*, come from Christ (q. 4, a. 3) Petr. de Andlo, I. c. 2.

104. See above, Note 40. The doctrine of the Karolingian time makes the Emperor *vicarius Dei*. Then during the Strife over the Investitures this is for the first time attacked; and then defended, e.g. by P. Crassus, p. 44, by Wenrich (Martene, Thes. Nov. Anecd. I. p. 220), and by the Kaisers and writers of the Hohenstaufen age. Comp. Dante, III. c. 16: solus eligit Deus, solus ipse confirmat; the Electors are merely *denuntiatores divinae providentiae* (though sometimes, being blinded by cupidity, they fail to perceive the will of God); sic ergo patet quod auctoritas temporalis monarchiae sine ullo medio in ipsum de fonte universalis auctoritatis descendit; qui quidem fons in arce suae simplicitatis unitus in multiplices alveos influit ex abundantia bonitatis. Bartol. prooem. D. nr. 14: Deus...causa efficiens. Ant. Ros. I. c. 47—8 and 56: the Electors, the Pope (in so far as he acts at all) and the Folk, are only *organa Dei*; so the Empire is *immediate a Deo*. Gerson, IV. p. 586.—Comp. Ockham, Octo q. II. c. 1—5, and IV. c. 8—9, and Dial. III. tr. 2, l. 1, c. 18 ff., where three shades of this doctrine are distinguished, for we may suppose (1) a direct gift by God, or (2) a gift *ministerio creaturae*, i.e. by the agency of the Electors (whose action may be likened to that of the priest in baptism, or that of a patron in the transfer of an office), or (3) a difference between the purely human heathen Empire and the modern Empire legitimated by Christ.

105. Joh. Saresb. v. c. 6: mediante sacerdotio. Aug. Triumph. I. q. 1, a. 1, II. q. 35, a. 1, q. 36, a. 4 (mediante papa), q. 45, a. 1. Alv. Pel. I. a. 37 D and DD, 41, 56, 59 E (a Deo...mediante institutione humana). Petr. de Andlo, II. c. 9: imperium a Deo...per subalternam emanationem. So in the Quaestio in utramque (a. 5) and the Somnium Virid. (I. c. 88, 180—1) the only dispute is whether kings are immediately or but mediately *ministri Dei*. See above, Note 22.

106.   See Dante, l. c.   Pet. de Andlo, I. c. 2 : regimen mundi a *Delega-tion by God of all Human Power.* summo rerum principe Deo eiusque divina dependet voluntate ; He institutes the pope as Vicar ; from the pope proceeds the *imperialis auctoritas* ; and from it again 'cetera regna, ducatus, principatus et dominia mundi subalterna quadam emanatione defluxerunt.'   Also II. c. 9.   Tengler, Laienspiegel, p. 14, 17, 56.

107.   Thom. Aq. De reg. princ. I. c. 2 : manifestum est quod *Monarchy and Unity.* unitatem magis efficere potest quod est per se unum quam plures ; and c. 5 ; Summa Theol. II. 1, q. 105, a. 1 ; II. 2, q. 10, a. 11 ; Summa cont. gentil. IV. 76 : optimum autem regimen multitudinis est ut regatur per unum ; quod patet ex fine regiminis, qui est pax : pax enim et unitas subditorum est finis regentis ; unitatis autem congruentior causa est unus quam multi ; Comm. ad Polit. p. 489 and 507 ; Aegid. Rom. De reg. princ. III. 2, c. 3 ; Dante, I. c. 5—9 and the practical arguments in c. 10—14 ; Joh. Paris. c. 1 ; Alv. Pel. I. a. 40 D and 62 C ; Ockham, Octo qu. III. c. 1 and 3 ; Dial. III. tr. 1, l. 2, c. 1, 6, 8, 9—11 ; Somn. Virid. I. c. 187 ; Gerson, IV. 585 (ad totius gubernationis exemplum, quae fit per unum Deum supremum) ; Nicol. Cus. III. praef. ; Laelius in Gold. II. p. 1595 ff. ; Anton. Ros. II. c. 5—7 ; Petrus de Andlo, I. c. 8 ; Patric. Sen. De regno, I. 1 and 13, p. 59 (unitas per imitationem ficta).   With some divergence and greater independence, Eng. Volk. I. c. 11—12 : now-a-days only a monarchy is able to unite wide territories and great masses of men.

108.   Dante, I. c. 15.   Similarly Pet. de Andlo, I. c. 3 : social *Singleness of Will in a Monarchy.* order depends on a sub-et-super-ordination of wills, as natural order upon a sub-et-super-ordination of natural forces.

109.   Thom. Aq. Summa cont. gentil. IV. q. 76 : the *regimen* *The Church a Monarchy.* *ecclesiae*, being of divine institution, must be *optime ordinatum*, and therefore must be such *ut unus toti ecclesiae praesit*.   Alv. Pel. I. a. 40 D and 54.   Joh. Par. c. 2.   Ockham, Dial. III. tr. 1, l. 2, c. 1, 3—11, 18—19, 29 ; also I. 5, c. 20—21.   Somn. Virid. II. c. 168— 179.   Ant. Ros. II. c. 1—7.

110.   Above all, Dante, lib. I. ; in c. 6, it is argued that the *Divine institution of Tem- poral Monarchy.* *ordo totalis* must be preferable to any *ordo partialis*.   Eng. Volk. De ortu, c. 14—15.   Ockham, Octo q. III. c. 1 and 3 ; Dial. III. tr. 2, l. 1, c. 1 and 9.   Aen. Sylv. c. 8.   Ant. Ros. II. c. 6.   Petr. de Andlo, I. c. 8.

111.   Above, Note 107.   Thom. Aq. l. c. ; it is so in every *populus* *Monarchy the Nor- mal Form of Govern- ment.* *unius ecclesiae*.   Compare his statements (in lib. IV. Sent. d. 17, q. 3, a. 3, sol. 5, ad 5) as to the relation of pope, bishop, and parson as the God-willed monarchical heads 'super eandem plebem immediate

constituti.' Dante, I. c. 6. Petr. de Andlo, I. c. 8. In particular, Ant. Ros. II. c. 6 (above, Note 64) as to the monarchical structure of the five *corpora mystica.*

References to Republics. 112. Thom. Aq. De reg. princ. I. c. 4. Eng. Volk. De reg. princ. I. c. 12—16. Petr. de Andlo, I. c. 8. Ant. Ros. II. c. 4 (on the other hand, c. 7, pp. 314—9).

Comparison of Forms of Government. 113. Ptol. Luc. II. c. 8, and IV. c. 8, goes so far as to hold that in the *status integer* of human nature the *regimen politicum* would be preferable; and even in the corrupt state of human nature the *dispositio gentis* may decide; thus e.g. the courage of the Italian race leaves no choice but republic or tyranny. Eng. Volk. I. c. 16. Ockham, Octo q. III. c. 3 and 7 (variances in accord with *congruentia temporum*); also Dial. III. tr. 2, l. 1, c. 5.

An Aristocratic World-State. 114. Ockham, Octo q. III. c. 3, 6, 8, and Dial. III. tr. 2, l. 1, c. 1, 4, 9, 13: it is possible that the form of government best suited to a part may not be the same as that best suited to the whole.

Necessity of Monarchy in the Church doubted. 115. Ockham, Dial. III. tr. 1, l. 2, c. 2, 12—4, 16—7, 25, 30. Even with an aristocratic constitution, unity is possible: pluralitas pontificum non scindit unitatem ecclesiae: what is good for a *pars* and *parvum* may not be always good for a *totum* and *magnum.* The divine institution of the primacy is expressly disputed by Marsilius, II. c. 15—22, III. concl. 32 and 41, and, among the Conciliar pamphleteers, by Randuf (De mod. un. eccl. c. 5) and others, who are opposed by d'Ailly, Gerson, and Breviscoxa (Gers. Op. I. p. 662, II. p. 88, and I. p. 872).

Preference of the Republican Form. 116. Patricius of Sienna in one place (De inst. reip. I. 1) expressly declares for a Republic; elsewhere (De regno I. 1) he gives a preference to Monarchy, but would pay heed to differences between various nations.

'Unitas principatus' in a Republic. Republican Assembly as a Collective Man. 117. Mars. Pat. I. c. 17 and III. concl. 11 (even for composite States). Ockham, Dial. III. tr. 2, l. 3, c. 17 and 22.

118. Aegid. Rom. III. 2, c. 3: plures homines principantes quasi constituunt unum hominem multorum oculorum et multarum manuum: but the good Monarch might become such a collective man by the association of wise councillors; and at any rate he is more *unus* than the Many can be 'in quantum tenent locum unius. —Mars. Pat. I. c. 17: 'quoad officium principatus' the *plures* must form a unit, so that every act of government appears as 'una actio ex communi decreto atque consensu eorum aut valentioris partis secundum statutas leges in his.'—So Ockham, Dial. III. tr. 2, l. 3, c. 17, with the addition that 'plures gerunt vicem unius et locum unius tenent.'—Patric. Sen. De inst. reip. I. 1 and III. 3: the ruling

assembly constitutes 'quasi unum hominem' or 'quasi unum corpus' with manifold members and faculties; I. 5: 'multitudo universa potestatem habet collecta in unum ubi de republica sit agendum, dimissi autem singuli rem suam agunt.'

119. Thus Dante, Mon. I. c. 6, sees in the Ruler 'aliquod unum quod non est pars.' So again Torquemada seeks to refute the whole Conciliar Theory by asserting that the very idea of a Monarch necessarily places him above the Community, like God above the world and the shepherd above the sheep: Summa de pot. pap. c. 26, 48, 83, 84; De conc. c. 29, 30, 44. *The Monarch above and outside the Group.*

120. Joh. Saresb. Policr. IV. c. 1: est...princeps potestas publica et in terris quaedam divinae maiestatis imago; V. c. 25, p. 391—5. Thom. Aq. De reg. I. c. 12—14: the erection of the State, being like unto God's creation of the world, and the government of the State, being like unto God's government of the world, are the affairs of the Ruler. *The Monarch represents Divinity.*

121. Gl. on c. 17 in Sexto 1, 6, v. *homini*: in hac parte non est homo sed Dei vicarius. Gl. on prooem. Cl. v. *papa*: nec Deus nec homo. Petr. Blesensis, ep. 141. Aug. Triumph. I. q. 6, a. 1—3 (identity of the Pope's sentence with God's, and therefore no appeal from the one to the other); q. 8, a. 1—3, q. 9, q. 18. Alv. Pel. I. a. 13 (non homo simpliciter, sed Deus, i.e. Dei vicarius), 37 y (Deus quodammodo, quia vicarius), 12 (unum est consistorium et tribunal Christi et Papae in terris). Bald. on l. ult. C. 7, 50. Ludov. Rom. cons. 345, nr. 6—8. Zenzelinus on c. 4, Extrav. Joh. XXII. nr. 14. Bertach. v. *papa*. *Apotheosis of the Pope.*

122. Already under the Hohenstaufen a formal apotheosis of the Emperor may be often found. See, e.g. Pet. de Vin. Ep. II. c. 7, and III. c. 44. Bald. I. cons. 228, nr. 7: imperator est dominus totius mundi et Deus in terra; cons. 373, nr. 2: princeps est Deus in terris. Joh. de Platea, l. 2, C. 11, 9, nr. 1: sicut Deus adoratur in coelis, ita princeps adoratur in terris; but only *improprie*. Theod. a Niem, p. 786: to the Emperor is due 'devotio tanquam praesenti et corporali Deo.' Aen. Sylv. c. 23: dominus mundi, Dei vicem in temporalibus gerens. Jason, II. cons. 177, nr. 11: princeps mundi et corporalis mundi Deus. *Apotheosis of the Emperor.*

123. Thus already in the Councils of Paris and Worms of 829 (M. G. L. I. p. 346 ff.) we find an exposition of the doctrine that the kingship is a 'ministerium a Deo commissum,' that the *Rex* is so called *a recte agendo*, that, ceasing to rule well, he becomes a tyrant. Similarly in Concil. Aquisgran. II. ann. 836 and Concil. Mogunt. ann. 888, c. 2 in Mansi XIV. p. 671 and XVIII. 62; cf. *Kingship is Office.*

Hefele IV. p. 91 and 546. Hincmar, Op. I. 693. Manegold v. Lautenbach, l.c., expressly uses the phrase *vocabulum officii.* John of Salisbury, IV. c. 1—3 and 5, says 'minister populi' and 'publicae utilitatis minister.' Hugh of Fleury, I. c. 4, 6, 7, 'ministerium, officium regis.' Thom. Aq. De reg. prin. I. c. 14. Alv. Pel. I. a. 62, I. Ptol. Luc. II. 5—16. Dante, I. c. 12 : princes are 'respectu viae domini, respectu termini ministri aliorum,' and in this respect the Emperor is 'minister omnium.' Eng. Volk. tr. II.—VII. Gerson, IV. p. 597. Ant. Ros. I. c. 64 : officium publicum ; like a tutor. Pet. de Andl. I. c. 3, II. c. 16—18.

Princes exist for the Common Weal. 124. In particular, Joh. Saresb. IV. c. 1—3, and 5. Thom. Aquin. De reg. Iud. q. 6 : Principes terrarum sunt a Deo instituti, non quidem ut propria lucra quaerant, sed ut communem utilitatem procurent ; Comm. ad Polit. p. 586. Ptol. Luc., III. c. 11 : regnum non est propter regem, sed rex propter regnum. Eng. Volk. De reg. princ. v. c. 9 : sicut tutela pupillorum, ita et procuratio reipublicae inventa est ad utilitatem eorum qui commissi sunt, et non eorum qui commissionem susceperunt ; II. c. 18, IV. c. 33—4. Dante, I. c. 12 : non enim cives propter consules nec gens propter regem, sed e converso consules propter cives et rex propter gentem. Ockham, Octo q. III. c. 4, and I. c. 6. Paris de Puteo, De synd. p. 40, nr. 21. Petrus de Andlo, I. c. 3.

Purpose of the Ruler. 125. Councils of Paris and Worms, an. 829 : to rule the Folk with righteousness and equity, to preserve peace and unity. Petr. Bles. Epist. 184, p. 476 : ut recte definiant et decidant examine quod ad eos pervenerit quaestionum. Dante, Mon. I. c. 12. Thom. Aq. Comm. ad Polit., p. 592, 595 ff. Eng. Volk. I. c. 10. Gerson, III. p. 1474. Ockham, Octo q. III. c. 5, declares a *plenitudo potestatis* incompatible with the best Form of Government, which should promote the liberty and exclude the slavery of the subjects ; and (VIII. c. 4) he opines that the Kaiser has smaller rights than other princes just because it behoves the Empire to have the best of constitutions.

Decline towards Tyranny. 126. Councils of Paris and Worms, an. 829. Council of Mainz, an. 888, c. 2. Nicolaus I. Epist. 4 ad Advent. Metens. : si iure principantur ; alioquin potius tyranni credendi sunt quam reges habendi. Petr. Bles. l. c. : Principatus nomen amittere promereretur qui a iusto iudicii declinat tramite. Hugo Flor. I. c. 7—8. Joh. Sar VIII. c. 17—24. Thom. Aq. De reg. princ. I. c. 3—11. Ptol. Luc. III. c. 11. Vinc. Bellov. VII. c. 8. Eng. Volk. I. c. 6 and 18. Alv. Pel. I. a. 62 D—H. Ockham, Dial. III. tr. 1, l. 2, c. 6 ff. ; Octo q. III. c. 14. Gerson, l.c. Paris de Puteo, l. c. pp. 8—51.

127. This principle was never doubted. See e.g. Pet. Bles. ep. 131, p. 388. Thom. Aq. Summa Theol. II. 1, q. 96, a. 4 (quia ad hoc ordo potestatis divinitus concessus se non extendit) and II. 2, q. 104, a. 5. To the same effect the 'Summists' [i.e. the compilers of Summae Confessorum, manuals for the use of confessors], e.g. Joh. Friburgensis, Sum. Conf. lib. 2, tit. 5, q. 204. — *God rather than Man is to be obeyed.*

128. Thus Hugh of Fleury, who therefore prescribes that tyrants be tolerated and prayed for, but that commands which contravene the law of God be disobeyed, and that punishment and death be borne in the martyr's spirit; I. c. 4, p. 17—22, c. 7, p. 31, c. 12, p. 44, II. p. 66.—Baldus also on l. 5, Dig. 1, 1, nr. 6—7, declares against any invasion into the rights of Rulers. — *Passive Resistance.*

129. Hug. de S. Victore, Quaest. in epist. Paul. q. 300 (Migne, vol. 175, p. 505): Reges et principes, quibus obediendum est in omnibus quae ad potestatem pertinent. Thom. Aq. Sum. Theol. II. 2, q. 104, a. 5: only in special circumstances or for the avoidance of scandal and danger, need a Christian obey the command of an usurper or even the unrighteous command of the legitimate ruler. So also Vincent Bellov. x. c. 87 and Joh. Friburg l. c. (Note **127**). Ockham, Dial. III. tr. 2, l. 2, c. 20: all men owe to the Emperor immediate but conditional obedience: to wit, 'in licitis' and 'in his quae spectant ad regimen populi temporalis,' so that, e.g. a prohibition of wine-drinking would not be binding. And compare c. 26 and 28. Nic. Cus. III. c. 5. Decius, Cons. 72, nr. 2: superiori non est obediendum quando egreditur fines sui officii. — *Nullity of Commands that are ultra vires statuentis.*

130. Already Manegold of Lautenbach (see Sitzungsber. d. bair. Akad. an. 1868, II. 325) teaches that the king who has become a tyrant should be expelled like an unfaithful shepherd. Similar revolutionary doctrines were frequently maintained by the papalistic party against the wielders of State-power. John of Salisbury emphatically recommends the slaughter of a tyrant 'qui violenta dominatione populum opprimit,' for a tyranny is nothing else than an abuse of power granted by God to man. He vouches biblical and classical examples, and rejects only the use of poison, breach of trust, and breach of oath. See Policr. III. c. 15, IV. c. 1, VI. c. 24—8, VIII. c. 17—20. Thomas of Aquino is against tyrannicide, but in favour of an active resistance against a *regimen tyrannicum*, for such a *regimen* is *non iustum*, and to abolish it is no *seditio*, unless indeed the measures that are taken be such that they will do more harm than would be done by tolerating the tyranny: Sum. Theol. II. 2, q. 42, a. 2, ad 3, q. 69, a. 4; De reg. princ. I. c. 6; Comm. ad Polit. p. 553. To the same effect, Aegid. Rom. De reg. princ. I. c. 6. — *Active Resistance and Tyrannicide.*

There is an elaborated doctrine of active resistance in Ockham, Dial. III. tr. 2, l. 2, c. 26 and 28 (it is *ius gentium*). Somn. Virid. I. c. 141. Henr. de Langenstein, Cons. pacis, c. 15. Gerson, IV. 600 and 624. Decius, Cons. 690, nr. 13. Bened. Capra, Reg. 10, nr. 42 : the execution of a tyrannical measure is an act of violence which may be violently resisted. Henricus de Pyro, Inst. I. 2, § 1 : iudici et ministris principum licet resistere de facto quando ipsi sine iure procedunt.—As to the thesis in which Jean Petit on 8 March, 1408 defended tyrannicide (Gerson, Op. V. pp. 15—42), the opposition of Gerson (Op. IV. 657—80) and the qualified condemnation of the thesis by the Council of Constance (sess. XV. of 6 July, 1415), see Schwab, Gerson, pp. 609—46. Wyclif (art. damn. 15 and 17) and Hus (art. 30) held that a Ruler who is in mortal sin is no true ruler.

The Pope's Plenitude of Power.

131.   The first to elaborate in idea and in phrase a 'plenitudo ecclesiasticae potestatis' vested by God in the Pope, whence all other ecclesiastical power has flowed and in which all other ecclesiastical power is still comprised, was Innocent III., although substantially the same doctrine had been taught by Gregory VII., lib. I., ep. 55ᵃ, ann. 1075. For Innocent III. see c. 13, X. 4, 17 ; c. 23, X. 5, 33 ; lib. I, ep. 127, p. 116, lib. 7, ep. 1 and 405, pp. 279 and 405, lib. 9, ep. 82, 83 and 130, pp. 898, 901 and 947. Compare Innocent IV. on c. 1, X. 1, 7 ; c. 10, X. 2, 2 ; c. 19, X. 2, 27, nr. 6. Durantis, Spec. I. 1 de legato § 6, nr. 1—58. Thom. Aquin. lib. 4, Sent. d. 20, q. 4, a. 3, ad 3, quaestiunc. 4, sol. 3 : Papa habet plenitudinem potestatis pontificalis quasi rex in regno, episcopi vero assumuntur in partem sollicitudinis quasi iudices singulis civitatibus praepositi. See also lib. 2, dist. et quest. ult. ; Summa Theol. II. 2, q. 1, a. 10 ; Opusc. cont. error. Graec. II. c. 34 and 38. Aegid. Rom. De pot. eccl. III. c. 9—12 : tanta potestatis plenitudo, quod eius posse est sine pondere, numero et mensura. Petr. Palud. in Raynald, a. 1328, nr. 30. The doctrine reaches the utmost exaltation in Augustinus Triumphus, I. q. 1, 8, 10—34, II. q. 48—75, but goes yet further in Alvarius Pelagius, I. a. 5—7, 11—12, 52—58 : potestas sine numero, pondere et mensura ; it is exceptionless, all-embracing, the basis of all power, sovereign, boundless and always immediate. Durantis, De modo eccl. conc. P. III. Turrecremata, Summa de eccl. II. c. 54, 65. Petrus a Monte, De primatu, f. 144 ff.

Limits to Papal Sovereignty.

132.   'Lex divina et lex naturalis, articuli fidei et sacramenta novae legis' were always recognized as limits. See Alex. III. in c. 4, X. 5, 19 and Innocent III. in c. 13, X. 2, 13. Joh. Sar. Ep. 198, p. 218. Thom. Aq. Summa Theol. II. 1, q. 97, a. 4, ad 3 ; Quodlib. IV. a. 13.

Aug. Triumph. I. q. 22, a. 1; Alv. Pel. I. a. 7 and 46. Comp.
Ockham, Dial. III. tr. 1, l. 1, c. 1, and tr. 2, l. 1, c. 23.

133. Ockham makes an elaborate attack on the doctrine which Limited
teaches that, at any rate in spiritual affairs, the Pope has a plenitude Monarchy
of power in the sight of God and man. This (he argues) would be Pope. of the
incompatible with 'evangelical liberty' for it would establish an
'intolerable servitude.' In all, or at any rate all normal, cases the
Pope's power is *potestas limitata.* Ockham, Octo q. I. c. 6, III.
c. 4—5, Dial. III. tr. 1, l. 1, c. 2—15, tr. 2, l. 1, c. 23. Compare
Joh. Paris. c. 3 and 6; Marsil. Patav. II. c. 22—30; Somn. Virid.
I. c. 156—161; Randuf, De mod. un. c. 5, 10, 23, 28; Greg. Heimb.
II. p. 1604.

134. Ockham, Octo q. I. c. 15 and III. c. 9: obedience is due Condi-
only 'in his quae necessaria sunt congregationi fidelium, salvis tional
iuribus et libertatibus aliorum'; if the Pope transcends his sphere of due to the
competence, every one, be he prelate, emperor, king, prince or Pope. The
simple layman, is entitled and bound to resist, regard being had to Necessity.
time, place and opportunity.—During the Great Schism the doctrine
of a right of resistance and rejection given by Necessity became
always commoner. See Matth. de Cracovia, Pierre du Mont de
St Michel and other Gallicans in Hübler, pp. 366, 370—2, 377;
also ib. p. 121, note 8; also ib. 373; Gerson, Trilogus, II. p. 83 ff.;
Theod. a Niem, De schism. III. c. 20 (resistance, as against a
bestia); Randuf, De mod. un. c. 9—10; Ant. Ros. II. c. 23, 27—30,
III. c. 4—6. Nicholas of Cues (Op. II. pp. 825—9) held to this
doctrine even after he had fallen away from the Conciliar party.

135. See the following sections.

136. Ockham refutes at large the opinion that the *lex divina vel* Limited
naturalis is the only limit to imperial power: on the contrary, Monarchy
'limitata est imperatoris potestas, ut quoad liberos sibi subiectos et Empire.
res eorum solummodo illa potest quae prosunt ad communem
utilitatem.' Dial. III. tr. 2, l. 2, c. 26—8: in relation to persons,
c. 20; in relation to things, c. 21—5. Gerson, IV. pp. 598, 601.
Nic. Cus. III. c. 5. See above, Notes 126—30.

137. See above, Note 16. Placentinus de var. actionum, I. 4. The State
Summa Rolandi, C. 23, q. 7, p. 96. Addition to the Gloss on § 5, of Nature.
Inst. 2, 1, v. *publicus* [which addition teaches that *communia* are
those things which by virtue of the *ius naturale primaevum* still
remain in their original condition as common to all]. Joh. Nider,
Tract. de Contr. (Tr. U. J. VI. p. 279), tr. v. K. Summenhard, De
contr. tr. 1, q. 8—11 [a German jurist, ob. 1502].—But Aquinas,
Summa Theol. I. q. 96, a. 4 and Ptolemy of Lucca, De reg. pr. III.

c. 9, and IV. c. 2—3, teach that *dominium politicum* would have come into existence even in the State of Innocence, though not *dominium servile*. [Elsewhere (D. G. R. III. 125) our author has spoken of the patristic doctrine that lordship and property are consequences of the Fall. He there refers to various works of Augustine and sends us for other patristic utterances to Hergenröther, Katholische Kirche und christlicher Staat, Freib. 1872, p. 461.]

Beginnings of the Original Contract.

138. Already in the course of the Investiture Quarrel, Manegold of Lautenbach (above, Note 130) asked: Nonne clarum est, merito illum a concessa dignitate cadere, populum ab eius dominio liberum existere, cum *pactum* pro quo constitutus est constat illum prius irrupisse? On the anti-papal side the only answer was that the People's Will when once uttered became a *necessitas*, and that therefore the grant of lordship was irrevocable. See the pronouncement of the Anti-Gregorian cardinals in Sudendorf, Registr. II. p. 41. Engelbert of Volkersdorf is the first to declare in a general way that all *regna et principatus* originated in a *pactum subiectionis* which satisfied a natural want and instinct: De ortu, c. 2. Marsil. Pat. I. c. 8, 12, 15. Ockham, Dial. III. tr. 2, l. 2, c. 24: the *ius humanum* which introduced lordship and ownership in place of the community of goods existent under divine and natural law, was a *ius populi* and was transferred by the *populus* to the Emperor, along with the *imperium*. Nic. Cus. III. c. 4. Aen. Sylv. c. 2.

Right of a People to choose a Superior.

139. Eng. Volk., De ortu, c. 10. Lup. Bebenb. c. 5 and 15. Ockham, Octo q. II. c. 4—5, V. c. 6, VIII. c. 3. Baldus, l. 5, Dig. I, 1, nr. 5 and 8; l. 2, Cod. 6, 3, nr. 3. Paul. Castr. l. 5, Dig. I, 1, lect. 1, nr. 5, and lect. 2, nr. 17—18.

The People as instruments of God.

140. Joh. Paris. c. 11 and 16: populo faciente et Deo inspirante. Mars. Pat. I. c. 9: where men institute a king, God is *causa remota*. Ockham, Dial. III. tr. 2, l. 1, c. 27: imperium a Deo, et tamen per homines, scil. Romanos. Ant. Ros. I. c. 56: imperium immediate a Deo, per medium tamen populi Romani, qui tanquam Dei minister et instrumentum eius iurisdictionem omnem in ipsum transtulit.—Somewhat divergently Almain, De auct. eccl. c. 1 (Gers. Op. II. pp. 978 and 1014): God gives the power to the *communitas* in order that this power may be transferred to the Ruler.

God and the People as the Source of Power.

141. Nicol. Cus. II. 19, III. praef. and c. 4, argues that all power in Church and State comes both from God and from Man, for the voluntary subjection of men gives the material power and God grants the spiritual force. Is it not divine, and not merely human, when an assembled multitude decides as though it were one heart and one soul (II. c. 5 and 15)?

142. [The famous text in question is l. 1, Dig. 1, 4 and Inst. The Lex Regia. 1, 2, 6 : Quod principi placuit legis habet vigorem : utpote cum lege regia, quae de imperio eius lata est, populus ei et in eum omne suum imperium et potestatem conferat.] Gloss on l. 9, Dig. 1, 3 ; l. 1, Dig. 1, 4 ; l. un. Dig. 1, 11 ; l. 2, Cod. 8, 53 ; l. 11, Cod. 1, 17 v. *solus imperator* ; and on 1. Feud. 26. Jac. Aren. Inst. de act. nr. 5, p. 277. Cinus, l. 4, Cod. 2, 54. Baldus, l. 1, Cod. 1, 1, nr. 1—12. Innoc. c. 1, X. 1, 7, nr. 1—2 : papa habet imperium a Deo, imperator a populo. Dante, III. c. 13—4. Lup. Bebenb. c. 5, p. 355 : olim tenuit monarchiam imperii populus urbis Romanae ; postea transtulit in ipsum imperatorem. Ockham, Octo q. II. c. 4—5 ; Dial. III. tr. 2, l. 1, c. 27—28. Aen. Sylv. c. 8. Ant. Ros. I. c. 32 and 36.

143. Thus Engelbert, Marsilius, Ockham and Æneas Sylvius, Voluntary Subjection the Ground of Lordship. as in Note 138. In particular, Nic. Cus. II. c. 12 : the binding force of all laws rests upon 'concordantia subiectionalis eorum qui ligantur' ; II. c. 13 : all power flows from the free 'subiectio inferiorum' ; III. c. 4 : it arises 'per viam voluntarie subiectionis et consensus' ; II. c. 8 and 10.

144. See above, Note 54.

145. Ockham, Dial. III. tr. 2, l. 1, c. 27, vouching Gloss on c. 6, X. 1, 2. Ant. Ros. v. c. 2 (true even for the Babylonian empire : with voucher of Dig. 3, 4, Innocentius and Bartolus).

146. See the letter of the Senatus Populusque Romanus to King Rights of the Burghers of Rome when the Empire is vacant. Conrad in Jaffé, Monum. Corbeiens. p. 332 (also Otto Fris. Gesta Frid. I. c. 28) : the Kaiser has the 'imperium a Deo,' but 'vigore senatus et populi Romani' : he ought to dwell 'in urbe quae caput mundi est.' Also Otto Fris. l. c. II. c. 21 ; letter of Wezel, ann. 1152, in Jaffé, l. c. p. 542 : set cum imperium et omnis reipublicae dignitas sit Romanorum et dum imperator sit Romanorum non Romani imperatoris,...quae lex, quae ratio senatum populumque prohibet creare imperatorem ?—Even the Hohenstaufen, however decisively they may assert their divine right as against such claims as these (cf. ep. an. 1152 in Jaffé, l. c. p. 449, and Otto Fris. III. c. 16, and IV. c. 3), treat Rome as the capital town of the Empire and the Roman townsfolk as in a special sense the imperial folk (cf. Petr. de Vineis, ep. I. c. 7, III. c. 1, 18, 72).

147. Lup. Bebenb. c. 12 and 17. Similarly Ockham, Dial. III. The People of Rome and the Roman People. tr. 2, l. 1, c. 30 : 'imperium Rom.' and 'dominium temporalium... principalissime spectat ad totam communitatem universalium morta- lium.' See also Dante, III. c. 16.

148. Joh. Paris. c. 16 : acclamante populo, cuius est se subicere The People's cui vult sine alterius praeiudicio. Marsil. Pat. Def. pac. II. c. 30 : the

Part in the
Transla-
tion of the
Empire.
Pope acted, if at all, as the delegate of the *legislator Romanus* [i.e. Roman people]. See also the changes made by Marsilius in Landulf's De transl. imp. c. 8, 9, 10, 12. Ockham, Octo q. II. c. 9, IV. c. 5 and 8 : auctoritate populi Romani, with the Pope as a part or mandatory or counsellor; Dial. III. tr. 2, l. 1, c. 20 : the Pope acted auctoritate et vice Romanorum...transferentibus consensit. Theod. a Niem, pp. 788—792. Aen. Sylv. c. 9 : concurrente summi pontificis consensu.

The
Roman
Citizens
and the
Transla-
tion.
149. Lup. Bebenb. c. 12, p. 385; comp. c. 1—4 and 8. Ockham, Dial. III. tr. 2, l. 1, c. 29—30, raises other doubts. Could the then *populus Romanus* surrender the *imperium* to the prejudice of the *populus sequens*? Could the whole *universitas mortalium* make the transfer *invitis Romanis*? To the last question the answer is Yes, if there were *culpa* on the part of the Romans, or other reasonable cause.

Right of
the People
during a
Vacancy
of the
Empire.
150. Lup. Bebenb. c. 5. Ockham, Octo q. II. c. 14, and Dial. III. tr. 2, l. 1, c. 22 : only by authorization of the *Romani* or the Electors can the Pope claim any right in this matter. Ant. Ros. I. c. 64 : the *populus Romanus* demises the imperial power as an *officium publicum*; on the Kaiser's death this reverts to the *populus*.

The Right
to choose
a Ruler.
151. See the citations in Note 138. Mars. Pat. I. c. 9 and 15. Lup. Bebenb. c. 5 : secundum ius gentium...quilibet populus potest sibi regem eligere; c. 15 : election or appointment by the Kaiser is, according to the common law, the only title whereby a *principatus* or *regnum* can be acquired. Ockham, Dial. III. tr. 2, l. 3, c. 5—6 : if once a departure has been made from the *Omnia communia* of pure Natural law, we have as a principle of the now modified Natural Law 'quod omnes quibus est praeficiendus aliquis habeant ius eligendi praeficiendum, nisi cedant iuri suo vel superior eis ordinet contrarium.' Nic. Cus. III. c. 4 : populus Romanus habet potestatem eligendi inperatorem per ipsum ius divinum et naturale ; for, according to God's very own will, all lordship, and in particular that of Kings and Kaisers, arises 'per viam voluntariae subiectionis et consensus.' Ant. Ros. I. c. 69.

Consen-
sual Origin
of Here-
ditary
Kingship.
152. Mars. Pat. I. c. 9. Eng. Volk. De ortu, c. 10. Lup. Bebenb. c. 15, p. 398. Ockham, Octo q. V. c. 6. K. Summenhard, De contr. tr. I. q. 11 : an hereditary kingship arises if those who first consented gave consent *pro se et suis*, an elective kingship if they only consented *pro se*, so that 'eo sublato, libere possunt se alteri submittere quem elegerint.' Custom, ordinance proceeding from a higher power, and conquest are mentioned as other titles to hereditary rule.

153. Thom. Aq. Comm. ad Polit. pp. 495 and 501. Aegid. Col.

III. 2, c. 5. Mars. Pat. I. c. 16. Bart. De reg. civ. nr. 23. Nic. Cus. III. praef. See also Miles in Somn. Virid. I. c. 187.

154. Otto Fris. Gesta, II. c. 1. Lup. Bebenb. c. 5. Ockham, Octo q. IV. c. 5 and 9, VIII. c. 3. Baldus, l. 5, Dig. I. 1, nr. 11—15. Nic. Cus. III. c. 4. According to Lupold, the *exercitus*, which 'repraesentabat totum populum Romanorum imperio subiectum,' used to make the election; afterwards it was made by the People itself; then by the Emperor who chose a successor; finally by the Prince Electors.

155. Mars. Pat. II. 26 (concessio populi is the basis) and III. concl. 9 and 10. Lup. Bebenb. c. 5 and 12: when the Karolings had died out, the princes and nobles of the Franks, Alamans, Bavarians and Saxons 'who represented the whole Folk of Germany' made the choice; then Otto III. 'by the express or at any rate the tacit consent' of the princes and people established the *Kurfürsten* (Prince Electors); and this was legitimate, for by the *ius gentium* every *universitas* may choose a king, and, in accordance with a general custom, may also confer upon him imperial rights, and moreover may delegate for ever to committees the right to make equally valid elections. Ockham, Octo q. VIII. c. 3. Nic. Cus. III. c. 4: the Electors were instituted in the time of Henry II. by the common consent of all the Germans and of all others who were subject to the Empire, and therefore 'radicalem vim habent ab ipso omnium consensu qui sibi naturali iure imperatorem constituere poterant.' Ant. Ros. I. c. 48: the 'collegium universale fidelium, et sic populus Romanus,' instituted the Electors.

156. Ockham, Dial. III. tr. 2, l. 1, c. 30: what the People has *de facto* conveyed to the Pope is knowable only by one who has seen all the papal charters, registers and authentic documents; but in principle the People might have transferred to the Pope power to constitute the Electoral College or even directly to make the election. Nic. Cus. III. c. 4 holds that it was merely as a subject of the Empire (for in temporals the Church is subject) that the Pope gave his consent, whereas the virtue (*vigor*) of the act flowed not 'ex suo sed ex communi omnium et ipsius et aliorum consensu.'—On the other hand, according to Lupold v. Bebenburg, c. 12, an authorization by the Church was requisite in order that the choice made by the Prince Electors might give a claim to imperial coronation and to imperial rights outside the realm of Charles the Great.

157. Mars. Pat. II. c. 26. Ockham, Octo q. VIII. c. 1—8, and IV. c. 8—9; Dial. III. tr. 2, l. 2, c. 29. Nic. Cus. III. c. 4.—So also Bebenburg, c. 5—6, but once more with an exception of imperial

[marginal notes:]
Elective Rulership is preferable. The Empire Elective.

Theory and the Prince Electors.

The Pope as a Popular Delegate.

Election, not Coronation, confers the

Imperial Rights.

rights beyond the limits of the 'immediate' *Reich.* Ockham justly urges that Bebenburg's own argument requires that the Electing Princes should represent the World-Folk, and not merely the folk of Charles the Great's lands.

Lex Regia: an irrevocable Conveyance.

158. Accursius in Gl. upon l. 9, Dig. 1, 3, v. *non ambigitur,* decides in favour of this view, while the Gl. upon l. 11, Cod. 1, 14, v. *solus imperator* mentions it but does not decide. So also Gl. upon 1. Feud. 26, v. *an imperatorem* (imperator maior populo). Hostiensis, De const. Bartolus, l. 11, Cod. 1, 14, nr. 3—4: omnis potestas est abdicata ab eis. Baldus, l. 8, Dig. 1, 3, nr. 5—11, says that the *populus Romanus* cannot depose the Emperor and is not *imperatori similis;* the *translatio* was an *alienatio pleno iure;* otherwise the Kaiser would be, not *dominus,* but *commissarius populi.* So Baldus in 1. Feud. 26, nr. 15 and 11. Feud. 53 § 1 (princeps maior populo); l. 8, Dig. 1, 14, nr. 1—3, and l. 11, eod. nr. 6: the populus can no longer make laws. Angel. Aret. § 6, 1. I, 2, nr. 5—6. Joh. de Platea, Inst. 1, 2, nr. 51. Marcus, Dec. 1. q. 187.

Lex Regia: a revocable Delegation.

159. See the counter opinions in the Glosses cited in the last note. Gl. on l. 2, Dig. de R. D. v. *littora*: the *protectio* of the *res communes omnium* is ascribed to the Roman people: Baldus substitutes *Caesaris* for *pop. Rom.* Also Cinus, l. 12, Cod. 1, 14: but he confesses that at the present day statutes made by the Roman people would find little observance outside the walls of Rome. Ockham, Octo q. IV. c. 8. Christof. Parcus § 6, Inst. 1, 2, nr. 4 (with elaborate proof). Zabar. c. 34 § *verum*, X. 1, 6, nr. 8. Paul. Castr. l. 8, Dig. 1, 3, nr. 4—6, and l. 1, Dig. 1, 4, nr. 4: he holds that there was a *concessio* of the *usus*, not a *translatio* of the *substantia*, but since Christ's advent the Church has taken the place of the People.

Absolute Monarchy and the Will of the People.

160. See e.g. the speech of the Abp of Milan to Frederick I. in Ott. Fris. IV. c. 4, and the letter of Frederick II. in Pet. de Vin. ep. V. c. 135.

Nullity of Monarch's Acts if they tend to impair his Fundamental Rights.

161. Oldradus and, following him, Baldus, Prooem. Feud. nr. 32, and II. Feud. 26 § 4 in generali, nr. 34. Picus a Monte Pico, 1. Feud. 7, nr. 7. Decius, Cons. 564, nr. 9—10. Franc. Curt. jun. Cons. 174, nr. 17.—Therefore to support the Donation of Constantine, an approval by Senate and People was supposed. Baldus, prooem. Dig. nr. 44—45, and II. Feud. 26 § 4, nr. 3; Aug. Triumphus, II. q. 43, a. 3; Ant. Rosellus, I. c. 69; Curtius, l. c. nr. 18.

Nullity of Acts subjecting the Empire to the Church.

162. Lup. Bebenb. c. 8, p. 367, and c. 12, p. 381, but esp. c. 14, pp. 395—7: since these concessions and confessions were made without the consent of the Prince Electors and the People of the realm and empire, the said Princes and other representatives of the People can contradict them, and this contradiction is to be received; so the

subditi may always raise objection if a *dominus* would subject himself and his land to another *dominus*; for according to the *ius gentium, civile et canonicum* whatever would prejudice a community 'debet ab omnibus approbari.' Similarly, Ockham, Dial. III. tr. ₹ l. 1, c. 30: a division or diminution of the Empire would be valid 'non absque consensu expresso vel tacito totius universitatis mortalium.'

163. See the Commentaries on l. 8, Cod. 1, 14; also Baldus, II. Feud. 26 § 1, nr. 13.

164. See e.g. Pet. de Vin. ep. I. c. 3, p. 105. Lup. Bebenb. c. 17, p. 406—7 : even were *rex maior populo*, the people must have a right to depose him in a case of necessity; 'necessitas enim legem non habet.' Ockham, Octo q. II. c. 7, VI. c. 2, III. c. 3; the Kaiser, albeit *ius a populo habet*, stands above the People, the King above the Realm, the General of an Order above all the friars : still in case of necessity the community may depose him. Anton. Ros. III. c. 16 : although the Kaiser stands as *caput* above the Assembly of the *Reich* and is judge in his own cause, an exception must be admitted if he is accused before that Assembly as 'tyrannus et scandalizans universale bonum imperii saecularis.' Comp. ib. c. 21 and 22, and above, Note 130.—On the other hand, already in the time of Henry IV. the Anti-Gregorian cardinals opine that, though the people can make a king, the will of the people, when once it is uttered, becomes a *necessitas*: see Sudendorf, Registr. II. 41. So also Baldus (Note 158); but comp. his Cons. V. c. 325—6.

The Right to depose a Ruler in a case of Necessity.

165. Thomas of Aquino attributes sovereignty sometimes to the People, sometimes to the Prince, regard being had to the different constitutions of different States. Summa Theol. II. 1, q. 90, a. 3 : ordinare aliquid in bonum commune est vel totius multitudinis vel alicuius gerentis vicem totius multitudinis; et ideo condere legem vel pertinet ad totam multitudinem, vel pertinet ad personam publicam, quae totius multitudinis curam habet. So also, q. 97, a. 3. In this matter later writers follow him : e.g. Joh. Friburg. II. t. 5, q. 209, and K. Summenhard, q. 11 : *potestas politica* exists 'duplici modo, uno modo in uno rege, alio in una communitate.' But as to the best constitution, Aquinas declares in favour of the mixed constitution which (so it is imagined) prevailed among the Jews. Summa Theol. II 1, q. 95, a. 4, and q. 105, a. 1 : 'Unde optima ordinatio principum est in aliqua civitate vel regno in quo *unus* praeficitur secundum virtutem qui omnibus praesit; et sub ipso sunt *aliqui* participantes secundum virtutem; et tamen talis principatus ad *omnes* pertinet, tum quia ex omnibus eligi possunt, tum quia etiam ab omnibus eliguntur: talis enim est omnis politia *bene commixta* ex *regno* in

The Mixed Constitution.

quantum unus praeest, ex *aristocratia* in quantum multi principantur secundum virtutem, et ex *democratia*, id est, potestate populi, in quantum ex popularibus possunt eligi principes et ad populum pertinet elecˑio principum.' In all cases he demands that Monarchy be subjected to limitations so that it may not degenerate into Tyranny : De reg. princ. I. c. 6. John of Paris, c. 20, p. 202, prefers to a pure Monarchy one mixed with Aristocracy and Democracy. So d'Ailly, De pot. eccl. II. c. 1, and Gerson, De pot. eccl. cons. 13. Eng. of Volkersdorf also (I. c. 14—16) portrays the advantages of mixed constitutions. Jason, l. 5, Cod. 1, 2, lect. 2, nr. 10—13, declares it to be a general maxim in Church and State, that, if there be *ardua negotia* concerned, the Head is bound to obtain the consent of a conciliar assembly. Almain, Comm. ad Occam, q. 1, c. 5 and 15, holds it to be compatible with the nature of a Monarchy that in State and Church respectively the *congregatio nobilium* or the Council is entitled to impose limits on the regal or papal power and to judge and depose the king or, as the case may be, the pope ; but then it is true that he elsewhere (Tract. de auct. eccl. c. 1, Gerson, Op. II. p. 977 ff.) declares that the Prince is above all individuals, but not above the community. John Mair, Disput. a. 1518 (Gerson, II. p. 1131 ff.) supposes two highest powers, that of the folk being the more unlimited.

166. See above, Note 159. Lup. Bebenb. c. 12 and 17. Ockham, Octo q. IV. 8.

Justice to be done upon the Ruler. 167. Mars. Pat. I. c. 15 and 18; II. c. 26 and 30. Lup. Bebenb. c. 17, p. 406. Ockham, Octo q. II. c. 8 (correctio imperatoris spectat ad Romanos). Miles in Somn. Virid. I. 141 : if a King imposes unjust taxes, denies justice, fails to defend the country, or otherwise neglects his duty, the People may depose him and choose another Ruler, and so the People of a part of the realm, if this part only has suffered neglect, may appoint a separate Ruler. Joh. Wiclif, art. 17 : populares possunt ad suum arbitrium dominos delinquentes corrigere. Nicol. Cus. III. c. 4.—Already in the course of the Investiture Quarrel, Manegold of Lautenbach deduced the right of deposition in case of breach of contract by the Ruler.— Innoc. c. 1, X. 1, 10, nr. 1—2 concedes a right of deposition only in the case of elective kings.

The Deposition of Kings. 168. Especially in relation to the deposition of the last Merovings and the exaltation of Pipin, it is asserted at length that 'non deposuit papa, sed deponendum consuluit et depositioni consensit,' 'non substituit sed substituendum consuluit et substituentibus consensit,' 'a iuramento absolvit, i.e., absolutos declaravit'; and reference is

made to Huguccio and Glos. ord. on c. *alius*, C. 15, q. 6. Joh. Paris.
c. 15. Mars. Pat. De transl. c. 6. Lup. Bebenb. c. 12, pp. 386—9:
the Pope merely declared a *dubium iuris*, the Franks deposed and
instituted. Ockham, Octo q. II. c. 8; VIII. c. 1 and 5; Dial. III. tr. 2,
l. 1, c. 18: so too Innocents III. and IV. acted *auctoritate Romanorum*, unless indeed their doings were usurpatory. Somn. Virid.
I. c. 72—73. Quaestio in utramque p. 106, ad 15—16. Nic. Cus. III.
c. 4: the Pope acted as a member of the *universitas*.

169. Lup. Bebenb. c. 12, p. 385, and c. 17, p. 406.

170. Marsil. Pat. I. c. 7—8, 12—13, 15, 18, II. c. 30, III. concl. 6.

171. Nicol. Cus. III. c. 4 and 41, and II. c. 12—13. The pro- The
posals made by Cusanus for the reformation of the Empire are Projects of
connected with these theories, and in a very remarkable fashion blend of Cues.
the forms of the medieval Land-Peace-Associations with the ideas of
Nature Right, III. c. 25—40. The Emperor continues to be the
monarchical Head of the Empire and is to take the initiative (c. 32).
A very complicated method is proposed for his election (c. 36—37).
The power of making laws for the Empire is wielded by an annually
assembled Imperial Diet (*Reichstag*) which consists of Prince-Electors,
Judges, Councillors and Deputies of Towns, and represents the
whole People (c. 35). Then below this stand annual Provincial
Assemblies of the three Estates (Clergy, Nobles and People) which
regulate the special affairs of the provinces, and depute standing
committees (provincial courts) with a strong executive power (c. 33).
Further and detailed reforms of the imperial army (c. 39), of the
finance and justice of the Empire, of the laws concerning the Land
Peace (c. 34), of ecclesiastical privileges (c. 40) and so forth are
proposed. As in the Empire, so generally in all territories the kings
and princes are to have by their sides an aristocratic *consilium quoti-
dianum* and an electing, legislating and deciding *consilium generale*
(c. 12).—Analogous reforms in the Church are proposed; II. c. 22—33.

172. See in particular the transactions of the French Estates of Popular
1484, and on them Bezold, Hist. Zeitschr. vol. 36 (1876) 361 ff., and reignty in
Baudrillart, Bodin et son temps, p. 10; the remarks of Philippe de France.
Comynes in Baudrillart, p. 11 ff.; the doctrine of Jacob. Almain,
Expos. ad Occam, q. I. c. 5 and 15; Tract. de auctor. eccl. c. 1
(Gerson, Op. II. p. 977 ff.); De dominio naturali etc. (ib. 964).

173. See the passages from the Canonists collected by v. Schulte, Papal
Die Stellung der Koncilien, p. 253 ff. Thom. Aq. Opusc. cont. err. General
Graec. II. c. 32—38. Innoc. c. 23, X. de V. S. nr. 3. Dur. Spec. Councils.
I. 1 de leg. § 5, nr. 10. Aegid. Rom. De pot. eccl. I. c. 2. Aug.
Triumph. I. q. 6, a. 6. Alv. Pel. I. a. 6 (printed in Hübler, Konst.

Ref. p. 361) and 17. Brief of Pius II. and Reply of Laelius in Gold. II. p. 1591 and 1595. Turrecremata, Summa de eccl. II. c. 54 and 65; III. c. 28, 32, 44, 47, 51, 55. Petrus de Monte in Tr. U. J. XIII. 1, p. 144 ff.

Papal Elections: Representative Character of the Cardinals.

174. If Aug. Triumphus, I. q. 3, a. 7—9, says that the electing college is not *maius papa*, since it is merely God's instrument for the *designatio personae*, makes the election *papae auctoritate*, and can confer no authority upon the pope, still in default of the college he attributes the right of election to the *Concilium Generale*, and connects this attribution with the doctrine that, during the vacancy of the see, the *collegium universalis ecclesiae* represents the Church, may assemble of its own motion or at the emperor's call, and, to this extent, possesses a 'potential superiority (*maioritas potentialis*)' which may be contrasted with the 'actual superiority (*maioritas actualis*)' of the pope. See I. q. 3, a. 2, q. 4, a. 1—8, q. 6, a. 6. However, during the vacancy the properly monarchical power, so far as its substance is concerned, lives on merely in Christ, and, so far as its use is concerned, lies dormant, for the Cardinals—here a departure from older theory—can at the most exercise the papal jurisdiction 'in minimis et quibusdam.' See also Alv. Pel. I. a. 20, Gl. on Cl. 2 de el. 1, 3, v. *non consonam*; Hinschius, Kirchenrecht, § 39.

175. See v. Schulte, Die Stellung der Koncilien, pp. 192—4 and p. 253 ff.

Deposition of an heretical Pope.

176. See c. 13, C. 2, q. 7, and c. 6, D. 40; also in v. Schulte, op. cit., the opinions of Gratian, Rufinus, Stephanus Tornacensis, Simon de Bisignano, Joh. Faventinus, Summa Coloniensis, Summa Parisiensis, Summa Lipsiensis, Huguccio, Bern. Papiensis, Joh. Teutonicus, Archidiaconus, Turrecremata, Goffr. Tranensis, Hostiensis, Joh. Andreae, Joh. de Imola, Joh. de Anania. Moreover, Gl. ord. on c. 9, C. 24, q. 1, v. *novitatibus*; Innoc. IV. on c. 23, X. de verb. sig. 5, 40, nr. 2—3; Host. de accus. nr. 7; Joh. de Anan. c. 29, X. 3, 5, nr. 9 ff.; Petrus a Monte, f. 148 ff.

The heretical Pope is deposed ipso facto.

177. This is suggested already by Joh. Teutonicus (l. c. nr. 310, p. 265), and is urged in particular by Aug. Triumphus, I. q. 5. a. 1, 2, 6 and q. 6, a. 6 (see also q. 1, a. 1, 3, q. 5, a. 3—4, q. 7, a. 1—4, q. 6, II. q. 6 and II. 45—46), and Alvarius Pelagius, I. a. 4—6 and 34, II. a. 10. Also by the Clerk in the Somnium Virid. II. c. 161 Ockham discusses the matter at length: Octo q. III. c. 8, VIII. c. 5—6, Dial. I. 6, c. 66—82.

In Matters of Faith the Pope is below

178. Already Huguccio (v. Schulte, p. 261) is of opinion that the heretical pope is 'minor quolibet catholico.' See the statement of this view in Ockham, Dial. I. 5, c. 27, and I. 6, c. 12—13, 57, 64:

in matters of faith the Council is 'maius papa' because it 'tenet the Council. vicem ecclesiae universalis.' Michael de Cesena, ep. a. 1331 (Goldast, II. p. 1237): in his quae ad fidem catholicam pertinent papa subest concilio. Henr. de Langenstein, Cons. pac. a. 1381, c. 13 and 15 in Gerson, II. p. 824, 832.

179. Thus already Huguccio and others; for *crimina notoria* Deposition of a schismatical or criminous Pope. comp. Ockham, Octo q. I. c. 17, II. c. 7, III. c. 8, VIII. c. 5—8; Dial. I. 6, c. 86. Letter of the University of Paris, an. 1394 (Schwab, pp. 131—2, Hübler, p. 362); for schism, Matth. de Cracovia (Hübler, p. 366—7). Pierre Plaoul, a. 1398 (Schwab, p. 147). Zabar., De schism. p. 697.

180. See above, Note 134. Henr. de Langenstein, l. c., c. 15. Rejection of a Pope in case of Necessity. Simon Cramaud, Pierre Plaoul and other Gallicans in Schwab, 146 ff. and Hübler, 368 ff. Opinion of the University of Bologna in 1409, in Martene, Ampl. Coll. VIII. 894. A practical application of this doctrine in the French Subtraction of Obedience (Schwab, p. 146 ff.) and Declaration of Neutrality (ib. 211).

181. Joh. Paris. c. 6, pp. 155—8, c. 14, p. 182, c. 21, p. 208, c. 25, p. 215—224.

182. Mars. Pat. II. c. 15—22, and III. concl. 32 and 41. All Marsilius on Pope and Council. other powers wielded by the popes have been usurped. The Council has authority, not only in matter of faith (II. c. 18, 20, III. c. 1 and 2), but also in matters of excommunication, punishment, legislation, raising tithes, licensing schools, canonization, establishment of festivals etc. (II. c. 7, 21, III. c. 5, 34—6).

183. See in Ockham, Dial. I. c. 5, c. 14—19, and III. tr. 1, l. 4, Divine Right of the Papal Primacy contested. the opinion that the papacy rests upon human ordinance; III. tr. 1, l. 2, c. 2, 12—14, 16—17 and 25, the reasons which can be urged against there being any single, human, monarchical head of the Church; III. tr. 1, l. 1, c. 1, the question how wide a power God has committed to the Pope. See also the references to such opinions in Petr. Alliac. (Gerson, Op. I. p. 662 ff.), Gerson (ib. II. p. 88, where it is said to be a common opinion that the pope is not *iure divino* Head of the Church) and Joh. Breviscoxa, Tract. de fide (ib. I. p. 808, esp. 878 ff.). The divinity of the primacy is decisively disputed by Nilus, arch. Thessalon., De primatu (Gold. I. pp. 30—39), Randuf, De mod. un., Wyclif, Hus, and so forth.—The *auctoritas conciliorum* is often mentioned by the older canonists as one of the forces which had constituted the primacy : e.g. Huguccio, l. c. p. 266. So d'Ailly (Gers. Op. II. p. 905) seems to favour the middle opinion : licet principaliter Rom. eccl. principatum habuerit a Domino, tamen secundario a concilio. In the same spirit, Gerson (II. p. 239 ff.) distin-

guishes those powers of the papacy that were divinely bestowed from those that have been acquired under human law.

Abolition of Papal Primacy suggested. 184. Ockham, Dial. III. tr. 1, l. 2, c. 20—27, treats the questions whether the Community of the Faithful possesses and might expediently use a power of changing the regal form of ecclesiastical government into an aristocratical, and *vice versa*. Also (c. 28) from the principle of autonomy (quaelibet ecclesia et quilibet populus Christianus propria autoritate ius proprium statuere pro sua utilitate potest) he deduces the right of every people to give itself a separate ecclesiastical head, in case the Pope be heretical, the papal see be long vacant, or access to Rome be impossible.

185. Ockham, Dial. III. tr. 2, l. 3, c. 4—13. And then to the like effect Henr. de Langenstein, Cons. pac. c. 14 and 15.

186. Ockham, Octo q. I. c. 15, III. c. 9; Dial. III. tr. 1, l. 1, c. 1 (where the fifth of the suggested opinions seems to be his own).

The Council may judge the Pope. 187. Ockham, Octo q. I. c. 17, III. c. 8; Dial. I. 5, c. 27; I. 6, c. 12—13, 57, 64, 69—72, 86. See Nilus, as in Note 183. Anonymus De aetat. eccl. c. 6, p. 28 : nemo primam sedem iudicare debet, sed hoc pertinet ad dominam et reginam sponsam Christi, cuius servus et dispensator est papa, quam universales synodi repraesentant. Somn. Virid. I. c. 161. Henr. de Langenstein, Cons. pac. c. 15.

Right of the Church to assemble and to constitute a Council. 188. Ockham, Dial. I. 6, c. 84 : this is but one instance of the general right of every autonomous *populus*, of every *communitas*, of every *corpus*, to assemble itself, or to constitute an assembly of deputies : potest aliquos eligere qui vicem gerant totius communitatis aut corporis absque alterius autoritate. So the Universal Church, when the holy see is vacant, might *per se convenire* were her size small enough, and, as it is, may assemble 'per aliquos electos a diversis partibus ecclesiae.' The impulse to such an assemblage may come from the temporal powers or from all the laity, in case the organs which in the first instance are entitled to give it, the prelates and divines, make default. Comp. Langenstein, l. c. c. 15 : Conrad de Gelnhausen, Tr. de cong. concil. (Martene, Thesaur. II. p. 1200).

Theory of the Conciliar Party. 189. Zabarella, De schism. p. 703, and upon c. 6, X. 1, 6, nr. 16 : id quod dicitur quod papa habet plenitudinem potestatis, debet intelligi non solus sed tanquam caput universitatis : ita quod ipsa potestas est in ipsa universitate tanquam in fundamento, sed in ipso tanquam ministro, per quem haec potestas explicatur. Petr. Alliac. de pot. eccl. (Gerson, Op. II. p. 949 ff.): the plenitude of ecclesiastical power is 'in papa tanquam in subiecto ipsam recipiente et ministerialiter exercente,...in universali ecclesia tanquam in obiecto ipsam causaliter et finaliter continente,...in generali concilio tanquam

in exemplo ipsam repraesentante et regulariter dirigente.' For Gerson
see the next note. Theod. a Niem, De schismate. Randuf, De
mod. un. especially c. 2, goes furthest: the Universal Church has
the power of the keys from God, the Roman Church has the exercise
thereof only in so far as this has been conceded to her by the
Universal Church.

190. See last Note. The whereabouts of ecclesiastical power
is more thoroughly discussed by Gerson than by others: Gers. II. Gerson's Theory.
225 ff.; Gold. II. 1384 ff. This power bestowed by Christ's mandate
must in all its elements be regarded from three points of view (c. 6).
'In se formaliter et absolute' (i.e. regarded abstractedly and according
to its simple essence) it is unchangeably and indestructibly in the
Church, thereby being meant the complete system of all essential
offices, among which offices the primacy is only one, so that it is a
part within the whole (c. 7). 'Respective et quodammodo materialiter' (i.e. regard being had to the 'subject' in which this power
resides) it is in the office-holders for the time being and to this extent
also in the Pope, but, if need be, can be changed or taken away
(c. 8). 'Quoad exercitium et usum' it is, in a yet more changeable
and more limited fashion, allotted among the various organs according to the Church's constitution (c. 9). In the first of these three
senses the power comes directly from Christ; in the second and third
senses 'mediante homine.'—Then as to the division of power among
ecclesiastical organs, the 'plenitudo' is both in the Pope and the
'ecclesia synodaliter congregata.' It is in the latter more aboriginally
and more fully in four respects (ratione indeviabilitatis, extensionis,
regulationis, generalis extensionis). Indeed it is in the Pope 'formaliter et monarchice'; but it is in the Church as in its final cause (in
ecclesia ut in fine) and as in its ordaining, regulating and supplementing wielder (ordinative, regulative et suppletive). It therefore
is exercised by the Pope, while the Council 'usum et applicationem
regulat,' and 'mortuo vel eiecto papa supplet' (c. 10—11; also '*concordia* quod plenitudo eccl. pot. sit in summo pontifice *et* in ecclesia,'
Op. II. p. 259 and Goldast, II. p. 1405). In its *latitudo*, on the other
hand, the ecclesiastical power is bestowed on *all* offices and therefore
in the highest degree on the Pope, but belongs to him only in so far
as respect is paid to the subordinate but independent power of other
offices and to the all-embracing power of the Council. (Hübler's
account of Gerson's trichotomy (p. 385 ff.) is not quite accurate.)

191. Zabarella, De schism. pp. 703, 709, and c. 6, X. 1, 6, nr. Practical
15—20: 'ipsa universitas totius ecclesiae' is to cooperate in arduous Powers of the
matters, to decide on good or bad administration, to accuse, to Council.

depose, and can never validly alienate these rights to the Pope. Gerson, De auferibilitate papae (Op. II. p. 209 and Gold. II. p. 1411) cons. 10 and 12—19, De unitate eccl. (Op. II. 113), De pot. eccl. c. 11 (comp. also Op. II. p. 275): the Church or the General Council representing the Church can repress abuses of power, can direct and moderate; can depose the Pope 'auctoritative, iudicialiter et iuridice,' not merely 'conciliative aut dictative vel denuntiative'; nay, can imprison him and put him to death: Aristotle teaches that every *communitas libera* has a like inalienable right against its *princeps*. See also Randuf, c. 5 and 9; Pierre du Mont de St Michel in Hübler, p. 380, and the doings at Constance, ib. 101—2 and 262.

Power of the Council to assemble. 192. Petr. Alliac. Propos. util. (Gerson, Op. II. p. 112): a right of the Council to assemble of its own accord is deduced both from the power given by Christ and (after Ockham's fashion) from the natural right of every *corpus civile seu civilis communitas vel politia rite ordinata* to assemble itself for the preservation of its unity. (Somewhat otherwise at an earlier date, ib. I. pp. 661—2.) Randuf, c. 3 (p. 164). Less unconditionally, Gerson, Propos. (Op. II. p. 123), De un. eccl. (ib. 113), De aufer. pap. (c. 11, ib. 211) and De pot. eccl. (ib. 249). Zabarella, De schism. pp. 689—694, attributes the right of summons to the Cardinals, and, failing them, to the Emperor 'loco ipsorum populorum,' since he represents the whole Christian people, 'cum in eum translata sit iurisdictio et potestas universi orbis': in the last resort, however, the Council may assemble itself according to the rules of Corporation Law.

Power of the Council during a Vacancy of the Holy See. 193. Gerson, De pot. eccl. c. 11. Zabar. De schism. pp. 688—9: with application to the case of a schism, for then the holy see is *quasi vacans.* Domin. Gem. Cons. 65, nr. 7.

The Cardinals are Representatives of the Whole Church. 194. Octo conclusiones per plures doctores in Italiae part. approb. ann. 1409 (Gers. Op. II. p. 110): veri cardinales in electione papae vices gerunt universalis ecclesiae Christianae. Zabarella, c. 6, X. 1, 6, nr. 9, and Panorm. eod. c. nr. 15. According to Gerson (Op. II. pp. 123, 293) the Council might institute another mode of election: according to Randuf (c. 9) it might itself elect.

An independent position assigned to the Cardinals. 195. Octo concl. l. c. Gerson, De pot. eccl. c. 7 and 11. Petr. Alliac. De pot. eccl. II. c. 1. Hübler, p. 74, and the Reform Decrees, ib. 129 and 218.

Mixed Government in the Church. 196. Gerson, De pot. eccl. c. 13: the organization of ecclesiastical power should share in the harmony and 'pulchra ordinis varietas' of *iura, leges, iurisdictiones* and *dominia*: therefore its *politia* must be compounded of the three good polities of Aristotle: the three degenerate forms also are possible in the Church. Pet. Alliac.

De pot. eccl. II. c. I (II. p. 946): the Church must have the best of constitutions, and therefore 'regimen regium, non purum, sed mixtum cum aristocratia et democratia.'

197. Zabar. De schism. pp. 703, 709. Octo concl. l. c.: delegated nature of all other powers. Pierre du Mont de St Michel, ann. 1406, in Hübler, p. 380. Gerson, De unit. eccl. (II. p. 113); Tract. quomodo et an liceat etc. (ib. 303 and Gold. II. 1515); De pot. eccl. 7 and 11: the Pope is only a *membrum* of the *corpus ecclesiae*, and is as little above the Church as a part is above the whole; much rather, if the General Council represents the Universal Church sufficiently and entirely, then of necessity it must include the papal power, whether there be a Pope, or whether he has died a natural or a civil death; but it will also include the power of the cardinals, bishops and priests. Randuf will allow to the Pope not a whit more power 'than is conceded to him by the Universal Church,' and only a power which is 'quasi instrumentalis et operativa seu executiva' (c. 2); the *concilium* is thoroughly 'supra papam,' and to it he owes obedience (c. 9); the Sovereignty of the Council is inalienable and all Canon Law to the contrary is invalid (c. 17; comp. c. 23). Add the famous decree of Session V. of the Synod of Constance, and Gerson, II. p. 275 thereon.

The Council above the Pope.

198. Gerson, De pot. eccl.: the 'congregatio totius universitatis hominum' could, it is true, establish the Empire, but could not, without Christ, have laid the foundation of the Church (c. 9); the Church is a system of offices, including the papacy, which were instituted by Christ and are indestructible (c. 7 and 9); the papacy, though as a function it is subject to alteration and may be temporarily dispensed with (c. 8), is as an institution indestructible (c. 11). Comp. De auferib. pap. c. 8 and 20, where this is made the distinctive difference between the constitution of the Church and civil constitutions. See also Op. II. pp. 130, 146, 529—30, and IV. p. 694.

Gerson on Divine Right of the Papacy.

199. See Randuf, l. c., c. 5.

200. In the Concordantia Catholica. See also his De auctor. praes. in Düx, I. p. 475 ff.

201. Gregory of Heimburg in his polemical writings touching the strife about the bishopric of Brixen: as to which see Brockhaus, Gregor v. Heimburg, pp. 149—259. [For this quarrel the English reader should refer to Creighton, Papacy, III. 237: Nicholas of Cusa and Gregory of Heimburg were concerned in it and Aeneas Sylvius was the then Pope, Pius II.] According to Heimburg the Council and only the Council represents the eternal, constant, infallible Church, realizes the Church's unity in a democratic form, and is

Popular Sovereignty in the Church.

greater than the monarchical Head (Gold. II. 1604 ff., 1615 ff.,
1626 ff.). Immediately from Christ it has power over the Pope in
matters of faith, unity and reform, and is his *superior*. From the
Pope lies an appeal to the Council, as in Rome an appeal lay from
Senate to People (ib. 1583, 1589, 1591, 1595, 1627); and a papal
prohibition of such an appeal is invalid (ib. 1591 and 1628). If no
Council be sitting, the appeal is to a future Council, since once in
every ten years the authority of the Church scattered throughout the
world—an authority which lies dormant during the intervals—should
become visible (ib. 1580—91).—Compare Almain, Expos. ad octo q.
I. c. 15, and Tract. de auctor. eccl. et conc. gen. (Gers. Op. II. p.
977 ff.): the Church is a Limited Monarchy, in which the Council
ratione indeviabilitatis stands above the Pope, sits in judgment on him,
receives appeals from him, restrains him by laws, can depose him,
and so forth.—Aeneas Sylvius, Comment. de gestis Basil. concilii
libr. II.: the comparison to the relationship between King and
People is consistently pursued.

Canonists and the Council.

202. Comp. Ludov. Rom., Panormitanus (e.g. upon c. 2, X. 1,
6, nr. 2: potestas ecclesiastica est in papa et in tota ecclesia, in papa
ut in capite, in ecclesia ut in corpore; c. 3, eod. nr. 2 --4; c. 6, eod.
nr. 15; c. 17, X. 1, 33, nr. 2), Decius (e.g. c. 4, X. 1, 6, nr. 1—22;
c. 5, eod. nr. 3; Cons. 151), Henr. de Bouhic (e.g. c. 6, X. 1, 6),
Marcus (e.g. Dec. 1. q. 935), and so forth.

The System of Antonius de Rosellis.

203. The Pope stands as Monarch (*caput*) above the Council:
but so soon as he prescribes anything against the Faith or the weal of
the Church or beyond his official competence, the Council stands
above him, judges him, and receives appeals from him (II. c. 13—22,
and III. c. 16—17). Although therefore he normally has the plenitude of power and his opinion has precedence over that of 'the
whole body mystical,' still the judgment of the whole Council takes
precedence 'in a matter of faith, or schism, or where the good of the
universal Church is in question' (III. c. 26—27), even if this good be
but some secondary good; for example, if there be question as to the
appointment of officers. When there is no pope or there are more
popes than one or the pope is heretical, then the Council has all
power (II. c. 24). The election of popes belongs to the Church
universal which has committed it to the cardinals (I. c. 48). Normally it is for the Pope to summon and authorize the Council
(III. c. 1 and 3): but he is bound to summon it for every arduous
affair of the whole Church or if he himself is to be called to judgment
(ib. c. 2). If he makes default, then the Cardinals, the Emperor, or
indeed any clerk or layman may call a Council, which then con-

stitutes itself of its own authority (II. c. 4 and 24, III. c. 3). Against a pope who has been condemned or who impedes or dissolves a Council which might depose him, there is a general right of resistance and renunciation (II. c. 23, 26—30, III. c. 4—6). To deal with 'mixed' affairs 'mixed' councils, to which the Church should submit, are to be summoned by the joint action of the spiritual and temporal powers (III. c. 15—18 and 21—22).

204. Turrecremata, De pot. pap. c. 38. So also Nicholas of Cues (Op. 825—9) in his later days: for Plurality is evolved out of Unity, and the Body out of the Head.—After as well as before the reaction in favour of the Papacy, the papalists admit the superiority of the Council in 'a cause of faith or of schism' (*contentio de papatu* and *causa contra papam*), but regard this as an exception. See, e.g., Card. Alexandr. c. 3, D. 21, c. 1, D. 23, summa, and c. 1, D. 15; Domin. Jacobatius Card. De consiliis, esp. IV. a. 7, nr. 29—31 and VI. a. 3, nr. 41 and 58—60, comp. with VI. a. 3, nr. 61; also Petrus de Monte and Turrecremata, in Schulte, Geschichte, II. p. 319 and 327. *Popular Sovereignty denied.*

205. As to the part assigned to delegates of Princes, Towns and Universities, see Hübler, p. 119, note 3, 120, note 5; Voigt, Enea Sylvio, I. p. 102 ff. Gerson, De pot. eccl. (II. p. 250), allows the laity only consultative voices. Even Nic. Cus. would allow them a real voice only under certain conditions, but lets all parishioners take part in the parochial synods, and the laity are to cooperate in the election of parsons and bishops (II. c. 16, III. c. 8—24). *Lay Representatives in the Councils.*

206. Gerson, Propos. coram Anglicis, ann. 1409 (Op. II. pp. 128 —130), De aufer. pap. (ib. 209 ff.), De pot. eccl. c. 7 and 9, Sermo in Op. II. p. 436 ff. So also Petr. Alliac. (ib. I. p. 666 ff. and 690) and Nic. Cus. (I. c. 7—10 and II. c. 19) regard the Priesthood as the essential and distinctive mark of the Church. As to Heinrich v. Langenstein, see his biography by O. Hartwig, I. pp. 56—57. [Dr Gierke here contrasts an idea of the Church which is *anstaltlich* with one which is *genossenschaftlich*. Some learning of a technically legal kind is implied by the employment of these words, and it cannot be briefly explained in English. But we shall not go far wrong if we contrast the idea of the Church as 'a corporation aggregate,' *congregatio fidelium*, with that of the Church as a system (*Inbegriff*) of personified offices, or (as we say in England) of 'corporations sole.'] *The Church an Institute rather than a Fellowship.*

207. So e.g. in Randuf, De mod. un. in Gerson, Op. II. p. 161 ff.

208. Ockham, Dial. I. 5, c. 1—35. So almost verbatim Petr. Alliac. (Gers. Op. I. p. 661 ff.) who, however, does not draw infer- *Fallibility of every*

Part of the ences as to the active participation of the laity in the constitution of
Church.
the Church. Comp. Randuf, c. 3.

The Laity
and the
Election
of Popes.

209. Ockham, Dial. III. tr. 2, l. 3, c. 4—15 : refuting opinions
which would attribute this right only to the Canons, or the Clergy, or
the Emperor.

The
Emperor's
part in
Papal
Elections.

210. Ockham, l. c., c. 5, 7, 12 (vice omnium eligeret) : not as
Emperor (c. 2, 3, 13), nor by the authority of the Pope (c. 5, 7).
Comp. Octo q. IV. c. 6 ; also III. c. 8, and I. c. 17.

The
Temporal
Magistrate
as Repre-
sentative
of the
Laity.

211. See e.g. Ockham, Octo q. III. c. 8, Dial. I. 6, c. 85,
91—100.—So too Wyclif and Hus, rejecting the severance of Clergy
and Laity, end by placing the ecclesiastical power in the hands of the
State. See Lechner, Johan v. Wiclif, I. p. 566 ff. and 597 ff.

The
Objectifi-
cation of
Office or
Dignity.

212. [Dr Gierke here refers to other parts of his work in which
he has given copious illustrations of this matter. The office or
dignity can be 'objectified,' i.e. conceived as a 'thing' in which
rights exist, and which remains the same while men successively
hold it ; and then again it can be 'subjectified' and conceived as a
person (or substitute for a person) capable of owning things. In the
present note he cites from Baldus 'dignitas...vice personae fungitur,'
and refers to a legal opinion touching a mitre which the deposed
John XXIII. was detaining from Martin V. and which was said to
belong to the (subjectified) Apostolic See.]

The
Prelate as
Repre-
sentative
of his
Church.

213. [Our author here refers to his treatment of this subject in
other parts of his book. It was generally agreed that, although the
Prelate was very often entitled solely to exercise those rights which
legal texts ascribed to his *ecclesia*, still he was not the *ecclesia*. Divers
analogies were sought. He acts 'sicut maritus in causa uxoris' ;
or again, he is the *tutor* and the *ecclesia* is his *pupillus*. They
all imply that, beside the Prelate, there is some other person concerned. Then practical inferences were drawn : e.g., a Prelate may
not be judge *in causa propria* ; but it is otherwise *in causa ecclesiae
suae*.]

Is the
Pope the
Church?

214. Only in this sense 'papa ipse ecclesia' (e.g. Huguccio, l. c.,
p. 263), 'papa est sedes apostolica' (Dur. Spec. I. 1 de leg. § 5, nr.
1), 'ecclesia intelligitur facere quod facit papa' (Joh. And. Nov. s.
c. 1 in Sexto, 2, 12, nr. 1). Comp. Domin. Gem. Cons. 93, nr. 12 ;
Cardin. Alex. in summa D. 15 (what the head does, the body does) ;
Jacobat., De conc. IV. a. 7, nr. 29—31, VI. a. 3, nr. 41 and 58 ff. : the
present Pope alone represents the whole church and is thus *ecclesia
corporalis* : such also is the case of a Bishop in those matters in
which the counsel, but not the consent, of the Chapter is requisite.

215. Ockham, Dial. I. 5, c. 25 : only within certain limits is

the Pope 'persona publica totius communitatis gerens vicem et
curam.' Zabar. c. 6, X. 1, 6, nr. 16 : non solus sed tanquam caput
universitatis. Gerson, De aufer. c. 8—20, De pot. eccl. c. 7. Nic.
Cus. I. c. 14—17, II. c. 27 ff. Ant. Ros. II. c. 20—24, III. c. 16—17.

216. Baldus, Rubr. C. 10, 1, nr. 12, 13, 18 : princeps repraesentat illum populum et ille populus imperium etiam mortuo
principe; but 'princeps *est* imperium, *est* fiscus,' because only in him
does the Empire live, will and act. Cons. III. c. 159, nr. 5 : 'ipsa
respublica repraesentata' can be bound by the acts of the Emperor.
Also Ockham, in Note 210 above, and Zabarella in Note 192.

217. Already Joh. Saresb. IV. c. 3 : the king 'gerit fideliter
ministerium,' if he 'suae conditionis memor, universitatis subiectorum se personam gerere recordatur'; compare c. 5. Thom. Aquin.
Summa Theol. II. 1, q. 90, ad 3 : Ordinare autem aliquid in bonum
commune est vel totius multitudinis vel alicuius gerentis vicem totius
multitudinis: et ideo condere legem vel pertinet ad totam multitudinem
vel pertinet ad personam publicam quae totius multitudinis curam
habet. So again ib. 97, a. 3. Mars. Pat. Def. pac. I. 15 : when the
rulers (*principantes*) act within the sphere constitutionally assigned
to them (secundum communitatis determinationem legalem), their
act is that of the whole community (hoc facientibus his, id facit
communitas universa). Baldus, Consil. 159, nr. 5 and especially
1 Feud. 14, pr. nr. 1 : 'The city of Bologna belongs to the Church!'
exclaims Baldus, 'Much rather to the Bolognese! For the Church
has no authority there, save as (*tanquam*) the Republic, of which
Republic it bears the name and image. Even so the city of Siena
belongs to the Kaiser, but more to the Sienese: for republic, fisc,
and prince are all one; the *respublica est sicut vivacitas sensuum*; the
fisc is the stomach, purse and fastness of the republic; therefore
the Emperor would be *quasi tyrannus* if he did not behave himself
as the Republic, and such are many other kings who seek their own
profit: for he is a robber, a *praedo*, who seeks his own profit and not
the profit of the owner.' [Dr Gierke gives this interesting passage in
Latin.] See also nr. 2 : the office of ruler (*dignitas*) is inalienable,
being 'totius universitatis decus.' Barth. Salic. l. 4, C. 2, 54 : the
civitas as such can demand a *restitutio in integrum*, even if the Ruler
who acted in its name profited by the transaction : and, despite
the *translatio*, this holds good of the *respublica imperii*. Jason, l. c.,
nr. 8. Nic. Cus., above in Note 171.

218. Baldus, Cons. III. c. 159, nr. 5 : loco duarum personarum
rex fungitur; I. c. 271, nr. 4 : bona propria...non tanquam rex, sed
tanquam homo et animal rationabile. Alex. Tart. l. 25 § 1, Dig. 29,

2, nr. 4: fiscalis res et Caesaris res est eadem, quia omnia iura fiscalia transferuntur in eum tanquam imperatorem non tanquam Titium : but with the 'patrimonium Caesaris' it is otherwise, for this he has 'tanquam Titius.' Marcus, Dec. I. q. 338, nr. 1—7. [Reference is made by Dr Gierke to other parts of his book where the dual personality of bishops and the like is discussed : a bishop, it was said, had two persons; one 'in quantum est episcopus'; the other 'in quantum est Petrus vel Martinus.']

King's Property and State's Property.
219. See last note. Also Ockham, Octo q. II. c. 2 : what the Kaiser had before he was Kaiser or afterwards acquired 'per se et non dignitati,' is his private property. On the other hand, the 'bona et iura imperii' exist 'propter bonum commune subditorum et non propter bonum proprium principatus.' Of these last he can dispose 'non nisi propter bonum commune seu utilitatem omnium subditorum,' and if he do otherwise he is bound to make restitution like anyone else who misapplies goods that have been entrusted to him.

Acts of the Prince and acts of the Man.
220. Baldus, Cons. I. 271, 326, 327; III. c. 159, 371. The question is whether and in what case a Prince, elective or hereditary, is bound by the acts of his predecessor, and Baldus always acutely reduces this to the question in what cases the State, or the Fisc, is bound by the acts of its highest organ. When it comes to particulars, he applies the ordinary rules of Corporation Law touching the liability of corporations for the contracts and torts of their governors; but in the case of Kings and more especially of hereditary Kings he supposes an unusually wide power of representation. A king is no mere 'legitimus administrator,' but stands 'loco domini' (nam regnum magis assimilatur dominio quam simplici regimini); and in particular his power to bind by contract extends to unusual as well as to usual affairs. In the same sense, Jason, Cons. III. c. 10, distinguishes the Ruler's 'pacta personalia,' and 'pacta realia nomine suae gentis inita' (c. 8), extends the principle to judicial acts (nr. 10), appeals to ecclesiastical analogies (nr. 15—19), and then declares that the successor is bound as successor 'si princeps faciat ea quae sunt de natura vel consuetudine sui officii' (nr. 21), or if the convention was made 'in utilitatem status' (nr. 14). Comp. Bologninus, Cons. 6. On the other hand Picus a Monte Pico, I. Feud. 3, nr. 1—3, and I. Feud. 7, nr. 1—17, once more throws the whole question into confusion.

221. Nic. Cus., above in Notes 171 and 209; Gerson, De pot. eccl. c. 10, and Concordia, p. 259.

Duties towards
222. See, e.g. Eng. Volk. De reg. princ. IV. c. 21—29 ; alongside the duties arising between individuals as men, as fellow countrymen,

as fellow burgesses, as kinsmen, as members of social groups, stand *Indivi-* their duties to the Whole which arise out of 'illa coniunctio qua *duals and Duties to* unusquisque privatus universitati sive reipublicae tanquam membrum *the Com-* corpori et tanquam pars toti consociatur.' Comp. VII. c. 8—12 as to *munity.* the different 'status personae.'

223. Mars. Pat. I. c. 12 : the *populus* is sovereign ; the *populus* *Rights of* is the *universitas civium* ; a *civis* is one who 'secundum suum *the Com-munity* gradum' takes part in public affairs ; excluded are 'pueri, servi, *exercised* advenae ac mulieres.' So Thom. Aq. Comm. ad Polit. p. 452 and *by its Active* 460 (comp. also Summa Theol. II. 1, q. 105, a. 1) and Patric. Sen. *Members.* De inst. reip. I. 3, p. 22 define *civis* in the Aristotelian way, so as to equate it with 'active citizen.'

224. Lup. Bebenb. c. 17, p. 406 : et intelligo populum Romani *Repre-* imperii connumeratis principibus electoribus ac etiam aliis prin- *sentation of the* cipibus, comitibus et baronibus regni et imperii Romanorum : nam *People as* appellatione populi continentur etiam patricii et senatores. And so *a System of Estates.* other writers.—Even the Radical Marsilius admits to the legislative assembly everyone 'secundum suum gradum'; tries to secure the influence of the *docti et sapientes* in the discovery and redaction of laws, and apparently would give no unconditional support to a system of equal votes, for the *valentior pars* which decides seems to be measured 'secundum politiarum consuetudinem honestam.' See Def. pac. I. 12—13 and 15; also De transl. imp. c. 6.

225. Mars. Pat. Def. I. pac. c. 12—13 : the *voluntas* of the *uni-* *Will of* *versitas civium* becomes law by being expressly declared in the *the People expressed* *congregatio generalis* ; I. c. 17 : the act is a single act though done by *by Assem-* many in common ; III. c. 6. So also Aegid. Col. II. 1, c. 3. *blies.*

226. From Corporation Law are deduced the exclusive right of *The Rules* the Pope to summon the Council (e.g. Card. Alex. c. 2, D. 17), and *of Cor-poration* by others a right of summons normally to be exercised by the Pope *Law are* (Jacobat. De Conc. IV. a. 7, nr. 24; Ant. Ros. III. c. 1—3), but *applied to Political* supplemented by a right of the Cardinals or such part of their body *Assem-* as does not make default (Zabar. De schism. p. 689; Ros. III. c. 3 ; *blies.* Decius, Cons. 151, nr. 13—22) and of the Kaiser (above, Note 48); and the right of the Council to assemble itself is similarly deduced (above, Notes 188, 192, 203). It is opined that if all the members, though unsummoned, were present, then, as in the case of other corporations, they might proceed to business (Ros. II. c. 4). If all are not present, then Zabarella (comp. De schismate, pp. 693—4) vouching Innocent [IV.] would require the presence of two-thirds, who would then have to summon the others and wait until they either appeared or could be declared guilty of contumacy. On the

other hand, Rosellus (III. c. 4) and Jacobatius (IV. a. 7, nr. 25—8) argue that in the case of the Council an *imminens periculum vel necessitas* may always be presupposed, and that, when this is so, even a minority can summon the others and preclude them, since, according to Corporation Law, the *pars in casu periculi non contumax* is in truth the *maior et sanior pars.* [In an earlier part of his book Dr Gierke has explored the formation of a law and theory of corporate assemblies. The legists, relying on certain texts which concerned the Roman *decuriones,* were inclined strictly to require the presence of two-thirds of the members. This requirement the canonists mitigated in divers fashions. They also held that if no meeting had been summoned, but two-thirds of the members were present, those present might proceed to business, but ought to summon the others unless there were danger (*periculum*) in delay. Then, according to the canonists, it was not a mere *maior pars* but a *maior et sanior pars* that could validly outvote a minority.]

Corporation Law and the General Council.

227. See especially Jacobat. IV. a. 7. He elaborately argues that l. 3 et 4, Dig. 3, 4 are not to be applied, and that, according to the canonical principle 'Vocati non venientes constituunt se alienos,' even a minority can act (nr. 1—16); also that the right of the *contempti* to re-open a question has no existence in this case, since a *citatio generalis* is sufficient (nr. 16—23); and so forth. Also Ros. III. c. 7—14 (in c. 14 the requirement of two-thirds is set aside). Card. Alex. c. 2, D. 17. [The Canonists had practically circumvented the requirement that two-thirds of the members should be present, by holding that those who failed to appear when duly summoned were in contempt, had 'made themselves alien' and were not to be counted.]

Majorities how reckoned.

228. Zabar. De schism. p. 689. Panorm. c. 26, X. 2, 27, nr. 13. Even in the Council the voice that prevailed was to be that of the greater 'and sounder' part (Card. Alex. c. 1, D. 15 in fine; Jacobat. IV. a. 3, nr. 1—41); and with this was connected the principle that matters of faith were not to be decided by mere majorities (Jacobat. l. c. nr. 7—12 and 25; Nic. Cus. I. c. 4). The words of Cusanus (II. c. 15) carry us back to old Germanic thoughts: quia quisque ad synodum pergens iudicio maioris partis se submittere tenetur... synodus finaliter ex concordia omnium definit. [The old Germanic thought is that unanimity is requisite, but that a minority ought to and can be compelled to give way.] Also we may see that the *iura singulorum* are to be protected against the vote of the majority (Jacobat. l. c. nr. 27—32). During the strife over the adjournment of the Council of Basel, an odd inference was drawn from this

principle, namely, that the minority or even any one member could resist an adjournment to another place on the ground of 'vested right' (*ius quaesitum*) : see Ludov. Rom. Cons. 352, nr. 10—24, and Cons. 522; Jacobat. l. c. nr. 36—39, and ib. a. 7, nr. 35. [Under the rubric *iura singulorum*, medieval law withdraws from the power of the majority rights of individual corporators which are more or less closely implicated in the property and affairs of the corporation. A modern example would be the shareholder's 'share': this does not lie at the mercy of a majority; a medieval example would be a canon's 'prebend.']

229. The plan of voting by Nations was justified by the rules that dealt with the conjoint action of divers *corpora* (Panorm. c. 40, X. 1, 6, nr. 6, Jacobat. IV. a. 3, nr. 52—57), while the opponents of that plan made much of the unity of the whole body of the Church (Card. Alex. c. 1, D. 15 in fine). See Hübler, p. 279, n. 60 and 316 ff. [The federalistic character of medieval groups gave rise to many elaborate schemes for securing a certain amount of unity and independence to those smaller bodies that were components of a larger body, e.g. the faculties and nations within an university.] *[margin: Majorities and Nations in the Council.]*

230. See e.g. Mars. Pat. Def. pac. I. c. 12, 13, 15, 17 : what the *valentior pars* does is 'pro eodem accipiendum' as that which the *tota universitas* does, for the 'valentior pars totam universitatem repraesentat.' Eng. Volk. De reg. pr. I. c. 5, 7, 10, 14. Lup. Bebenb. c. 6 and 12. Ockham and Ant. Ros. as above, in Note 145. *[margin: The Majority as a Representation of the Whole.]*

231. Ockham, Dial. III. tr. 2, l. 1, c. 29—30 : quaecunque universitas seu communitas particularis propter culpam suam potest privari quocunque honore et iure speciali; and therefore for *culpa* the Romans may be deprived of their lordship in the Empire; and so with other nations; and so for their *culpa* whole portions of mankind can be deprived of their active rights in the World-State, and many think that this has happened to the Jews and Heathen, their share in the Empire having 'devolved' to the Christians. But, according to l. 2, c. 5, there ought to be a formal *sententia* of the *universitas mortalium* or its representatives. Whether the papal 'translatio a Graecis in Germanos' was founded on this principle and whether that act was rightful or wrongful could, says Ockham (Octo q. II. c. 9), be known only to one who possessed all the documents of that age. *[margin: Corporate Torts of the Roman People.]*

232. See the definition given by Konrad v. Gelnhausen, De congreg. conc. temp. schism. an. 1391 (in Martene II. p. 1200) : concilium generale est multarum vel plurium personarum rite con- vocatarum repraesentantium vel gerentium vicem diversorum statuum, *[margin: Representative Character of the Council.]*

ordinum et personarum totius Christianitatis venire aut mittere volentium aut potentium ad tractandum de bono communi universalis ecclesiae in unum locum communem congregatio. Gerson, De aufer. c. 10; De pot. eccl. c. 7 ff. Nic. Cus. De auctor. praes. (in Düx, I. p. 475 ff.): the Pope is the remotest, the General Council the directest and surest representative of the Universal Church. Decius, c. 4, X. 1, 6, nr. 21.

The Council a mere Representative.

233. See Ockham, Dial. I. 5, c. 25—28: even the representative Council is only *pars ecclesiae*; it stands below the 'communitas fidelium si posset convenire'; is summoned by human agency and can be dissolved; and it can err, so that resistance to, appeal from, and accusation against it are not inconceivable. Similarly at some points, Petr. Alliac. in Gers. Op. I. p. 688 ff., and again at the Synod of Constance (Sess. I. in Mansi, XXVII. p. 547).—So Breviscoxa (Gers. Op. I. p. 898) speaks with hesitation about the Council's infallibility.—On the other hand, Gerson and Cusanus (II. c. 15—16) maintain its infallibility, its representation of the Church being absorptive.

Election and Representation.

234. Nic. Cus. I. c. 15 and II. c. 18: it is on the ground of election that 'praesidentes figurant suam subiectam ecclesiam' and that Councils of such prelates represent the larger circles of the Church; and so on up to a representation of the Church Universal. Ant. Butr. c. 17, X. 1, 33, nr. 27—28: at the Provincial Councils the Prelates and 'Rectores' do not appear as individuals, but 'quilibet praelatus vel rector tenet vicem universitatis.' Zabar. c. ult., X. 3, 10, nr. 1—3. Panorm. c. 17, X. 1, 33, nr. 2: in the General Council 'praelati totius orbis conveniunt et faciunt unum corpus, repraesentantes ecclesiam universalem'; so the *praelati et maiores* of the province represent their *universitates*, and so in their Provincial Assembly they represent the *universitates ecclesiarum* of the province; and again 'in una dioecesi...praelati et capitula repraesentant totum clerum'; and so also is it in the constitution of Universities.

Election of Lay Representatives.

235. Ockham, Dial. I. 6, c. 84 (above, Note 209): he appeals to the general right of every people, every commune. every *corpus*, to assemble, not only in proper person but also 'per aliquos electos a diversis partibus,' for every body 'potest aliquos eligere qui vicem gerant totius communitatis aut corporis.'

Representation in Temporal Assemblies.

236. See above, Notes 161—3, 168, 172. Marsil. Pat. I. c. 12—13: vicem et auctoritatem universitatis civium repraesentant. Nic. Cus. III. c. 12 and 25. Men thought that certain texts in the Corpus Juris assigned a similar position to the Roman Senate. [Our author is referring in particular to certain words of Pomponius (l. 2, § 9,

Dig. 1, 2) which, he says, exercised a marked influence on Political
Theory; deinde quia difficile plebs convenire coepit, populus certe
multo difficilius in tanta turba hominum, necessitas ipsa curam
reipublicae ad senatum deduxit. He here remarks that already in
the Brachylogus—a manual of Roman law which he is inclined to
ascribe to Orléans and the twelfth century—these words of Pomponius
are supposed to record a formal transfer of power by the *populus* to
the senate.]

237. See the formulation of the general principle in Ockham
(above, Note 235) and Mars. Pat. l. c.

238. Nic. Cus. III. c. 12 and 25 : elected governors are to The
represent communities; assemblies of such governors are to repre- Represent the lands and provinces; and an *universale concilium imperiale* Parlia-
is to represent the *Reich*: in this council 'praesides provinciarum of
suas provincias repraesentantes ac etiam universitatum magnarum Nicholas
rectores ac magistri' and also men of senatorial rank are to meet; of Cues.
they will compose the 'corpus imperiale cuius caput est Caesar, et
dum simul conveniunt in uno compendio repraesentativo, totum im-
perium collectum est.'

The Representative Parliamentarism of Nicholas of Cues.

239. Mars. Pat. I. c. 12—13; he says in c. 12: sive id fecerit The
universitas praedicta civium aut eius pars valentior per se ipsam Radical-
immediate, sive id alicui vel aliquibus commiserit faciendum, qui Marsilius.
legislator simpliciter non sunt nec esse possunt, sed solum ad aliquid
et quandoque ac secundum primi legislatoris auctoritatem.

The Radicalism of Marsilius.

240. Lup. Bebenb. c. 5, p. 352—3 and c. 6, p. 357—8 : the The Prince
Prince Electors make the election 'repraesentantes in hoc omnes Electors
principes et populum Germaniae, Italiae et aliarum provinciarum et sentatives.
terrarum regni et imperii, quasi vice omnium eligendo.' Were it not
for their institution, the 'universitas ipsa' would have to make the
choice; but, as it is, the Electors choose 'vice et auctoritate universitatis.' When therefore they have made the choice, 'proinde est ac
si tota universitas principum et populi...fecisset'; to prove which
voucher is made of l. 6 § 1, Dig. 3, 4, and c. ult. in Sexto *de prae-*
bendis. See also the participation of the Electors in the deposition
of an Emperor, c. 12, p. 386—7, and in the alienation of rights of
sovereignty, c. 14, p. 396.—Comp. Ockham, Octo q. VIII. c. 3 :
'repraesentantes universitatem.' Zabar. c. 34 § *verum* X. 1, 6, nr. 8.
Nic. Cus. III. c. 4 : 'qui vice omnium eligerent.' Gregor. Heimb.
ın Gold. 1. p. 561. Ant. Ros. I. c. 48.

The Prince Electors as Representatives.

241. See above, Notes 174 and 194. Ockham, Dial. I. 5, c. 6 The
and 8. Nic. Cus. I. c. 14, 17, II. c. 14 (repraesentant); Ant. Ros. Cardinals
I. c. 48 : ab universali ecclesia, quam cardinales et electores in hoc sentatives.

The Cardinals as Representatives.

ipsam totam repraesentant.—Nic. Cus. II. c. 14—15 desires therefore
to extend to the Cardinals the elective principle, which is in his eyes
the only conceivable foundation for a mandate in political affairs.
The Cardinals ought to be elected provincial deputies forming an
Estate and constituting in some sort the aristocratic Upper House of
a parliamentarily organized Spiritual Polity.

Corporation Law and Imperial Elections.

242. Hostiensis, Johannes Andreae (c. 34, X. 1, 6, nr. 25) and
others opined that the Prince Electors made the choice as individuals, 'ut singuli.' Lup. Bebenb. c. 6, pp. 356—8, and c. 12, pp. 379
—80, argues that much rather they are representatives of an *universitas*, and must themselves meet 'tanquam collegium seu universitas'
and make the choice *communiter*. Therefore he would here apply
the principle of the 'ius gentium, civile et canonicum' which teaches
that an election made by an absolute majority is 'electio iuris inter-
pretatione concors' and exactly equivalent to an unanimous election.
So too Zabarella (c. 34 § *verum*, X. 1, 6, nr. 8) who cites Leopold: in
all respects the same procedure should be observed as 'in aliis
actibus universitatum': thus, e.g., the requirement of the presence
of two-thirds of the members, the preclusion of those who do not
attend, and so forth. Comp. also Cons. 154, nr. 6. Felinus, c. 6,
X. 1, 2, nr. 29. Bertach. Rep. v. *maior pars*, nr. 27. Petrus de
Andlo, II. c. 1—4, treats the Election of an Emperor at great length,
and in detail subjects it to Roman and canonical rules for the
election of prelates which are stated by Johannes Andreae, Antonius
de Butrio, Johannes de Anania, Baldus and Panormitanus. Thus
it is in the matter of summons and presidency, form of scrutiny,
decision with absolute majority, *accessio*, self-election; so also in the
matter of the demand for and grant of examination and approbation
on the part of the Pope, and the devolution or lapse of the election
to the Pope; and so again as to the requirement of an *actus communis*, the right of objection of *unus contemptus*, the privation of *scienter
eligentes indignum*. For he opines that 'these Electors have suc-
ceeded to the place of the Roman People, who *ut universitas* elected
an Emperor, and so the Electors must be conceived to act in the
same right [i.e. *ut universitas*], since a surrogate savours of the
nature of him whose surrogate he is.'

Corporation Law and Papal Elections. The Universal Church and the Particular Churches as Corporations.

243. See Innoc., Host., Ant. Butr., Zabar., Panorm., Dec. on
c. 6, X. 1, 6; Aug. Triumph. 1. q. 3; Alv. Pel. 1. a. 1; Ludov. Rom.
Cons. 498, nr. 1—22 (applying the whole of the law about decu-
rions); Ant. Ros. II. c. 8—10; Bertach. v. *gesta a maiori parte*.

244. [Dr Gierke here refers to other parts of his work where he
has dealt with the Canonists' conception of every church as a *corpus*.]

245. Baldus s. pac. Const. v. *imp. clem.* nr. 4: the Emperor, The Empire or State as a Corporation. Baldus explains, is speaking 'de ista magna universitate, quae omnes fideles imperii in se complectitur tam praesentis aetatis quam succes- sivae posteritatis.' Prooem. Feud. nr. 32: non potest rex facere deteriorem conditionem universitatis, i.e. regni. Rubr. C. 10, 1, nr. 11: Respublica as an 'Object' means publica res, as a 'Subject' ipsa universitas gentium quae rempublicam facit. Zabar. c. 13, X. 5, 31, nr. 1—7 brings in the learning of Corporations, defines *corpus* or *collegium* as 'collectio corporum rationabilium constituens unum corpus repraesentativum,' distinguishes 'collegia surgentia naturaliter,' which so soon as they have come into being are also 'necessaria,' and 'collegia mere voluntaria'; in the former class he reckons com- munes, provinces and realms, and therefore brings in at this point the learning of the six Aristotelian forms of government, and the doctrine of the World-Monarchies and their relation to the Church.

246. Baldus, Cons. III. c. 159. Comp. ib. c. 371, and I. c. 326 Perpetuity of the State. —327 and c. 271 (respublica et fiscus sunt quid aeternum et per- petuum quantum ad essentiam, licet disponens saepe mutetur). Comp. also Jason, Cons. III. c. 10, where in nr. 14 we already meet the phrase 'conventio facta in utilitatem *Status.*'

247. Baldus, Rubr. C. 10, 1, nr. 15—16.

248. See above, Notes 212 and 218—20; also 190 and 206.

249. See above, Notes 213—7.

250. See above, Note 118.

251. See above, Notes 221—231.

252. Expressly d'Ailly, Gerson (De pot. eccl. c. 10) and Mere Col- lectivism in the Concept of the Church. Nicholas of Cues (II. 34) vest all the rights of the Church in the 'omnes collective sumpti.' But also Marsilius, Randuf and others leave no room for doubt that for them the Church, considered as the Congregation of the Faithful, is coincident with the sum of indi- viduals. And if Ockham in one passage (Octo q. I. c. 11) names as the receiver of the divine mandate the 'persona communitatis fide- lium,' still his whole system, as set forth above, and most unambigu- ously his discussion of the whereabouts of the Church's infallibility, prove that he is not thinking of a single personality which comes to light in organization, but of a personified collective unit. See above, Notes 188 and 208.

253. Turrecrem. De pot. pap. c. 71—72: where the power of the The Church as a 'Subject' of Rights. keys is ascribed to 'the Church,' this means in truth that she has it in some of her members and the whole of it only in her head.

254. See in particular Nic. Cus. as above in Note 171, also III. The People a c. 4 (vice omnium), 12 and 25; Mars. Pat. I. c. 12—13; Lup.

Collective Unit.

Bebenb. c. 5—6; Ockham, Dial. i. 6, c. 84; Patric. Sen. De inst. reip. i. 1, 5 (multitudo universa potestatem habet collecta in unum,... dimissi autem singuli rem suam agunt).

255.   See above, Notes 215—8, 228, 230, 232—42.

The Law of Nature and the Essence of Law.

256.   That there was a Law of Nature was not doubted, nor that it flowed from a source superior to the human lawgiver and so was absolutely binding upon him.   Such was the case whatever solution might be found for that deep-reaching question of scholastic controversy which asks whether the essence of Law is Will or Reason.   In any case God Himself appeared as being the ultimate cause of Natural Law.   This was so, if, with Ockham, Gerson and d'Ailly, men saw in Natural Law a Command proceeding from the Will of God, which Command therefore was righteous and binding.   It was so, if, with Hugh de St Victor, Gabriel Biel and Almain, they placed the constitutive moment of the Law of Nature in the Being of God, but discovered dictates of Eternal Reason declaring what is right, which dictates were unalterable even by God himself.   Lastly, it was so, if, with Aquinas and his followers, they (on the one hand) derived the content of the Law of Nature from the Reason that is immanent in the Being of God and is directly determined by that *Natura Rerum* which is comprised in God Himself, but (on the other hand) traced the binding force of this Law to God's Will.   Aquinas (Summa Theol. ii. 1, q. 90—92), when he has discussed the nature, kinds and operations of a *Lex* in general, and has defined it (q. 90, a. 4) as 'quaedam rationis ordinatio ad bonum commune, et ab eo, qui curam communitatis habet, promulgata,' proceeds to put at the head of his Philosophy of Law the idea of *Lex Aeterna*.   And this, he says, as being 'ipsa ratio gubernationis rerum in Deo sicut in Principe universitatis existens,' and 'summa ratio in Deo existens,' is identical with the Being of God (*non aliud a Deo*), but at the same time is a true *Lex*, absolutely binding, and the source of every other *Lex* (omnis lex a lege aeterna derivatur); l. c. q. 91, a. 1, q. 93, a. 1—6. Immediately from this he derives the *Lex Naturalis* which is grounded in the participation by Man, as a reasonable being, in the moral order of the world (participatio legis aeternae in rationali creatura) and is perceived by the light of Natural Reason (lumen rationis naturalis) entrusted to us by God (q. 91, a. 2, q. 94).   It is a *lex promulgata*, for 'Deus eam mentibus hominum inseruit naturaliter cognoscendam' (q. 90, a. 4); it exists *in actu* and not merely *in habitu* (q. 94, a. 1); it is in its principles a true, everywhere identical, unalterable and indestructible rule for all actions (q. 94, a. 3—6).

[Dr Gierke here cites a note in his tract on Johannes Althusius

(p. 73) in which he has dealt with the same matter and from which we take the following sentences, though they reach beyond the Middle Age.]

The older view, which is more especially that of the Realists, explained the *Lex Naturalis* as an intellectual act independent of Will—as a mere *lex indicativa*, in which God was not lawgiver but a teacher working by means of Reason—in short, as the dictate of Reason as to what is right, grounded in the Being of God but unalterable even by him. (To this effect already Hugo de S. Victore Saxo, in the days of Calixtus II. and Henry V., Opera omnia, Mog. 1617, III. p. 385, de sacramentis I. p. 6, c. 6—7; later Gabriel Biel, Almain and others.) The opposite opinion, proceeding from pure Nominalism, saw in the Law of Nature a mere divine Command, which was right and binding merely because God was the law-giver. So Ockham, Gerson, d'Ailly. The prevailing opinion was of a mediating kind, though it inclined to the principle of Realism. It regarded the substance of Natural Law as a judgment touching what was right, a judgment necessarily flowing from the Divine Being and unalterably determined by that Nature of Things which is comprised in God; howbeit, the binding force of this Law, but only its binding force, was traced to God's Will. Thus Aquinas, Caietanus, Soto, Suarez. In like fashions was decided the question, What is the constitutive element of Law [or Right] in general? Most of the Schoolmen therefore held that what makes Law to be Law is 'iudicium rationis quod sit aliquid iustum.' So with even greater sharpness Soto, De iustitia et iure, Venet. 1602 (first in 1556), I. q. 1, a. 1, and Molina, Tract. v. disp. 46, §§ 10—12. Compare also Bolognetus (1534—85), De lege, iure et aequitate, Tr. U. J. 1. 289 ff. c. 3; Gregorius de Valentia, Commentarii theologici, Ingoldst. 1592, II. disp. 1, q. 1, punct. 2. The opposite party taught that Law becomes Law merely through the Will that this or that shall pass for Law and be binding; or they laid all the stress on a Command (*imperium*) given to subjects. Others, again, declared that *intellectus* and *voluntas* were equally essential. Only Suarez, who reviews at length all the older opinions, distinguished at this point between Positive Law and Natural Law, and in the case of the former sees the legislative Will (not however the law-giver's command) as the constitutive, while Reason is only a normative, moment (I. c. 4—5 and III. c. 20). In the later Philosophy of Law the derivation of all Law from Will and the explanation of both Natural and Positive Law as mere Command was well-nigh universal. Only Leibnitz (1646—1716), who in so many directions went deeper than his contemporaries, and who, perhaps for this reason, so often turned his eyes backwards towards medieval ways of thought, disputed this 'Will-Theory' with powerful words directed against Pufendorf and Cocceji. He denied the essentialness of the idea of Compulsion in the idea of Law, and argued that *Recht* was prior to *Gesetz.* 'Das Recht is nicht Recht weil Gott es gewollt hat, sondern weil Gott gerecht ist.' See Opera, ed. Dutens, Genev. 1768, IV. 3, pp. 275—83, also p. 270 ff. § 7 ff. and § 13.

[In another note Dr Gierke (Joh. Althusius, p. 74) cites the following passage from the German, Gabriel Biel (ob. 1495). In his Collectorium Sententiarum, Tubing. 1501, lib. II. dist. 35, q. un., art. 1, he says: Nam si per impossibile Deus non esset, qui est ratio divina, aut ratio illa divina esset errans, adhuc si quis ageret contra rectam rationem angelicam vel humanam aut aliam aliquam si qua esset, peccaret. Et si nulla penitus esset recta ratio, adhuc si quis ageret contra id quod agendum dictaret ratio recta si aliqua esset, peccaret. 'Already' Dr Gierke adds, 'medieval Schoolmen had hazarded the saying, usually referred to Grotius, that there would be a Law of Nature, discoverable by human reason and absolutely binding, even if there were no God, or the Deity were unreasonable or unrighteous.']

Nullity of Laws contravening the Law of Nature.

257. Thom. Aquin. Sum. Theol. II. 1, q. 91, art. 2, q. 94, a. 1—6, q. 97, a. 1 (the whole people bound); II. 2, q. 57, a. 2. Aegid. Rom. De reg. princ. III. 2, c. 29: the *rex* stands below the *lex naturalis.* Vincent. Bellovac. VII. c. 41 ff. and X. c. 87: ipso iure non valent leges quia nulla lex potest valere contra Deum. Joh. Friburg. II. t. 5, q. 204—6, t. 7, q. 43 ('leges permittentes usuras' are null). Ockham, Dial. III. tr. 1, l. 2, c. 6, and tr. 2, l. 2, c. 26—8 (as to Kaiser and Pope), ib. c. 29 (as to the *universitas populi*), and tr. 2, l. 1, c. 30 (even an unanimous decision of the *universitas mortalium* could not wholly abolish the Roman Empire). Baldus, I. Feud. 1 § 3, nr. 2 (potentius est ius naturale quam principatus), and l. 1, Cod. 1, 1, nr. 24 ff. (therefore Kaiser and Pope could not, e.g., make usury lawful). Gloss on the Sachsensp. I. a. 25 and 55. Bened. Capra, Regula 10, nr. 20—43 and 53 (as to *princeps, papa, imperator, populus seu universitas* with *iurisdictio* and *imperium*). Felinus Sand. c. 7, X. 1, 2, nr. 19—25 (as to Pope) and nr. 26 ff. (as to *imperator, princeps, populus liber*). Petr. Alliac. in Gers. Op. 1. p. 652 ff. Nic. Cus. III. c. 5. Ant. Ros. IV. c. 2—14. As to the Pope, see above, Note 132, and as to the Council, see Gerson in Note 198.

Revealed Law and

258. So in particular Thom. Aquin. Sum. Theol. II. 1, q. 91, art. 1—2 and 4—5; he thereafter (q. 98—105) treats at length of

the *lex vetus*, and (q. 106 ff.) of the *lex nova*.   Comp. Aegid. Rom. Natural
De reg. princ. III. 2, c. 24—9 (*lex naturalis*) and c. 30 (*lex divina*). Law.
Gerson, IV. p. 652—4.   See also the passages cited in the last Note,
in which the force of the *lex divina* is placed on a level with that of
the *lex naturalis*, this principle being applied, e.g., when statutes that
permit usury are pronounced void.

259.   See e.g. Thom. Aquin. l. c. q. 95, a. 2 and 4: the *lex* Nature of
humana carries into detail the *principia legis naturalis*, partly as *ius* the Ius
gentium by way of mere *conclusiones*, partly as *ius civile* by way of Gentium
determinationes.   See also ib. II. 2, q. 57, a. 3.   Aegid. Rom. III. c. 2,
c. 25 and c. 29: si dicitur legem aliquam positivam esse supra
principantem, hoc non est ut positiva, sed ut in ea reservatur virtus
iuris naturalis.   Lup. Bebenb. c. 15, p. 401.   Ockham, Dial. III. tr.
2, l. 2, c. 28: the *ius gentium*, in accordance with which the highest
power is subject to the common weal, 'non est imperatorum vel
regum per institutionem, sed solum per approbationem et observa-
tionem.'   Baldus, I. Feud. I § 3, nr. 2.   Hieronymus de Tortis, Consilium for Florence, nr. 25: Papa et imperator non sunt supra ius
gentium; therefore (nr. 20—32) a papal sentence, if not preceded by
citation, is null.

260.   Thus Thom. Aquin. l. c. q. 94, a. 4—6, distinguishes the Principles
prima principia of the *lex naturalis*, which are everywhere identical, and
immutable, ineradicable, and the *praecepta secundaria* of the same Secondary
lex which are mutable and, in consequence of the depravity of Rules of
human reason, 'in aliquo' destructible.   Generally it is said that the Law of
the *ius naturale* is immutable and can never be abrogated (*tolli*) by Nature.
the *ius civile*; but that derogation from it 'quoad quid' is possible,
and that 'ex causa' additions to and detractions from it can be made.
See Lup. Bebenb. c. 15, p. 401.   Ockham, Dial. III. tr. 2, l. 2, c. 24.
Gloss on Sachsensp. I. a. 55.   Anton. Rosell. IV. c. 7: the 'ius
naturale divinum' is wholly unalterable; on the other hand, the
'ius naturale homini commune cum animalibus' cannot indeed be
abrogated by the law-giver, but can 'ex causa' be interpreted and
confined.—This limitation was unavoidable, for, according to
general opinion, the very existence of lordship and ownership implied
a breach of the pure Law of Nature, and even Thomas Aquinas,
Sum. Theol. II. 2, q. 66, a. 2, was of opinion that 'proprietas possessi-
onum non est contra ius naturale, sed iuri naturali superadditur per
adinventionem rationis humanae.'   Compare I. q. 96, a. 1—4; and
K. Summenhard, Tr. I. q. 8—11, who speaks at length.

261.   Anton. Ros. IV. c. 2—6 says that, though John de Lignano Positive
denies this, the legists are all agreed that though the *ius divinum* Modifica-
tions of

the Law of God. cannot be abrogated (*tolli*) it can be distinguished, limited and restrained in proper cases, and that additions can be made to it; but this holds good only of such *ius divinum* as is not *de necessitate.* Comp. Ockham, Dial. III. tr. 2, l. 2, c. 24. Such limitations become all the more necessary when men are beginning to regard Positive Canon Law as *ius divinum.*

Primeval and Secondary Ius Gentium. 262. Very usual is a distinction between the 'ius gentium primaevum' which has existed ever since men were in their original condition and the 'ius gentium secundarium' which is of later growth. According to Anton. Rosell. IV. c. 7, the law-giver can not abrogate, though he may interpret, the former, while the latter he may abrogate 'ex causa.'

Mutability of Positive Law. 263. Thom. Aquin. Sum. Theol. II. 1, q. 90, a. 2 and 3, q. 91, a. 3, q. 95, a. 2, q. 96, a. 5: but he maintains that a law has a *vis directiva* for the legislator who made it. Also q. 97, a. 1—4. Aegid. Rom. De reg. princ. III. 2, c. 24, 26—28, 31: already we see here a comparison between law and language; like language, the *lex positiva* varies according to 'consuetudo, tempus, patria et mores illius gentis.' Mars. Pat. I. c. 12—13: a quite modern definition of a law as the expressly declared will of a sovereign community. Patric. Sen. De inst. reip. I. 5.

The Prince and Positive Law. 264. Thom. Aquin. l. c. q. 90, a. 3, q. 97, a. 3; also Comm. ad Polit. p. 477, 491, 499, 518. Aeg. Rom. III. 2, c. 29: 'positiva lex est infra principantem sicut lex naturalis est supra'; the Prince stands in the middle between Natural Law and Positive; the latter receives its *auctoritas* from him and he must adapt it to the particular case. Ptol. Luc. II. c. 8, III. c. 8 and IV. c. 1: the essential difference between the *principatus regalis* and the *principatus politicus* lies in this, that the latter is a responsible government according to the laws, while in the former the *lex* is 'in pectore regentis,' wherefore he can at any time produce as law from this living fount whatever seems expedient to him. Engelb. Volk. I. c. 10—11: the *rex* as *lex animata*; and such a *lex*, since it can suit itself to the concrete case, is better than a *lex inanimata.* Joh. Saresb. IV. c. 2. Ockham, Dial. III. tr. 1, l. 2, c. 6. Petr. de Andlo, I. c. 8.

Potestas legibus soluta. 265. As to the Pope, see Boniface VIII. in c. 1 in Sexto 1, 2 (qui iura omnia in scrinio pectoris censetur habere); Aug. Triumph. I. q. 22, a. 1; Alv. Pel. I. a. 58; Laelius in Gold. II. p. 1595 ff.; Aen. Sylv. a. 1457 (Voigt, II. p. 240 ff.); Nic. Cus. after his change of opinion (Op. 825 ff.). Then as to the Emperor, see the doctrine of all civilians; the theories of the Hohenstaufen; Frederick I. in Otto Fris. III. 16 and IV. 4; Wezel, l. c.; Ep. Freder. II. in ann.

1244 and 1245 in Huillard, Hist. dipl. Frid. II. vol. VI. pp. 217, 258, and Pet. de Vin. Ep. II. c. 8 (quamquam enim Serenitati nostrae... subiaceat omne quod volumus etc.); III. c. 9, V. c. 1 ff.; Höfler, p. 70 ff.; Ficker, II. pp. 495, 539 ff., 554 ff.; Gloss on Sachsensp. I. a. 1, III. a. 52—54, 64, Lehnrecht, a. 4; the summary in Ockham, Dial. III. tr. 2, l. 2, c. 26 and tr. 1, l. 2, c. 6; Aen. Sylv. praef. and c. 19—21; Petr. de Andlo, II. c. 8 (but how does this agree with the doctrine, II. c. 10, that the Emperor can be tried by the Palsgrave?).

266. Comp. Thom. Aq., Ptol. Luc., Engelb. Volk., Ockham, Petr. de Andlo, as above in Note 264. Aegid. Rom. III. 2, c. 2: it is so in the Italian towns, where despite the existence of a Lord (*dominus*) or Podesta (*potestas*), 'totus populus magis dominatur,' since the People makes statutes 'quae non licet dominum transgredi.' Pat Sen. De inst. reip. I. 5 (lex tantum dominatur) and III. 1 (the Magistrates rule over the People and the Laws over the Magistrates). *Only in a Republic is the Ruler below the Laws.*

267. See above Notes 159, 166, 169—71, 186—7, 200. Most decisively Mars. Patav. I. c. 7—11, 14—15 and 18; with him the 'legislator' is in all cases the People, and the 'principans' is bound by the 'forma sibi tradita a legislatore.' Nicol. Cus. II. c. 9—10 and 20, III. praef. and c. 41: all the binding force of the laws rests on the will of the whole community; the Pope is bound by the 'canones,' the Emperor by the 'leges imperiales,' and the laws are to allow for governmental and judicial acts a no wider field of activity than is absolutely necessary. Gregor. Heimb. II. p. 1604 ff. Comp. Ockham, Dial. III. tr. 1, l. 2, c. 6: he remarks that perhaps in the whole world there is no instance of a regal form of government in the sense of a lordship unrestrained by laws, and that such a form would not deserve approbation except in the case, never found in practice, of an absolutely virtuous ruler. With this Aquinas agrees in so far that he prefers a monarchy limited by law.—Naturally those who advocated the supremacy of the laws appealed at this point to the 'lex *digna*.' In that text their opponents saw no more than that a purely voluntary observance of the laws on the part of the Princeps was promised by him as a praiseworthy practice. [This famous text (l. 4, Cod. 1, 14) runs thus: Digna vox maiestate regnantis legibus alligatum se principem profiteri.] *The Ruler is always below the Laws.*

268. In particular Mars. Pat. I. c. 11, 14, 15 and 18 and Nic. Cus. develop modern thoughts at this point. It is to be observed, however, that all the writers mentioned in Note 266 suppose that in a Republic there will be a separation of legislative from executive power, such as they do not allow in a Monarchy, and thereby they make this separation the distinguishing trait of a Republic. [The *The 'Rechts-staatsidee.'*

translator of these pages believes that in German controversy the common contrast to the *Rechtsstaat* has been the *Beamtenstaat.* Perhaps the nearest English equivalent for the former term would be the Reign of Law. But not all theorists would allow that the Reign of Law exists in England where the State or Crown cannot be made to answer in Court for its wrongful acts.]

Popular Assemblies above the Laws. 269. In relation to the Assembly of the People, this comes out most plainly in the doctrine of Marsilius. In relation to the General Council of the Church the freedom from the restraints of Positive (canon) Law comes out in the doctrine of Epieikia which finds its clearest expression in Henr. de Langenstein, Cons. pac. c. 15, Randuf, De mod. un. c. 5 (Gerson, Op. II. p. 166) and in particular Gerson, De unit. eccl. (ib. p. 115, also p. 241 and 276).

Omnia Principis esse intelliguntur. 270. See the statement and refutation of this doctrine in Georg Meyer, Das Recht der Expropriation, Leipz. 1868, p. 86 ff.

Eminent Domain. 271. See Accursius in Gl. on l. 3, Cod. 7, 37, v. *omnia principis* and l. 2, Dig. de rer. div. v. *littora* (the Princeps has *iurisdictio vel protectio* not *proprietas*). Jac. Aren. Dig. prooem. nr. 1—7. And. Is. II. Feud. 40, nr. 27—29. Bart. Const. I. Dig. pr. nr. 3; l. 4, Dig. 50, 9, nr. 12; l. 6, Dig. 50, 12: throughout a distinction is maintained between 'dominium mundi ratione iurisdictionis et gubernationis' and 'dominium ratione proprietatis.' Baldus, l. 2, Dig. de rer. div., Const. I. Dig. pr. nr. 10—11: a double 'dominium' in 'singulae res,' but 'diversa ratione': ius publicum Caesaris, privatum privatarum personarum. Baldus, II. Feud. 51, pr. nr. 1—4: territorial lordship and ownership distinguished in the case of a city that has been given away or has subjected itself. See also Alv. Pel. II. a. 15 (*administratio* contrasted with *dominium*) and a. 57 and 63 (Christ had no *dominium particulare*, but he had *dominium generale*). Ockham, Dial. III. tr. 2, l. 2, c. 21—25, discusses all opinions at some length. He rejects both that which asserts and that which denies that the Emperor is 'dominus omnium temporalium,' and teaches the mediating doctrine of a 'dominium quodammodo' vested in him by conveyance from the People. This is evidently the 'dominium eminens' of later times, for, on the one hand, it is a 'dominium,' though 'minus pingue,' and yet is compatible with the ownership of the 'res privatorum' by private individuals and with the ownership of the 'res nullius' by the 'totum genus humanum.' Somn. Virid. II. c. 23—30 and 366: 'dominium universale' of Emperor and Pope contrasted with 'dominium appropriatius et specialius' of individuals. Ant. Ros. I. c. 70. Petr. de Andlo, II. c. 8. Almain, Expos. ad q. I. c. 6, and II. c. 2. Decius, Cons. 538, nr. 8—11: in the case of every City, as well as in the case of the Emperor, we must distinguish 'iurisdictio et imperium' over the 'districtus et territorium,' which is a 'superioritas coercitionis,' from 'proprietas et dominium'; for 'proprietas et imperium nulla societate coniunguntur.'

272. See the work of Georg Meyer, as above in Note 270. [Dr Gierke remarks that his own notes on this subject, which had already appeared in his tract on Althusius, are supplemental to the learning collected by Meyer.]

The Right of Expropriation.

273. Accursius in Gl. on l. 3, Dig. 1, 14, v. *multo magis* and other passages in G. Meyer p. 88; Gloss. Ord. on c. 1, D. 22, v. *iniustitiam*; Jac. Arena, Dig. prooem. nr. 1—7; And. Isern. 11. Feud. 40, nr. 27—29; Host. Summa de rescript. nr. 11 ff.; Oldradus, Cons. 224 and 257; Bart. l. 4, Dig. 50, 9, l. 6, Dig. 50, 12, l. 6, Cod. 1, 22 and Const. 1. Dig. pr. nr. 4—6 (neither *rescribendo* nor yet *legem condendo*); Raphael Fulgosius, Cons. 6, nr. 46—47, Cons. 21, nr. 12 and 28; Paul. Castr. l. 23, Dig. 41, 2, l. 6, Cod. 1, 22, Const. 1. c. 229; Jason, l. 3, Dig. 1, 14, nr. 24—34 and Const. 111. c. 86, nr. 14; Anton. Butr. c. 6, X. 1, 2, nr. 20—22; Panorm. eod. c. nr. 6; Bologninus, Cons. 58; Alex. Tart. Cons. 11. c. 190 (esp. nr. 13) and c. 226, nr. 18; Franc. Curtius sen. Cons. 20, 49, 50, 60; Christof. de Castellione, Cons. 8, nr. 16—18; Joh. Crottus, Cons. 11. c. 156, nr. 28—44; Ant. Ros. 1v. c. 8 and 10. Ockham, Dial. 111. tr. 2, l. 2, c. 23—5 mentions as an outcome of the 'dominium quodammodo' which he allows to the Emperor, a right to quash or appropriate to himself or transfer private ownership, and to forbid the occupation of 'res nullius'; but such acts as these are not to be done 'ad libitum' but only 'ex causa et pro communi utilitate' in so far as general utility is to be preferred to 'privata utilitas.' And at the same time it is Ockham who most emphatically teaches (ib. c. 27) that this is not merely a limit set to the power of the Monarch but a limit set to the power of the State itself; for, according to him, the limitation of imperial rights by the rights of individuals rests upon the fact that the *Populus*, which transferred its power to the *Princeps*, had itself no unbounded power, but (in accordance with c. 6, X. 1, 2) was entitled to invade the sphere of private rights by the resolutions of a majority only at the call of necessity (*de necessitate*).

No Expropriation without Just Cause: an absolute Rule of Law.

274. To this effect, despite a strong tendency towards absolutism, Jacob. Buttrig. l. 2, Cod. 1, 19; Alber. Rosc. Const. 1. Dig. v. *omnis*, nr. 5 ff.; l. 15, Dig. 6, 1; l. 2, Cod. 1, 19; Baldus, Const. 1. Dig. pr. nr. 11; l. 7, Cod. 1, 19; l. 6, Cod. 1, 22; l. 3, Cod. 7, 37. For some intermediate opinions see Felinus Sandaeus c. 7, X. 1, 2, nr. 26—45; Decius eod. c. nr. 19—24 and Cons. 191, 198, 269, nr. 4—5, 271, nr. 3, 352, nr. 1, 357, nr. 3, 361, nr. 7, 250, nr. 5—6, 588,

No Expropriation without Just Cause: a good general Rule.

606, nr. 8, 699, nr. 8; Riminald. Cons. I. c. 73. Ludov. Rom. Cons. 310 (a just cause necessary in case of a 'lex specialis' but not in case of a 'lex universalis'); Bened. Capra, Reg. 10, nr. 30 ff.

Compensation for the Expropriated.
275. As to the fluctuations of the Glossa Ordinaria, see Meyer, op. cit. p. 92—94. Decidedly in favour of compensation are Baldus, l. 2, Cod. 7, 13; Decius, l. 11, Dig. de Reg. Iur. and Cons. 520 (recompensatio); Jason, l. 3, Dig. 1, 14 and Cons. III. c. 92, nr. 11 (si causa cessat debet res illa restitui si potest); Paul. Castr. l. 5 § 11, Dig. 39, 1, nr. 4, l. 10, Cod. 1, 2, nr. 3; Lud. Rom. Cons. 310, nr. 4; Bertach. Rep. v. *civitas*, nr. 88 and 96; Fel. Sand. c. 6, X. 1, 2, nr. 2 and c. 7, eod. nr. 28—29. Aeneas Sylvius, c. 18 (if practicable, 'ex publico compensandum est'); Crottus, Cons. II. c. 156, nr. 27 (princeps propter favorem publicum si auferat dominium alicui, debet pretium solvere) nr. 28—29 (expropriatory acts of towns), nr. 31 (the Pope).— On the other side, Alber. Rosc. l. 14 § 1, Dig. 8. 6.

No Compensation in case of General Expropriatory Law.
276. Decius, Cons. 520: a law may take away rights 'generaliter' even 'sine compensatione privatorum'; on the other hand, if the law does this 'particulariter alicui subdito' then it must be 'cum recompensatione.' Jason, l. 3, Dig. 1, 14, nr. 44; Paris de Puteo, De synd. p. 41, nr. 24 and Ant. Ros. IV. c. 8 and 10.

No Compensation in a Case of Necessity.
277. So, e.g., Aen. Sylv. c. 17—18: in case 'reipublicae necessitas id expostulat,' though 'aliquibus fortasse durum videbitur et absurdum.'

Proprietary Rights proceed from the Ius Gentium.
278. Thus already the Glos. Ord. on l. 2, Cod. 1, 19, and l. 6 Cod. 1, 22; also Hostiensis, Jac. de Arena, Oldradus, Fulgosius, Iserna, Bartolus, Paul. Castrensis, Jason, Ockham, as in Note 273; also, but with less protection for property, Rosciate, Baldus, Decius and Bened. Capra, as in Note 274. See also Joh. Paris. c. 7, where private ownership is placed outside the sphere of the Public Power, temporal and spiritual, by the more specific argument that such ownership originates in the labour of an individual and thus is a right that arises without any relation to the connexion between men or to the existence of a society with a common head (commune caput). Paris de Puteo, De synd. p. 41, nr. 22—24; Somn. Virid. I. c. 156—161; Bertach. v. *plenitudo potestatis*; Pet. de Andlo, II. c. 8; Gerson, IV. p. 598; Ant. Ros. IV. c. 8 and 10 (the source of private property is *ius gentium*, but *ius gentium secundarium*, and so it is destructible).— When the objection was raised that it was only Property as an institution that existed *ex iure gentium*, and that this was not infringed if particular owners were robbed, the reply was that the *distinctio dominorum* and the permanent establishment of certain modes of acquisition were attributable to the *ius gentium*.

279. Baldus 1. Feud. 7 (God subjected the laws, but not con- Sacred-
tracts, to the Emperor); Ludov. Rom. Cons. 352, nr. 15—25; ness of
Christof. Castell. Cons. 8, nr. 25; Jason, Cons. 1. c. 1 and c. 56, 11. c. made by
223, nr. 16 ff. and 226; Decius, Cons. 184 nr. 2, 286 nr. 5, 292 nr. 8, the State.
404 nr. 8 (for 'Deus ipse ex promissione obligatur'), 528 nr. 6, 689
nr. 7—27. But, once more, 'ex iusta causa' breach of contract is
permissible: Jason, Cons. 1. c. 1, nr. 12 and 29 ff., 11. 226, nr. 43,
l. 3 Dig. 1, 14, nr. 34; Bened. Capra, Reg. 10, nr. 43 ff.; Ant. Ros.
IV. c. 14. Therefore the old moot question, whether a city can
revoke the freedom from taxation which it has promised to a settler,
is generally answered in the negative, on the ground that such an act
would be a breach of contract; but exceptions are allowed 'ex causa,'
e.g., when there is the punishment of a delict, or if the city's existence
is at stake; Jason, Cons. 1. c. 1, nr. 21—30; Ant. Ros. IV. c. 15.

280. Thus the Gloss. Ord. on l. 2 Cod. 1, 19 and l. 1 Cod. 1, Rights
22 holds that private rights are suspended if the *ius civile* comes into on Positive
collision with them, and that they are abolished by a simple rescript, Law are at
if the intent to abolish them be clearly expressed; but many, it is of the
added, hold that in the case last mentioned the rescript to be effectual State.
must contain the clause 'non obstante lege.' Then the last of these
opinions is developed by Hostiensis, Paulus Castrensis, Jason and
others. Bartolus allows that private rights arising *ex iure civili* can
be abolished 'without cause,' but only by legislation, and not (unless
the damage be inconsiderable) by way of rescript. On the other
hand, Baldus, Decius and others hold that such rights can be withdrawn unconditionally and in every form. Innocent IV., Alb. Rosciate and others think that the State cannot take away the right of
ownership (*dominium ipsum*), but can make it illusory by taking
away the rights of action which flow merely from Positive Law.
Anton. Ros. III. c. 14 and Bened. Capra, Reg. 10, nr. 43—52 discuss
at length the withdrawal of 'iura mere positiva.'

281. Jason, Cons. 1. c. 1, nr. 20, c. 56, nr. 1, 2, 7, 8, 21, 11. Revoca-
c. 226, nr. 43—49: 'privileges' granted gratuitously may be revoked 'Privi-
'sine causa'; those granted for value 'ex causa.' Felinus Sand. c. 7 leges.'
X. 1. 2, nr. 48—52: for the *princeps* can 'ius auferre, cuius ipse fuit
causa ut acquireretur.' Bened. Capra, l. c., excepts the case of 'non
subiecti.' Aen. Sylv. c. 15: privileges may be revoked if they be
reipublicae damnosa.—In the Disput. inter mil. et cler. p. 686, and
the Somnium Viridarii I. c. 33—34 the knight already applies this
doctrine in such wise that the State 'pro ardua necessitate reipublicae
vel utilitate manifesta' can withdraw all ecclesiastical privileges,
since every privilege must be deemed to comprise a clause to the
effect that it is not to impair the 'salus publica.'

282. See above Notes 2, 87, 125—30; Dante, Mon. I. c. 3; Ockham, Dial. III. tr. 2, l. 2, c. 28.

Nullity of the 'Donation of Constantine.'

283. Already in the Gloss. on Auth. Coll. I. tit. 6, prooem. v. *conferens*, there is a suggestion of the arguments which the legists afterwards developed by way of proof that the Donation of Constantine was void, because the imperial power is inalienable and no 'expropriatio territorii, dignitatis vel iurisdictionis' is possible. For full discussions of this matter, see Bartol. on prooem. Dig. nr. 13—14 and Baldus eod. nr. 36—57, and prooem. Feud. nr. 32—33. Compare Dante, Mon. III. c. 10 : 'nemini licet ea facere *per* officium sibi deputatum quae sunt *contra* illud officium'; the Emperor cannot destroy the Empire, which exists before he exists, and whence he draws his imperial rights (ab eo recipiat esse quod est); the seamless garment would be rent; in every grant or infeudation by the Emperor there is a reservation of 'superius illud dominium cuius unitas divisionem non patitur.' Lup. Beb. c. 13, p. 391—3. Quaestio in utramque, p. 106, ad 14. Ockham, Octo q. I. c. 12, III. c. 9, VIII. c. 1, Dial. III. tr. 2, l. 1, c. 27. Gloss on Sachsensp. III. a. 63. Damasus, Broc. M. III. br. 19. Greg. Heimb. I. p. 560. Anton. Ros. I. c. 64 —70 ('officium publicum'; 'imperium indivisibile et inalienabile'; 'corpus mysticum'; 'ecclesia non capax'; 'populus Romanus liber, non in commercio').—These arguments are not attacked by the other party. The defenders of the Donation are for making an exceptional case of it. The gift was really made to God and therefore was not subject to the ordinary restrictions. So Bartolus, l. c., whose chief reason, however, is that he is teaching in the papal territory: so also Baldus and others. In particular, however, the papal party develop the doctrine that the Pope was already 'verus dominus iure divino,' and that therefore the donation bore the character of a 'restitutio.' So Innocent IV., Ptol. Luc. III. c. 16; Alv. Pel. I. a. 13 E, 43 D—E, 24 S, 56 M, 59 H, II. a. 29; Aug. Triumph. I. q. 1, a. 1, II. q. 36, a. 3, 38, a. 1, 43, a. 1—3; comp. And. Isern. I. Feud. 1, nr. 10 and Petr. de Andlo I. c. 11, and II. c. 9.—The opinion that the whole donation was a fable had never quite died out in the days before the forgery was exposed by Nic. Cusanus (III. c. 2) and Laur. Valla (ann. 1439 in Schard, p. 734—80). This is shewn by the bold words of Wezel, ann. 1152, in Jaffé, Mon. Corb. p. 542, and the mention of this opinion by Lup. Bebenb. c. 13.

Inalienability of Public Power.

284. See above, Note 58. In particular Lupold von Bebenburg (c. 15, pp. 398—401) in this context sharply formulates the general proposition that the 'imperium,' since it is 'ob publicum usum

'assignatum,' stands 'extra commercium' like any other 'res in publico usu.'

285. Among the jurists and publicists we may see an always more definite apprehension of the rule that every contract which purports to sacrifice an essential right of the State is void, and that no title can give protection against that claim to submission which flows from the very idea of State-Power. (Compare the passages cited in Note 283.) Therefore contracts made by the Princeps are not binding on his successor if thereby 'monarchia regni et honor coronae diminui possit,' or 'magna diminutio iurisdictionis' would ensue, or 'regalia status' would be abandoned. See Bart. l. 3, § 2, Dig. 43, 23, nr. 5; Bald. I. Cons. 271, nr. 3; Joh. Paris. c. 22; Somn. Virid. II. c. 293; Picus a Monte Pico, I. Feud. 7, nr. 10; Jason, Cons. III. c. 10, nr. 6—9, 16, 24—25; Crottus, Cons. II. c. 223, nr. 11 and 21—22; Bertach. v. *successor in regno.* So a contract by a city purporting to exempt a man from taxation might be valid if entered into with a new settler, but would be invalid if made with one who was 'civis iam subditus': Bart. l. 2, Dig. 50, 6, nr. 2 and 6; to the contrary, Gal. Marg. c. 30, nr. 11 and Dur. Spec. IV. 3, de cens. § 2, nr. 12.

[margin: Nullity of Acts tending to diminish the State's Power.]

286. See Notes 283—5. Dante, III. c. 7: Emperor or Pope, like God, is powerless in one point, namely, 'quod sibi similem creare non potest: auctoritas principalis non est principis nisi ad usum, quia nullus princeps seipsum autorizare potest.' Aen. Sylv. c. 11—12.

[margin: Inalienability of Sovereignty.]

287. Most definitely Nicol. Cus. (above, Note 171); but also Mars. Pat. I. c. 12 (in the words 'nec esse possunt'). As regards the Church, see above, Notes 189 and 200. According to Ockham, Dial. III. tr. 1, l. 1, c. 29, there were some who held that a renunciation of the lordship of the world by the 'Populus Romanus' was impossible and would not bind the 'populus sequens'; but this opinion is refuted, reference being made to the merely 'positive' character of the Romans' right to preeminence, and also to the doctrine about the binding force of resolutions passed by a corporation.

[margin: An indestructible Sovereignty of the People.]

288. Bart. Rubr. C. 10, 1, nr. 3—5 and 9—10. The idea of the Fiscus includes only 'quicquid ad commodum *pecuniarium* imperii pertinet: alia vero, quae ad iurisdictionem et honores imperii pertinent et non commodum pecuniarium et bursale, continentur nomine *reipublicae* et non fisci.' Baldus, II. Feud. 51, pr. nr. 4: a city which subjects itself to lordship thereby conveys the *iurisdictio* over the town mills, for this the city had possessed 'sicut ipsa

[margin: Essential Rights of the State and casually acquired Rights of the Fisc.]

civitas,' but it does not convey the ownership of the mills, for this it had 'iure privato.' Compare Bald. Rubr. C. 10, nr. 11, Cons. I. c. 271, nr. 2, but especially l. 1, Cod. 4, 39, nr. 4, and above all l. 5, Cod. 7, 53, nr. 13: a distinction between 'res universitatis in commercio' and 'extra commercium': in things of the latter class—and to this class belong all public rights—'tenuta capi non potest' [a tenure cannot be created]; therefore, e.g., the right to impose a tax 'cum sit publicum auctoritate et utilitate et sit meri imperii' is inalienable, and can never 'privato concedi vel in tenutam dari'; only the *commoditas* [profit] of this right can be sold, given, let to farm, in such wise that the 'civitas ipsa' will still 'impose' the tax, though the buyer or lessee 'exacts' it; also the city can appoint for itself a *capitaneus* or *conservator*, who, as its proctor, will impose taxes and exercise other rights of ownership; 'et sub hoc colore perdunt civitates suas libertates, quae de decreto vendi non possunt.' See further the separation of the sovereign rights and fiscal rights of the Empire in Ockham, Dial. III. tr. 2, l. 2, c. 23: also the distinction between the *commodum pecuniarium*, which is involved in the idea of the *fiscus*, and the *regalia* which are involved in the idea of the *respublica*, in Vocab. Iuris, v. *fiscus*, in Paul. Castr. l. 4, Cod. 2, 54, Marcus, Dec. I. q. 338, nr. 8—10 and 17, Martinus Laudensis, De fisco, q. 141.

Gradual apprehension of the Distinction between Ius Publicum and Ius Privatum.

289. See the passages cited above in Notes 284, 285 and 288.— A certain, but a very distant, influence was exercised at this point by the distinctions drawn by the Philosophers between the various sorts of *iustitia*. So, in particular, the Thomistic distinction between (1) the *iustitia particularis*, which is (a) commutative, regulating the relationships of man to man, or (b) distributive, dividing among individuals what is common, and (2) the *iustitia generalis s. legalis*, which limits the rights of individuals in accordance with the demands of the *bonum commune*. See Thom. Aquin. Sum. Theol. II. 2, q. 58 ff.; also II. 1, q. 105, a. 2. Also Aegid. Rom. above, Note 83.

Nullity of the Sovereign's Acts if they conflict with Natural Law.

290. So, to some extent, all the writers mentioned in Note 257. And so in connexion with attacks on vested rights made without *iusta causa*, all the authors named in Note 273: see especially Gloss. Ord. on l. 2, Cod. 1, 19 and l. 6, Cod. 1, 22, Host. l. c., Jacob. Aren. l. c. (for the Emperor, if he orders anything contrary to law, 'quasi non facit ut imperator'), Raphael Fulgosius l. c. (the opinion that the Emperor, though he does unright, does a valid act, would practically subject everything to arbitrary power). Comp. Bened. Capra, Reg. 10, nr. 35—42.—Then Bartolus draws, and others

accept, the distinction between invasions of right (1) legem condendo, (2) iudicando, (3) rescribendo, and he is inclined to allow
greater force to an act of legislation than to acts of other kinds;
still it is just he who expressly declares that in conflict with Natural
Right, strictly so-called, even laws are void.—See also above, Note
259 *in fine.*

291. See above, Notes 129—130 and 134.

292. This is the core of the doctrine that the lack of a *iusta* Tribunals
causa for any invasion of vested rights by the Sovereign can be must give
Effect to
supplied by the deliberateness (*ex certa scientia*) with which he Acts of the
exercises his *plenitudo potestatis*: deliberateness which can be mani- Sovereign
if done de-
fested by such a clause as 'lege non obstante.' This doctrine, which liberately.
first appears in a rough form in Durantis, Speculum, I. tit. interd. leg.
et sedi Apost. reserv. nr. 89 (cf. G. Meyer, op. cit. p. 101), is attacked
by the jurists cited in our Note 273 (though Jason in Cons. II. c. 233,
c. 236, n. 12—13 and IV. c. 107, nr. 4, makes large concessions) and
is defended, though to a varying degree, by the jurists mentioned
in our Note 274. See in particular Alber. Rosc. l. c. where practically all difference between Positive and Natural Right disappears
and the same formal omnipotence is claimed both for rescripts and
for acts of legislation. Baldus, l. c.; Felin. Sand. l. c. nr. 60—66
(despite nr. 45—52); Riminald. Cons. I. c. 73; Capra, Reg. 10,
nr. 48—52, 56—59; Decius, c. 7, X. 1, 2, nr. 27—28, Cons. 198,
nr. 7, 269, nr. 4—5, 271, nr. 3, 640, nr. 6—7, and esp. 588, nr. 1—
14; also Aen. Sylv. c. 16—17.—The rejection of the right of active
resistance is a logical consequence; see above, Note 127.

293. This is made externally visible by the treatment as two dif- Natural
Law is not
ferent subjects of (1) the '*lex* naturalis et divina,' which is binding on reduced to
rulers as on others, but like all other 'leges' is concerned with the level
of mere
'actus exteriores,' and (2) that Instruction for the Virtuous Prince, in Ethics.
the development of which medieval publicists expend much of their
pains.

294. Already John of Salisbury, IV. c. 1, 2 and 4, speaks of a Coercive
and
'*lex* iustitiae,' to which the Ruler remains subject, since the 'aequitas Directive
et iustitia,' of which the 'lex' is the 'interpres,' should govern his Force of
Law.
will. Then in Aquinas there comes to the front the formula that the
Prince, in so far as the rules of law have no 'vis coactiva' against
him, is still bound by them 'quantum ad vim directivam'; comp.
Sum. Theol. II. 1, q. 96, a. 5, also q. 93, a. 3. With Thomas himself
it is only the 'lex humana' which is reduced to the exercise of a
merely directive force over the Prince; in this province unrighteous
laws (e.g. those which proceed 'ultra sibi commissam potestatem,'

which impose unjust taxes and unjust divisions of burdens, or which are 'contra commune bonum') have formally the force of laws, though they are not binding 'in foro conscientiae': comp. ib. q. 90, a. 2, and q. 96, a. 1—4. Similarly Joh. Friburg. c. II. t. 5, q. 204. On the other hand, those who unconditionally maintain the formal sovereignty of the legislator and in so doing refuse even to Natural Law any 'coactive force' against him, are unanimous in allowing to it at least a 'directive force.' See also Ptol. Luc. De reg. princ. IV. c. 1. Ockham, Dial. III. tr. 2, l. 2, c. 28. Gerson, IV. p. 593 ff. esp. 601.

Legal Limit to the Duty of Obedience.

295. See above, Notes 127—8. The limit to the duty of obedience is steadily represented as a matter for Jurisprudence, and is deduced from the nature of *lex* or *ius*.

Unjust Acts of Sovereignty to be interpreted into Rightfulness.

296. See, e.g., Gloss. Ord. on l. 2, Cod. 1, 19, and l. 1, Cod. 1, 22; Baldus, as cited in Note 274; Jason, Cons. II. c. 233, nr. 9, III. c. 24, nr. 21, IV. c. 166, nr. 9; Franc. Aret. Cons. 15, nr. 9; Franc. Curt. sen. Cons. 20, 49, 50; Domin. Gem. Cons. 99, nr. 7—8, c. 104, nr. 4; Decius, Cons. 292, nr. 3 and 9, 373 nr. 10, 606 nr. 17. In case of need men were ready to feign that the Sovereign's act had been induced by subreptio, circumventio, etc.

Discharge of the Sovereign from the Moral Law.

297. For the benefit of the omnipotent Council, Randuf teaches that, if the weal of the Church requires it, the Council may disregard the Moral Law: De mod. un. c. 6, 16, 20 and 22 (Gerson, Op. II. pp. 170, 182, 188, 190). Gerson (IV. p. 671) protests against this: the Law of Morality must not be transgressed even for the sake of the common weal; perjury should not be committed even to save the whole people.

298. In my book 'Joh. Althusius und die Entwicklung der naturrechtlichen Staatstheorien' I have submitted just this side of the medieval doctrine to closer inspection, and have traced the later development of those germs that were planted in the Middle Age.

299. See above, Notes 16, 137 and 260 *in fine*.

300. See above, Notes 16, 138—9, 142—5.

301. See above, Notes 140—1.

Natural Growth of the State.

302. Aegid. Rom. De reg. princ. III. 1, c. 6, supposes three possible origins of a State: the first is the purely natural way of a gradual growth from out the Family; the second is the 'concordia constituentium civitatem vel regnum' and this is partially natural, owing to a 'naturalis impetus' which impels to this concord; the third is the way of mere violence, compulsion and conquest. Marsil. Pat. I. c. 3 combines the thought of natural increase and differentiation with the notion of a creative act of human activity.

303. Already Aquinas, however great may be the stress that he lays on man's nature as 'animal politicum et sociale in multitudine vivens' (De reg. princ. I. c. 1 and Sum. Theol. I. q. 96, a. 4), makes mention of the 'ratio constituens civitatem' (above, Note 98). Comp. Ptol. Luc. III. c. 9, and IV. c. 2—3. Aegid. Rom. III. 2, c. 32 says expressly: 'sciendum est quod civitas sit aliquo modo *quid naturale,* eo quod naturalem habemus impetum ad civitatem constituendam; non tamen efficitur nec perficitur civitas *nisi ex opera et industria hominum.*' Comp. III. 1, c. 1 (opus humanum) with c. 3—5 (homo est naturaliter animal civile et civitas aliquid secundum naturam). Engelb. Volk. De ortu, c. 1: ratio imitata naturam. Joh. Paris. c. 1. Gerson, IV. p. 648. Nic. Cus. III. praef. Aen. Sylv. c. 1, 2 and 4: human reason, 'sive docente natura sive Deo volente, totius naturae magistro,' invented and instituted the State, Lordship, Empire. Already Patric. Sen. De reip. inst. I. 3 speaks of all the manifestations of social life—living in company, making strongholds, language, the arts, the laws, the State—as 'inventions' to which mankind 'duce naturae' came by giving thought to general utility (de communi utilitate cogitare). According to III. 5, the State may be so erected that it cannot perish.

Rational Origin of the State.

304. The ecclesiastical theory that the constitutive principle of the State was violence and compulsion (see above, Note 16) was still maintained by Ptolemy of Lucca, IV. c. 3, and such an origin seemed at least possible to Aegidius Romanus (above, Note 302). On the other hand, Aquinas traces the founding of the State to the office of the King (above, Note 98).

The State erected by Violence.

305. See Mars. Pat. I. c. 15 as to the 'anima universitatis vel eius valentioris partis' as the 'principium factivum' of the State (above, Note 98). And so in relation to the World Empire (above, Note 145).

The State founded by Incorpora- tion.

306. Of special importance was the acceptance of Cicero's definitions of the State as a *societas.* See, e.g. Thom. Aquin. Sum. Theol. II. 1, q. 105, a. 1, II. 2, q. 42, a. 2; Vincent Bellov. VII. c. 6—7; Dom. Gem. c. 17 in Sexto, 1, 6, nr. 7; Randuf, De mod. un. c. 7, p. 171; Theod. a Niem, Nemus Unionis, tr. v. p. 261. So also the acceptance, in c. 2 § 2 D. 8, of the words of St Augustine: 'generale quippe *pactum* est *societatis* humanae obedire regibus.' The separation of the Social Contract from the Contract which institutes the ruler is suggested by John of Paris, c. 1, and is effected in clear outline by Aeneas Sylvius, who treats (De ortu, c. 1) of the grounding of a *societas civilis* by men who theretofore wandered wild in the woods, and then (c. 2) of the establishment of a

The Social Contract.

regia potestas in consequence of the transgressions of the Social Contract that men were beginning to commit. See also Aegid. Rom. above in Note 302 ; Patric. Sen. I. 3. [The passages in Cicero's works referred to in this note are given by Dr Gierke elsewhere (D. G. R. III. p. 23). De off. I. 17, where the State appears among the *societates*. De republ. I. 25, 39 : 'populus autem non omnis hominum coetus quoquo modo congregatus, sed coetus multitudinis iuris consensu et utilitatis communione sociatus'; ib. 26, 41 ; ib. 32, 49 : 'lex civilis societatis vinculum, ius autem legis aequale ; quid enim est civitas nisi iuris societas?'; ib. III. 31 : 'neque esset unum vinculum iuris nec consensus ac societas coetus, quod est populus'; ib. 33 ; ib. 35, 50 ; ib. IV. 3 : 'civium beate et honeste vivendi societas'; ib. VI. 13 (Somn. Scip.) : 'concilia coetus-que hominum iure sociati, quae civitates appellantur.' In another place Dr Gierke (D. G. R. III. p. 124), discussing the influence of the patristic writings, remarks that certain pregnant sentences of Cicero's long-lost *De republica* were known in the Middle Age through Lactantius and Augustine and exercised a powerful influence. In yet another place (D. G. R. III. p. 125) the words 'generale quippe pactum est societatis humanae obedire regibus' are cited from August. Confess. III. 8 ; but it is there remarked that Augustine is wont to give to the State a sinful origin in violence.]

Voluntary Subjection the Ground of Obedience. 307. See the derivation of the binding force of laws from a self-binding of individuals, in Mars. Pat. I. c. 12 (lex illa melius observatur a quocumque civium, quam sibi quilibet imposuisse videtur ;...hanc quilibet sibi statuisse videtur ideoque contra illam reclamare non habet) ; in Ockham, Dial. III. tr. 2, l. 2, c. 26—28 ; in Nic. Cus. II. 8, 10, 12 (concordantia subiectionalis eorum qui ligantur), 13 (sub-iectio inferiorum), III. c. 14 (per viam voluntariae subiectionis et consensus). Add to this the supposition that the isolated individual is historically prior to the community : Aen. Sylv. l. c., and Patric. Sen. l. c.

The terms of the Contract of Subjection. 308. Already Ockham, Dial. III. tr. 2, l. 2, c. 26, says that many derive the Emperor's 'plenitudo potestatis' from Original Contracts, since 'humana societas servare tenetur ad quod se obligavit' : 'sed societas humana obligat se ad obediendum generaliter regibus et multo magis imperatori'; this appears from the words of Augustine [above, Note 306]. Ockham himself, however, opines (c. 28 *in fine*) that this *pactum* secured obedience only 'in his quae ad utilitatem communem proficiunt.' Comp. Aen. Sylv. l. c.

309. See Dante, I. c. 3 ; Ockham, Dial. III. tr. 2, l. 2, c. 28.

Limitation of the Work of 310. So when Dante (above, Note 6) makes the institution of an 'universalis pax' the aim and object of the Empire. So when

Engelbert of Volkersdorf (De ortu, c. 7—13) finds the object of the
State in the 'felicitas regni,' and, having mentioned its components,
finally (c. 14) sums them all up in the one idea of 'pax,' and elsewhere (c. 19) simply identifies the 'ordinatio et conservatio pacis et
iustitiae' with the object of the State.   So also when Gerson, IV.
p. 649, does the like.   And so, again, when Petrus de Andlo, II.
c. 16—18, mentions the 'cura totius reipublicae' as the State's object,
but, when it comes to particulars, mentions only the administration
of justice, the preservation of the peace and the protection of
religion. *the State to the Mainten-ance of Peace and Law.*

311.   See, e.g., Thom. Aquin. De reg. princ. I. c. 14: the object
of the State is life according to virtue; but the 'virtus humana' of
the 'multitudo,' which is to be realized by the 'regimen humanum,'
is itself but means to that other-worldly purpose which the Church
has to promote by realizing the 'virtus divina.'   See also c. 7—15,
and Sum. Theol. II. 1, q. 90, a. 2.   On the other hand, in his
Commentary on the Politics he simply follows Aristotle: see Op. XXI.
pp. 307 ff., 400, 402, 424, 469, 634 ff., 678 ff.   Compare Ptol. Luc.
III. c. 3, and IV. c. 23; Aegid. Rom. III. 1, c. 1—2, III. 2, c. 8 and
32; Eng. Volk. De reg. princ. II. c. 2—4; Anton. Ros. I. c. 46
and 56. *Final Causes of State and Church.*

312.   Joh. Paris. c. 18: since the virtuous life (vivere secundum
virtutem) is the object of the State, it is untrue 'quod potestas regalis
sit corporalis et non spiritualis et habeat curam corporum et non
animarum.'   Somn. Virid. I. c. 154—5.   Gerson, in Schwab, p. 88 ff.—
For the rest, even Alvarius Pelagius, I. a. 56, confesses that the
temporal power, since its object is the 'vita virtuosa,' has to work
upon the 'anima,' and to that extent is 'spiritualis': it works,
however, only 'secundum naturam,' while the spiritual power works
'secundum gratiam' and therefore is 'spiritualis' by preeminence. *Extension of the State's Province in a Spiritual Direction.*

313.   Mars. Pat. I. c. 4—6 ascribes to the State a solicitude for
the 'bene vivere' both on earth and in heaven, and therefore a
widely extended care for morals and general welfare.   Patric. Sen.
De inst. reip. claims for the government the whole 'vita familiaris'
(allotment of land and settlement of families, lib. IV.), the 'vita
civilis' of every citizen (lib. V.), the ordering of the Estates of men
(lib. VI.), nay, even the duty of seeing that the citizens receive none
but beautiful (of course they would be classical) names (lib. VI. 7,
pp. 298—304). *Spiritual Aims of the State.*

314.   See Thom. Aquin. De reg. princ. I. c. 1; Engelb. Volk.
De reg. princ. I. c. 1—4; Dante, I. c. 5; Alv. Pelag. I. a. 62 B;
Joh. Paris. c. 1.

Lessons in
the Art of
Government.

315. Such lessons are given *ex officio* by John of Salisbury, Aquinas, Vincent of Beauvais, Engelbert of Volkersdorf, Aegidius Romanus, Patricius of Siena.

The
Forms of
Government.

316. See the doctrine, deriving from Aristotle, of the Forms of Government in Aquin. l. c. I. c. 1—3; Aegid. Rom. III. 2, c. 2; Mars. Patav. I. c. 8—9 (with five sub-forms of Monarchy); Ockham, Dial. III. tr. 1, l. 2, c. 6—8; Patric. Sen. De inst. reip. I. 4; Almain, Expos. ad q. 1, c. 5 and 15. See also Engelb. Volk. l. c. I. c. 5—18 who supposes four fundamental forms: *democratia, aristocratia, olicratia* (sic!) and *monarchia,* each with specific *principium* and *finis,* and four degenerate forms, *tyrannis, olicratia* (degenerate *aristocratia*), *clerotis* and *barbaries.* See also above, Notes 131, 135, 264—5, 283—6.

317. See above, Notes 269 and 287.

318. See above, Notes 293—6.

Possible
Limitation
of Mon-
archy.

319. See above, Notes 136, 161 and 165. At this point we may also mention the theory that a 'consilium principis' is necessary and that the law-courts should be independent: see Eng. Volk. III. c. 1—45; Aegid. Rom. III. c. 2, c. 1 ff. (the *princeps* to maintain, the *consilium* to contrive, the *iudices* to apply, the *populus* to observe, the laws).

Mixed
Constitu
tions.

320. See above, Note 165. Engelbert of Volkersdorf (I. c. 7—8 and 14—16) is the most independent teacher of this doctrine; out of his four fundamental forms he constructs six that are doubly, four that are triply, and one that is simply compounded, and then of his fifteen forms he gives highly interesting examples from the political life of his time.

321. See above, Note 268.

322. See above, pp. 65 ff.

Growth
of the
Modern
State. The
Taxing
Power.

323. A characteristic example is given by the doctrine of the right to tax. At first this is viewed as a power of Expropriation founded on and limited by the good of the public. [In another part of his work (D. G. R. III. 389) our author has spoken of the view taken by the legists: taxation is a form of expropriation, and therefore there should be a *iusta causa* for a tax.] Thom. Aquin. De reg. Iud. q. 6—7: the State may impose taxes for the 'communis populi utilitas'; but, beyond the 'soliti redditus' (accustomed revenues), only 'collectae' which are moderate or are necessitated by such emergencies as hostile attacks should be levied: if these bounds are exceeded, there is unrighteous extortion. Vincent. Bellov. x. c. 66—69. Ptol. Luc. III. c. 11: the king, because of his duty of caring for the common weal, has a right of taxation, which however is limited by

the purpose for which it exists : always therefore 'de iure naturae'
he may demand 'omnia necessaria ad conservationem societatis
humanae'; but never any more. Joh. Paris. c. 7 deduces the right
of taxation from the fact that private property needs the protection of
the State and its tribunals, and therefore should contribute; but it
may be taxed only 'in casu necessitatis' and proportionately.
Similarly Somn. Virid. I. 140—1 : taxes which exceed traditional
practice can only be imposed in those cases (they are specified) in
which the 'necessitas reipublicae' requires them; they must be
moderate and can only be demanded if the Ruler's own means are
insufficient; and they must be rightly applied; all other taxation is
sin; the Church should punish it 'in foro conscientiae' and, if
possible, secure redress; and it gives the people a right to refuse
payment and even to depose the ruler. Gerson, IV. p. 199 and 616 :
taxes should be imposed only for the purposes of the State and
should be equal for all. See Decius, Cons. 649, nr. 4: the prohibition of the imposition of new taxes does not extend to sovereign
cities.

324. In quite modern fashion Patric. Sen. I. 6 proclaims the
equality of all before the law (aequalitas iuris inter cives), nay, their
equal capacity for all offices and their equal civic duties. *Equality before the Law.*

325. See the statements of civic duty, to sacrifice life and goods
for the 'salus publica'—statements influenced by classical antiquity
—in Aen. Sylv. c. 18, and Patric. Sen. v. 1—10. Also Thom.
Aquin. Summa Theol. II. 1, q. 90, a. 2 : 'unus autem homo est pars
communitatis perfectae,' therefore all private good is to be regulated
only 'secundum ordinem ad bonum commune,' for 'omnis pars
ordinatur ad totum'; ib. a. 3, so in relation to the *domus*; ib. II. 2,
q. 58, a. 5: 'omnes qui sub communitate aliqua continentur, com-
parantur ad communitatem sicut partes ad totum; pars autem id
quod est totius est; unde et quodlibet bonum partis est ordinabile in
bonum totius.' Joh. Friburg. II. t. 5, q. 204: duty of paying taxes
incumbent on every one as 'pars multitudinis' and therefore 'pars
totius.' *State and Citizen. Influence of Antiquity.*

326. Marsilius in his Defensor Pacis expressly declares that the
Church is a State Institution and that the *sacerdotium* is 'pars et
officium civitatis' (I. c. 5—6). Sovereign in things ecclesiastical is
the 'universitas fidelium,' which, however, coincides with the 'universitas civium' and in this respect, as in all other matters, is
represented by the *principans* whom it has instituted, so that the line
between Spiritual and Temporal is always a line between two classes
of affairs and never a line between two classes of persons (II. c. 2, 7, *The Marsilian Absorption of Church in State.*

14, 17, 18, 21). The State Power imposes conditions for admission to the *sacerdotium*, regulates the functions of the priesthood, fixes the number of churches and spiritual offices (II. c. 8 ; III. concl. 12 and 21). It authorizes ecclesiastical foundations and corporations (II. c. 17). It appoints the individual clergyman, pays him, obliges him to a performance of duties, removes him, nay, its consent is necessary to every ordination (II. c. 17, 24 ; III. 21, 40, 41). It watches over the exercise of every spiritual office, to see that it is strictly confined to purely spiritual affairs (I. 19 ; II. 1—10). All *iurisdictio* and *potestas coactiva* are exercised immediately and exclusively by the wielder of temporal power, even if clerical persons are concerned, or matrimonial causes, dispensations, legitimations or matters of heresy (II. c. 8 ; III. c. 12 and 22). Interdicts, excommunications, canonizations, appointments of fasts and feasts, require, at the very least, authorization by the State (II. c. 7, 21 ; III. c. 16, 34, 35). Only on the ground of express commission from the State is it conceivable that the churches should have any worldly powers or the decretals any worldly force (I. c. 12 ; II. c. 28 ; III. c. 7, 13). Education is exclusively the State's affair (I. c. 21 ; III. c. 25). Appeals and complaints to the State Power are always permissible (III. c. 37). All Councils, general and particular, must be summoned and directed by the State (II. c. 8, 21 ; III. c. 33). Church property is in part the State's property, and in part it is *res nullius* (II. c. 14). In any case it is at the disposal of the State, which thereout should provide what is necessary for the support of the clergy and for the maintenance of worship, and should collect and apply the residue for the relief of the poor and other public purposes (II. c. 14 ; III. c. 27, 38, 39). The State therefore may freely tax it, may divert the tithes to itself, may give and take benefices at pleasure, and for good cause may secularize and sell them, 'quoniam sua sunt et in ipsius semper potestate de iure' (II. c. 17, 21 ; III. c. 27). Only what has come from private foundations should, under State control, 'conservari, custodiri et distribui secundum donantis vel legantis intentionem' (II. c. 14, 17 ; III. c. 28).

Attitude of the State towards the Church. 327. Joh. Paris. c. 21, pp. 203—5 : 'est enim licitum principi abusum gladii spiritualis repellere eo modo quo potest, etiam per gladium materialem : praecipue ubi abusus gladii spiritualis vergit in malum reipublicae, cuius cura regi incumbit.'

Church Property and Public Property. 328. Thus in Disput. inter mil. et cler. pp. 682—6 and Somn. Virid. c. 21—22, where the confiscation of church property is justified (with a strong premonitory suggestion of the 'proprieté de la nation'), since the weal and peace of Christian folk certainly are 'pious uses.'

Comp. Joh. Wiclif, Trial p. 407 ff. art. 17, and Joh. Hus, Determinatio
de ablatione temporalium a clericis, in Gold. I. pp. 232—42, where the
right to secularize church property, at all events in case of abuse, is
deduced from the nature of government and the subjection of the
clergy. Joh. Paris. c. 20, p. 203; Nic. Cus. III. c. 39 and others
argue in the same manner for the State's right to tax ecclesiastical
property. So too Quaest. in utramque part. p. 106, ad 17, touching
statutes of mortmain.

329. Comp. Nic. Cus. III. c. 8—24, 33 and 40: the temporal
power is to take in hand ecclesiastical affairs and to demand and
control their reformation, for (II. c. 40) to the State belongs the care
of all things pertaining 'ad bonum publicum,' and this is so 'etiam
in ecclesiasticis negotiis.' Gregor. Heimb. in Gold. I. pp. 559—60.
Peter Bertrand ib. II. pp. 1261—83. Patric. Sen. III. 4. As to the
practical treatment of the Reform of the Church as an affair of the
State, see Hübler, op. cit. pp. 281—8 and 318—22. *The State's Right to reform the Church.*

330. The maxim 'ius publicum est in sacris, sacerdotibus et
magistratibus' was applied by the prevailing doctrine as a proof of
the state-like nature of the Church; see Thom. Aquin. Sum. Theol.
II. 1, q. 95, a. 4. But already Ockham, Octo q. IV. c. 6, says that
many infer from this text that the Emperor 'possit ordinare apostoli-
cam sedem et archiepiscopos et episcopos,' and also that no
renunciation of such a 'ius publicum' can have been valid. *Ius Sacrum is part of Ius Publicum.*

331. See above, Notes 62—64.

332. Thom. Aquin. De reg. princ. I. c. 1 in fine, Summa Theol.
II. 1, q. 90, a. 2—3 (civitas est communitas perfecta), Comm. ad
Polit. p. 366 ff.; Aegid. Rom. III. 1, c. 1 (principalissima communitas), c. 4, III. 2, c. 32; Joh. Paris. c. 1; Eng. Volk. De reg.
princ. II. c. 2—3; Mars. Pat. I. c. 4 (perfecta communitas omnem
habens terminum per se sufficientiae); Ockham, Dial. III. tr. 1, l. 2,
c. 3—5. *Definition of the State.*

333. Thus Thom. Aquin. De reg. pr. I. c. 1 sees civitas, provincia, regnum, in an ascending scale of self-sufficiency (per se
sufficiens esse). Ptol. Luc. III. c. 10—22 and IV. c. 1—28 places
the priest-kingly, the kingly (including the imperial), the 'political,'
and the domestic as four grades of Lordship, and in so doing applies
the name *politia* to the *civitates* which have been expressly defined
(IV. c. 1) as cities that in some points are subject to the Emperor or
King; but he then proceeds to use *civitas* now in this and now in a
more general sense. The procedure of Aegidius Romanus is clearer:
for him the *civitas* is the 'principalissima communitas' only 'respectu
domus et vici'; the 'communitas regni' is yet 'principalior,' being *State, Realm, Empire, Civitas.*

related to *civitas* as *civitas* to *vicus* and *domus* (III. 1, c. 1); also he declares it highly necessary that, to secure their internal and external completion (finis et complementum), various *civitates* should be united in the body of one *regnum* or in a *confoederatio sub uno rege* (III. 1, c. 4—5; compare II. 1, c. 2 and III. 2, c. 32). Similarly Ockham, Dial. III. tr. 1, l. 2, c. 5: the 'civitas' is 'principalissima omnium communitatum,' but only of those 'simul in eodem loco habitantes'; for the rest, it is subordinated to some *ducatus* or some *regnum*, which in its turn may be subordinate. In the passages cited in Note 64 Dante, Engelbert of Volkersdorf, Augustinus Triumphus and Antonius Rosellus presuppose as matter of course that the *civitas* will be completed by some *regnum* and this by the *imperium.*

The Imperium as the only true Civitas.

334. See above, Notes 199 ff. Lupold of Bebenburg at this point adheres closely to the legists; for him (c. 15) kings are 'magistratus maiores' who differ from 'praesides provinciae' merely by being hereditary, and who in strictness owe their places to an imperial appointment made by way of 'tacit consent': so also all lower 'magistratus' and the governors of 'universitates, castra, villae.'

Legal Definitions of Civitas.

335. See the definition of *civitas* along with *urbs, oppidum, villa, castrum,* etc. in Joh. And. c. 17 in Sexto 5, 11 and c. 17 in Sexto 1, 6, nr. 7; Dom. Gem. c. 17 in Sexto, 5, 11, nr. 3—4; Phil. Franch. cod. c. nr. 4—5; Archid. c. 56, C. 12, q. 2; Barth. Caep. l. 2, pr. Dig. de V. S. nr. 1—28; Vocab. Iuris v. *civitas*; Baldus, l. 5, Dig. 1, 1; Barthol. l. 1, § 12, Dig. 39, 1; Ludov. Rom. l. 1, § 12, Dig. 39, 1, nr. 12—17; Jason, l. 73, § 1, de leg. 1. nr. 1—9; Marcus, Dec. 1. q. 365 and 366. The favourite definitions of *civitas* leave quite open the question whether the State or a commune is intended: thus, e.g., 'civium unitas' or 'hominum multitudo societatis vinculo adunata ad simul iure vivendum' or 'humanae multitudinis coetus iuris consensu et concordi communione sociatus,' and so forth.

City and Republic.

336. Baldus, Const. 1. Dig. pr. nr. 8: the *respublica* is sometimes Rome, sometimes 'totum imperium,' sometimes 'quaelibet civitas'; Cons. v. c. 336; Jason, l. 71, § 5, Dig. de leg. 1. nr. 29; Barth. Salic. l. 4, Cod. 2, 54; Decius, Cons. 360, 403, 468, 564, 638; Joh. de Platea, l. un. Cod. 11, 21, nr. 5; Bertach. v. *respublica.* Men help themselves out of difficulties by the confession that they are using words 'improprie.' [Dr Gierke refers to earlier pages in his book in which he has dealt with the usage of the glossators (D. G. R. III. 201) and later legists (ib. 358). Of the glossators he says that they endeavour to regard the Empire as the only true *respublica* and to maintain that all smaller communities stand 'loco privatorum'; but, under the shelter of a use of words which they admit to be

'improper,' they practically concede political rights to civic communities.]

337. This is the procedure of John of Paris, c. 1, and other Frenchmen, who treat 'the Realm' (*regnum*) as the abstract State and utterly deny the *imperium mundi* (above, Note 61). So also Mars. Pat. and Patric. Sen. (1. 3 ff.) without further definition. *The State cutting itself loose from the Empire.*

338. [At this point Dr Gierke refers to earlier parts of his book in which he has illustrated the slow emergence in legal theory of a line similar to that which moderns draw between State and Commune. The process takes the form of a division of corporations into two classes : namely, those that do and those that do not 'recognize a superior.' He cites (D. G. R. III. p. 382) the following passage from Bartolus, l. 7, Dig. 48, 1, nr. 14 : cum quaelibet civitas Italiae hodie, praecipue in Tuscia, dominum non recognoscit, in seipsa habet liberum populum et habet merum imperium in seipsa et tantam potestatem habet in populo quantam Imperator in universo. Then the 'universitas superiorem non recognoscens' began to be regarded as being *de facto*, if not *de iure*, the *respublica* and the *civitas* (or, in modern terms, the State) of the Roman texts. But the process was gradual. The *universitas* which does 'recognize a superior' will have *iurisdictio*, and *imperium* can be acquired by privilege or prescription. After the days of Bartolus, says our author, we are often given to understand that little importance is attached to the old dispute as to whether communities can acquire sovereignty *de iure* as well as *de facto*. He cites Panormitanus (c. 7, X. 1, 2, nr. 6) for the admission that sovereign kings and cities have imperial rights in their territories.] *Communities which do and Communities which do not recognize a Superior.*

339. Paul. Castr. on l. 1, §§ 1—3, Dig. 3, 4, nr. 1, l. 5, Dig. 1, 1, lect. 2, l. 86, Dig. 29, 2, nr. 3, expressly says that, according to modern law, every 'populus superiorem non recognoscens' has a real and true *respublica* of its own, and other communes have 'largo modo rempublicam,' while other *collegia* are only 'partes reipublicae,' though they have a certain likeness (*similitudo*) to republics. Similarly Jason, l. 19, Cod. 1, 2, nr. 15, and l. 1, Dig. 2, 1, nr. 18. Therefore the notion of a *fiscus* is claimed for every community which does not recognize a Superior and denied to other groups. Baldus, l. 1, Dig. 1, 8, nr. 19, l. 1, Cod. 4, 39, nr. 22 ; Hippol. Mars. l. ult. Cod. 3, 13, nr. 189 ; Lud. Rom. Cons. 111 ; Bertach. v. *fiscus dicitur* and v. *civitas*, nr. 23, 46, 133, 135—7 ; Marcus, Dec. 1. q. 234 and 339. *No Community above The State and only Communes below The State.*

340. As to the lack that there is in medieval theory of any concept of a Federal State (*Bundesstaatsbegriff*), see S. Brie, der *Federal States.*

Bundesstaat, I. Leipz. 1874, p. 12 ff. If, besides alliances, mention is made of permanent 'ligae et confoederationes' between 'corpora' and 'universitates' (Bartol. on l. 4, Dig. 47, 22, nr. 6—11; Baldus, s. pac. Const. v. *ego*, nr. 1; Angel. Cons. 269, nr. 1—2) these are considered to have no political quality but to belong to the domain of Corporation Law.

Resistance to the Centralizing Idea of The State.

341. In the Church the writers of the Conciliar Party resist the centralizing trend which is to be seen in the doctrine of the Pope's Universal Episcopate (as set forth, e.g., by Augustinus Triumphus, I. q. 19, Alvarius Pelagius and Turrecremata, De pot. pap. c. 65), and in the derivation of the rights of all other Churches from the right of the Roman Church (Dom. Gem. Cons. 14, nr. 2—4 and 74, nr. 3—6), and in the assertion of the Pope's power of disposition over the rights of all particular Churches (Decius, Cons. 341, nr. 8—9: papa potest dominium et ius quaesitum alicui ecclesiae etiam sine causa auferre), and so forth. See Joh. Paris. c. 6; Petr. de Alliac. in Gers. Op. I. pp. 666 ff. and 692 and De eccl. pot. II. c. 1; Gerson, II. p. 256, for the defence on principle of the rights of the particular Churches; and, for profounder treatment, see Nic. Cus. II. c. 13, 22—28; also above, Notes 89, 90. In the State, besides Dante, Cusanus and Ant. Rosellus (above, Notes 62—64), who hold fast the medieval thought of a Community comprising All Mankind, even Marsilius, II. c. 24, upholds both in State and Church the principle of mediate organic articulation (above, Note 89). According to Ockham, Dial. III. tr. 2, l. I. c. 30, even 'ipsa tota communitas Romanorum' ought not to invade the 'iura partialia Romanorum personarum vel congregationum seu collegiorum aut communitatum particularium.' Comp. ib. 1, 2, c. 28: 'quaelibet privata persona et quodlibet particulare collegium est pars totius communitatis, et ideo bonum cuiuslibet privatae personae et cuiuslibet particularis collegii est bonum totius communitatis.' See also Paris de Puteo, Tr. de Synd. p. 40, nr. 20: Princeps sine causa non tollit universitati publicum vel commune sicut nec rem privati : it would be *rapina*. Also we often hear, as part of Aristotle's teaching, that the suppression of 'sodalitates et congregationes' is a mark of Tyranny, whereas the 'verus rex' would have his subjects 'confoederatos et coniunctos': Aegid. Rom. III. 2, c. 10; Thom. Aquin. De reg. princ. I. c. 3; Somn. Virid. c. 134; Gerson, IV. p. 600.

Political Theory and Feudalism.

342. Of the writers of this group Ptolemy of Lucca is the only one who comes to close quarters with Feudalism : he develops the thought that while salaried offices are best adapted to a Republic, infeudated offices suit a Monarchy: II. c. 10; and compare III. c. 21—22.

343. Towards this result both the doctrine of the Prince's 'plenitude of power' and the doctrine of Popular Sovereignty were tending. Aeneas Sylvius, c. 14—23, gives to it its sharpest form for the Kaiser's benefit. He goes so far as to declare that an appeal from Emperor to Emperor and Princes is impossible, and the attempt is *laesa maiestas*; for the 'imperator cum principibus' can do no more than the 'imperator solus':—'amat enim unitatem suprema potestas.'

All other Power is derived by Delegation from Sovereign Power.

344. See the notion of office entertained by the Emperor Frederick II. as formulated in Petr. de Vin. III. 68 : For the fulfilment of our divine mission we must appoint officers, 'quia non possumus per universas mundi partes personaliter interesse, licet simus potentialiter ubique nos'; the officers are rightly 'ad *actum* deducere...quod in *potentia* gerimus per eos velut ministros.' See also ib. V. c. 1 ff., 100—2, VI. c. 19, 21—23. As to the transformation by the Hohenstaufen of the infeudated offices in Italy see Ficker, Forschungen, II. pp. 277, 472 ff., 477 ff. See also the notion of *officium* in Thom. Aquin. De reg. princ. I. c. 15 ; Mars. Pat. I. c. 5, 7, 15 (the institution of offices and the definition of spheres of official competence are matters for the legislature ; the appointment, correction, payment of officers are matters for the executive power). Patric. Sen. III. 1—12.

Early Official-ism.

345. Thus, e.g., Petr. de Andlo, I. c. 12, relying on the maxim 'contra absolutam potestatem principis non potest praescribi,' expressly says that the Emperor can withdraw all public powers from any commune or corporation, no matter the longest usage. He recommends that this be done in the case of jurisdictional rights, more especially in matters of life and limb, vested in 'plures communitates, imo castella et exiguae villae terrarum, ubi per simplicissimos rusticos ius reddi consuevit.'—Compare also the rejection of 'autonomy' in Aegid. Rom. III. 2, c. 27, and indirectly in Thom. Aquin. Summa Theol. II. 1, q. 90, a. 3 ; also the power that Marsilius accords to the State over ecclesiastical *collegia* (II. c. 21 and III. c. 29) and foundations (II. c. 17, 21, and III. c. 28). And see above, Note 324.

All Power proceeds from and is revocable by the State.

Idea

"god" — parody of James

Villains criticize
Machievels   Gonzalo

head vs. ass body

they no greater father
        King's two bodies

nominalism

utopianism vs. Machievels